CROSSING THE ROCKY MOUNTAINS IN WINTER.

[See p. 232.

THIRTY YEARS

OF

ARMY LIFE ON THE BORDER.

COMPRISING

DESCRIPTIONS OF THE INDIAN NOMADS OF THE PLAINS;

EXPLORATIONS OF NEW TERRITORY;

A TRIP ACROSS THE ROCKY MOUNTAINS IN THE WINTER;

DESCRIPTIONS OF THE HABITS OF DIFFERENT ANIMALS FOUND IN THE WEST, AND THE METHODS OF HUNTING THEM;

WITH INCIDENTS IN THE LIFE OF DIFFERENT FRONTIER MEN,

&c., &c.

BY COLONEL R. B. MARCY, U. S. A.,

AUTHOR OF "THE PRAIRIE TRAVELER."

With Numerous Illustrations.

NEW YORK:

HARPER & BROTHERS, PUBLISHERS,

FRANKLIN SQUARE.

1866.

INTRODUCTORY.

IN this age of many books, it is hardly possible that any new publication can need an apology or an explanation. I have been persuaded by many friends that the contents of the book which is herewith presented to the public are not without value as records of a fast vanishing age, and as truthful sketches of men of various races, whose memory will shortly depend only on romance, unless some one who knew them shall undertake to leave outlines of their peculiar characteristics.

More than thirty years of service in the United States Army, a large portion of the time on the frontiers, on the prairies, or among the far Western mountains, have given me some experience in the life of the frontiersman, as well as made me the frequent companion of the hardy trappers, the pioneers, the advance-guards of civilization, while it has been necessary for me to meet on either friendly or hostile terms nearly all the aboriginal tribes of the prairies.

If any excuse were needed for the publication of sketches somewhat desultory and disconnected as these will prove, I am persuaded that excuse may be found in the simple fact that all these subjects of my description—men, conditions of life, races of aboriginal inhabitants, and adventurous hunters and pioneers—are passing away. A few years more, and the prairie will be transformed into farms, the mountain ravines will be the abodes of busy manufacturers, the aboriginal races will have utterly disappeared, and the gigantic power of American civilization will have taken possession of the land from the great river of the West to the very shores of the Pacific. It can not be entirely in vain that any one contributes that which he knows from personal experience, however little, to aid in preserving the memory of the people and the customs of the West in the middle of the nineteenth century. The wild animals that abound on the great plains to-day will soon be as unknown as the Indian hunters who have for centuries pursued them. The world is fast filling up. I trust I am not in error when I venture to place some value, however small, on every thing which goes to form the truthful history of a condition of men incident to the advance of civilization over the continent—a condition which forms peculiar types of character, produces remarkable developments of human nature—a condition, also, which can hardly again exist on this or any other continent, and which has therefore especial value in the sum of human history. This is the only apology which I have to offer for the anecdotes of persons and the sketches of frontier life which I have ventured to make a part of this volume. Such people will probably not again be found in the future life of the race, and unless some record be made of them, it is by no means certain that generations to come will not regard them as solely the creatures of fiction, in whose pages they have for the most part hitherto been described.

The portions of the volume devoted to relations of personal adventure, as well as those which refer to the general characteristics of the Western country, to modes of travel and life on the prairies, the advice I have given to those who may be called, either in public service or for private purposes, to cross the great plains, the accounts of hunting, and descriptions of Western game and the methods of pursuing and killing it—all these parts of the volume are offered to the public in the hope that they may have practical value, and be of public as well as private benefit.

CONTENTS.

CHAPTER I.

THE INDIANS OF THE PLAINS.

CHAPTER II.

COMANCHE INDIANS.

CHAPTER III.

INDIAN WARFARE.

CHAPTER IV.

PUEBLO INDIANS.

CHAPTER V.

RED RIVER EXPEDITION.

CHAPTER VI.

CHAPTER VII.

INDIAN RESERVATIONS.

CHAPTER VIII.

WINTER EXPEDITION OVER THE ROCKY MOUNTAINS.

CHAPTER IX.

RETURN TRIP TO UTAH.

CHAPTER X.

UNEXPLORED TERRITORY.

CHAPTER XI.

HUNTING.

CHAPTER XII.

PIONEERS OF THE WEST.

CHAPTER XIII.

MOUNTAINEERS.

CHAPTER XIV.

CAPTAIN MARTIN SCOTT.

THIRTY YEARS OF ARMY LIFE ON THE BORDER.

CHAPTER I.

THE INDIANS OF THE PLAINS.

The Indians of the Plains not described in Bancroft's History.—Different in Habits from the Eastern Tribes.—First discovered by Coronado.—Similarity in Habits with the Arabs.—Pantomimic Language.—Characteristics of different Tribes.

In the third volume of Bancroft's History of the United States may be found a very circumstantial, comprehensive, and reliable account of the aborigines, who, from the time of the advent of Europeans, have inhabited that portion of our territory lying east of the Mississippi River, and the author, in this connection, has presented many highly interesting facts relative to their habits, languages, institutions, and religions; but, with the exception of a brief allusion to the partially civilized eastern Sioux or Dacotahs, he as yet has said nothing concerning the Comanche, Kioway, Cheyenne, and other numerous and warlike tribes that range over the great plains west of the Mississippi.

Several years' service in the district of country frequented by this peculiar type of the Indian race has frequently thrown me in contact with different tribes, and thereby afforded me good opportunities for observing their peculiarities and habits, and for collecting the facts which follow.

Whatever common anatomical or phrenological characteristics physiologists may have detected in the skulls of the great families of the Algonquin, Iroquois, Cherokee, or

Catawba tribes, and those of the natives on the Pacific Coast, yet between the habits, languages, and institutions of the Red Men who roam over the Plains, and those of the Indians so elaborately described by our distinguished historian, there exists as wide a contrast as can be found between the Bedouins of the desert and the denizens of London, Paris, or New York.

The earliest information we have of the prairie tribes is contained in Castenada's account of the daring expedition of Coronado, which was sent out from Cicuya, New Mexico, in search of the "golden city" of Quivera, during the summer of 1541.

After marching for several days, the party encountered "an Arab people called *Querechos*, who lived in buffalo-skin tents, and subsisted exclusively on the raw flesh of those animals." Continuing their march in an easterly direction, the Spaniards reached extensive plains, covered with countless herds of buffalo and their erratic enemies, the Indian nomads of the prairies. These people had no horses then, but they possessed great numbers of dogs, which were used to transport their luggage as they followed the migrations of the buffalo. They were a mild, peaceable race of people, who extended to the Spaniards the warmest hospitality and friendship, and they were not addicted to those horrible practices which prevailed among some of the Indians in New Mexico and Sonora. They "jerked" or dried the meat, and made the pemmican, at that early period, in precisely the same manner as it is prepared at the present day by the half-breeds upon the Red River of the North, and they still continue to use the dogs as pack animals.

From this it appears that the Indians seen by the Spanish explorers were the same type of aborigines as are now found roaming over the vast prairies of North America, and with the exception of the changes incident to the introduction of the horse, their habits and manner of living in the sixteenth century were precisely the same as they are at the present moment. The whimsical caprices of fashion hold no tyrannical sway over their beaux and belles. They are not obliged to send three thousand miles to ascertain what particular colored ribbon would be authorized to adorn a bonnet during the succeeding month, or what special style of neck-tie would meet the approbation of the *beau monde* in Paris. The material and cut of their garments to-day are precisely the same as they were three hundred years ago; indeed, so uniform and permanent is their method of conducting all the affairs of life, that an expert has only to examine the remains of an old camp-fire, or even a moccasin, in order to determine what particular tribe of Indians passed that way.

The habits of all the prairie tribes assimilate very closely to each other in some respects, as, for example, they all follow the buffaloes; use the bow and arrow, lance and shield; take the war-path, and fight their battles mounted on horseback, in the open prairie; transport their lodges and all their worldly effects wherever they go; never till the ground, but subsist exclusively on fresh-meat diet. All use the sweat or medicine lodges, and religiously believe in the efficacy of incantations and jugglery in curing diseases, preparing for war, the chase, etc. On the contrary, the natives of the Eastern States, from the time of the first discovery of the country, lived in permanent villages, where they cultivated fields of corn, and possessed strong attachment for their ancestral abodes and sepulchres. Seldom wandering far from home, they did not use horses, but always made their war and hunting expeditions on foot, and sought the cover of trees on going into action.

In their treatment of prisoners of war there has been

also a very marked dissimilarity. The Eastern aborigines, although they put their victims to tortures of the most appalling character, seldom, if ever, violated the chastity of the females; while, on the contrary, the prairie Indians do not put their prisoners to death by prolonged tortures, but invariably compel the females to submit to their lewd embraces. I have known of several well-authenticated instances where their barbarous treatment of females has proved this conclusively.

As there seems to be a most striking physical similitude between the deserts of Arabia, and the steppes of Central Asia, and the prairie *mesas* of our own country, a marked resemblance is also observed in the habits and customs of the respective inhabitants. The Arabs of the desert, the Tartar tribes, and the aboriginal occupants of the prairies, are alike wanderers, having no permanent abiding-places, transporting their lodges or tents wherever they go, and where these are pitched there are their homes. They alike permit no authorities to control them but such as receive the unanimous sanction of the masses, and the rule of their leaders is guided by the counsels of their wise old men, who in many instances allay dissensions and curb the impetuosity of ambitious younger warriors, whose thirst for fame would otherwise involve the nation in protracted wars. Their government is essentially patriarchal, guided by wise and fraternal councils. They are insensible to the wants and luxuries of civilization, and know neither poverty nor riches, vice or virtue, and are alike exempt from the deplorable vicissitudes of fortune. Theirs is a happy state of social equality, which knows not the perplexities of political ambition or the crimes of avarice. They are alike the most expert horsemen in the world, and possess the same fond attachment for the animal. I once made an effort to purchase a favorite horse from a chief of one of the bands of the Southern Comanches (Se-na-co), and offered him a large price, but he could not be persuaded to part with him. He said the animal was one of the fleetest in their possession, and if he were to sell him it would prove a calamity to his whole band, as it often required all the speed of this animal to insure success in the buffalo chase; that his loss would be felt by all his people, and he would be regarded as very foolish; moreover, he said (patting his favorite on the neck), "I love him very much."

The like estimation in which the horse is held among the Eastern nomads is illustrated in a very interesting story related by Mr. W. C. Prime in his "Boat Life in Egypt and Nubia." He says: "Speaking of horses as we rode along, one of the governor's officers told me a story of an old sheik of the Bedouins that I have seen in print in two or three forms, but never precisely in this:

"He was old and poor. The latter virtue is common to his race. He owned a tent, a Nubian slave, and a mare; nothing else. The mare was the fleetest animal on the desert. From the Nile to the Euphrates fame of this animal had gone out, and kings had sought in vain to own her. The love of the Bedouin for his horse is not that fabled affection that we read of in books. This love is the same affection that an American nabob has for his gold, or rather that a poor laborer has for his wages. His horse is his life. He can rob, plunder, kill, and destroy *ad libitum* if he have a fleet steed. If he have none, he can do nothing, but is the prey of every one who has. Acquisition is a prominent feature of Arab character, but accumulation is not found in the brain of a son of Ishmael. The reason is obvious. If he have wealth he has nowhere to keep it. He would be robbed in the night. He would, indeed, have no desire to keep it; for the Bedouin who murders you for a shawl, or a belt, or some gay trapping, will give it away the next day.

"Living this wandering life, the old sheik was rich in this one mare, which was acknowledged to be the fleetest horse in Arabia.

"Ibrahim Pasha wished the animal, as his father had wished before him. He sent various offers to the old sheik, but in vain. At length he sent a deputation, with five hundred purses (a purse is five pounds), and the old man laughed at them.

"'Then,' said Ibrahim Pasha, 'I will take your mare.'

"'Try it.'

"He sent a regiment into the desert, and the sheik rode around them, and laughed at them, and the regiment came home.

"At last the sheik died from a wound received in a fray with a neighboring tribe. Dying, he gave to his Nubian slave all that he had—this priceless mare—and the duties of the blood revenge.

"The faithful slave accepted both, and has ever since been the terror of the Eastern desert. Yearly he comes down like a hawk on the tents of that devoted tribe, and leaves a ball or a lance in man or woman. No amount of blood satisfies his revenge; and the mare and the black rider are as celebrated in Arabia as the wild huntsman in European forests, and much better known."

The only property of these people, with the exception of a few articles belonging to their domestic economy, consists entirely in horses and mules, of which they possess great numbers. These are mostly pillaged from the Mexicans, as is evident from the brand which is found upon them. The most successful horse-thieves among them own from fifty to two hundred animals.

In their political and domestic relations there is also a similarity to the Old World nomads. They are governed by a chief, the tenure of whose office is hereditary so long as his administration meets the approbation of his followers. He leads them to war, and presides at their deliberations in council; but should he disgrace himself by any act of cowardice or maladministration, they do not hesitate to depose him and place a more competent man in his stead. Their laws are such as are adapted to their peculiar situation, and are sanctioned by the voice of the people. Their execution is vested in the subordinate chiefs, or captains, as they are called, and they are promptly and rigidly enforced. In respect to the rights of property, their code is strictly Spartan. They are perhaps as arrant freebooters as can be found upon the face of the earth; and they regard stealing from strangers as perfectly legitimate and honorable, and that man who has been most successful in this is the most highly honored by his tribe; indeed, a young man who has not made one or more of these expeditions into Mexico is held in but little repute. In evidence of this, I was told by an old chief of the Northern Comanches, called Is-sa-keep, that he was the father of four sons, who he said were as fine young men as could be found; that they were a great source of comfort to him in his old age, and could steal more horses than any young men in his band.

As these forays are often attended with much toil and danger, they are called "war expeditions." It not unfrequently happens that but six or eight young men set out upon one of these adventures, and the only outfit each requires is a horse, with the war equipments, consisting of the bow and arrows, lance and shield, with occasionally a gun. Thus prepared, they set out upon a journey of a thousand miles or more, through a perfectly wild and desolate country, dependent for subsistence wholly upon such game as they may chance to find. They make their way to the northern provinces of Mexico, where they lie in wait near some hacienda until a favorable opportunity offers to sweep down upon a solitary herdsman, and, with the most terrific yells, drive before them all the animals they desire. Wo to the panic-stricken ranchero who fails to make a precipitate retreat, as they invariably kill such men as offer the slightest impediment to their operations, and take women and children prisoners, whom they hold in bondage of the most servile character. They are sometimes absent from their tribes two years or more before their success is sufficient to justify their returning with credit to themselves.

The use of the bow, which is the favorite arm and constant appendage of the prairie Indian, and which he makes use of exclusively in hunting the buffalo, is taught the boys at a very early age; and by constant and careful practice, they acquire a degree of proficiency in the art that renders them, when grown up to manhood, formidable in war, as well as successful in the chase. Their bows are made of the tough and elastic wood of the "bois d'arc," or Osage orange (*Maclura aurantiaca*), strengthened and re-enforced with the sinews of the deer wrapped firmly around them, and strung with a cord made of the same material. They are not more than one half the length of the old English long-bow, which was said to have been sixteen hands' breadth in length. The arrows are twenty inches long, of flexible wood, with a triangular point of iron at one end, and two feathers, intersecting each other at right angles, at the opposite extremity. At short distances the bow, in the hands of the Indian, is effective, and frequently throws the arrow entirely through the huge carcass of the buffalo. In using this instrument, the Indian warrior protects himself from the missiles of an enemy with a shield of circular form, covered with two thicknesses of hard, undressed buffalo hide, separated by a space of about an inch, which is stuffed with hair; this is fastened to the left arm by two bands, in such a manner as not to interfere with the free use of the hand, and offers such resistance that a rifle-ball will not penetrate it unless it strikes perpendicular to the surface. They also make use of a war-club, made by bending a withe around a hard stone of about two pounds weight, which has been previously prepared with a groove in which the withe fits, and is thereby prevented from slipping off. The handle is about fourteen inches long, and bound with buffalo hide.

The men are about the medium stature, with bright, copper-colored complexions and intelligent countenances, in many instances with aquiline noses, thin lips, black eyes and hair, with but little beard. They never cut the hair, but wear it of very great length, and ornament it upon state occasions with silver and beads. Their dress consists of leggins and moccasins, with a cloth wrapped around the loins. The body is generally naked above the middle, except when covered with the buffalo robe, which is a constant appendage to their wardrobe. The women are short, with crooked legs, and are obliged to crop their hair close to their heads. They wear, in addition to the leggins and moccasins, a skirt of dressed deer-skin. They also tattoo their faces and breasts, and are far from being as good looking as the men.

Notwithstanding these people are hospitable and kind to strangers, and apparently amiable in their dispositions, yet, when a warrior conceives himself injured, his thirst for revenge knows no satiety. Grave and dignified in his deportment, and priding himself upon his coolness of temper and the control of his passions, yet, when once provoked, he, like the majority of his race, is implacable and unrelenting; an affront is laid up and cherished in his breast, and nothing can efface it from his mind until ample reparation has been made. He has no idea of forgiveness:

the insult must be atoned for by blood. With other tribes, quarrels can often be settled by presents to the injured party; but with the prairie Indians, the law of equity is such that no reconciliation can take place until the reproach is wiped out with the blood of their enemy. They make no use of money except for ornaments. Like other tribes, they are fond of decking themselves with paint, beads, and feathers; and the young warrior often spends more time at his toilet than the most conceited coxcomb that can be found in civilized life. Bright red and blue are their favorite colors; and vermilion is an important article in the stock of goods of one of their traders. This they always carry about their persons; and whenever they expect to meet strangers, they always (provided they have time) make their toilet with care, and paint their faces. Some few of their chiefs who have visited their Great Father at Washington have returned strongly impressed with the numerical power and prosperity of the whites; but the great majority of them, being entirely ignorant of every thing that relates to us, and a portion of them having never even seen a white man, believe the prairie Indians to be the most powerful people in existence; and the relation of facts which conflict with this notion, by their own people, to the masses of the tribes at their prairie firesides, only subjects the narrator to ridicule, and he is set down as one whose brain has been turned by the necromancy of the pale-faces, and is thenceforth regarded as wholly unworthy of confidence.

The Northern and Middle Comanches, as well as the Kioways, Cheyennes, Sioux, and other tribes, subsist almost exclusively upon the flesh of the buffalo, and are known among the Indians as "buffalo eaters;" and they are generally found upon the trails of those animals, migrating with them from place to place, as the seasons come around, over those vast and inhospitable plains of the West, which are, for the most part, not susceptible of cultivation, and seem destined in the future, as in the past, to be the abode of these wandering savages. This barren district, however, exhibits one characteristic which compensates for many of its asperities, as, perhaps, no part of the habitable globe is more favorable to health and the continuation of human existence than this. Free from marshes, stagnant water, great bodies of timber, and all other sources of poisonous malaria, and open to every wind that blows, this immense grassy expanse is purged from impurities of every kind, and the air imparts a force and vigor to the body and mind which repays the occupant in a great measure for his deprivations. Nature, which almost every where exhibits some compensation to man for great hardships, has here conferred upon him health, the first and best of her gifts. It is a fact worthy of remark that man, in whatever situation he may be placed, is influenced in his modes of existence, his physical and moral condition, by the natural resources of climate, soil, and other circumstances around him, over the operations of which he has no control. Fortunately, such is the flexibility of his nature that he soon learns to adapt himself to the hardest and most untoward circumstances, and, indeed, ultimately becomes not only reconciled to his lot, but persuades himself that his condition is far preferable to that of most others.

The example of our Western-border settlers is illustrative of this fact, as they continue to move farther and farther west as the settlements encroach upon them, preferring a life of dangerous adventure and solitude to personal security and the comforts and enjoyments of society; and what was at first necessity to them becomes in time a source of excitement and pleasure.

The nomadic Indian of the prairies demonstrates the position still more forcibly; free as the boundless plains over which he roams, he neither knows nor wants any luxuries beyond what he finds in the buffalo or the deer around him. These serve him with food, clothing, and a covering for his lodge, and he sighs not for the titles and distinctions which occupy the thoughts and engage the energies of civilized man. His only ambition consists in being able to cope successfully with his enemy in war, and in managing his steed with unfailing adroitness. He is in the saddle from boyhood to old age, and his favorite horse is his constant companion. It is when mounted that the prairie warrior exhibits himself to the best advantage; here he is at home, and his skill in various manœuvres which he makes available in battle—such as throwing himself entirely upon one side of his horse, and discharging his arrows with great rapidity toward the opposite side from beneath the animal's neck while he is at full speed—is truly astonishing. Many of the women are equally expert, as equestrians, with the men. They ride upon the same saddles and in the same manner, with a leg upon each side of the horse. As an example of their skill in horsemanship, two young women of one of the bands of the Northern Comanches, while we were encamped near them, upon seeing some antelopes at a distance from their camp, mounted horses, and, with lassos in their hands, set off at full speed in pursuit of this fleetest inhabitant of the plains. After pursuing them for some distance, and taking all the advantages which their circuitous course permitted, they finally came near them, and, throwing the lasso with unerring precision, secured each an animal, and brought it back in triumph to the camp. Every warrior has his war-horse, which is the fleetest that can be obtained, and he prizes him more highly than any thing else in his possession, and it is seldom that he can be induced to part with him at any price. He never mounts him except when going into battle, the buffalo chase, or upon state occasions. On his return from an excursion he is met at the door of his lodge by one of his wives, who takes his horse and attends to its wants with the utmost care. The prairie warrior performs no menial labor; his only occupation is in war and the chase. His wives, who are but little dearer to him than his horse, perform all the drudgery. He follows the chase, he smokes his pipe, he eats and sleeps; and thus he passes his time, and in his own estimation he is the most lordly and independent sovereign in the universe.

The mode of life of the prairie tribes, owing to their unsettled and wandering habits, is such as to render their condition one of constant danger and apprehension. The security of their numerous animals from the encroachments of their enemies, and their constant liability to attacks, make it imperatively necessary for them to be at all times upon the alert. Their details for herdsmen are made with as much regularity as the guard details at a military post; and even in times of the most profound peace, they guard their animals both night and day, while scouts are often patrolling upon the adjoining heights to give notice of the approach of strangers, when their animals are hurried to a place of security, and every thing made ready for defense. The manner in which they salute a stranger is somewhat peculiar, as my own reception at one of their encampments will show. The chief at this encampment was a very corpulent old man, with exceedingly scanty attire, who, immediately on our approach, declared himself a great friend of the Americans, and persisted in giving me evidence of his sincerity by an embrace, which, to please him, I forced myself to submit to, although it was far from agreeable to my own feelings. Seizing me in his brawny arms while we were yet in the saddle, and laying his greasy head upon my shoulder, he inflicted upon me a most bruin-like squeeze, which I endured with a degree of patient fortitude worthy of the occasion; and I was consoling myself upon the completion of the salutation, when the savage again seized me in his arms, and I was doomed to another similar torture, with his head on my other shoulder, while at the same time he rubbed his greasy face against mine in the most affectionate manner; all of which proceeding, he gave me to understand, was to be regarded as a most distinguished and signal mark of affection for the American people in general, whom, as he expressed it, he loved so much that it almost broke his heart; and in particular for myself, who, as their representative, can bear testimony to the strength of his attachment. On leaving his camp, the chief shook me heartily by the hand, telling me at the same time that he was not a Comanche, but an American; and as I did not feel disposed to be outdone in politeness by an Indian, I replied in the same spirit that there was not a drop of Anglo-Saxon blood in my veins, but that I was wholly and absolutely a Comanche, at which he seemed delighted, duly understanding and appreciating the compliment. These people are hospitable and kind to all with whom they are not at war; and on the arrival of a stranger at their camps a lodge is prepared for him, and he is entertained as long as he chooses to remain among them. They are also kind and affectionate to each other, and as long as any thing comestible remains in the camp, all are permitted to share alike; but with these exceptions, they are possessed of but few virtues. Polygamy is sanctioned, and is very common among them, every man being allowed as many wives as he can support.

A few years ago the Comanches (for what reason I could not learn) took an inveterate dislike to the negroes, and massacred several small parties of those who attempted to escape from the Seminoles and cross the Plains for the purpose of joining Wild Cat upon the Rio Grande. Upon inquiring of them the cause of their hostility to the blacks, they replied that it was because they were slaves to the whites; that they were sorry for them. I suspect, however, that they were actuated by other motives than they cared about acknowledging, and that instead of wishing to better their condition by sending them to another world, where they would be released from the fetters of bondage, they were apprehensive, if they permitted them to pass quietly, that in time Wild Cat's followers upon the Rio Grande would augment to such a degree that he would interfere with their marauding operations along the Mexican borders. These people, who are so extremely jealous of their own freedom that they will often commit suicide rather than be taken prisoners, are the more prone to enslave others, and this dominant principle is carried to the greatest extreme so far as regards their women. A beast of burden and a slave to the will of her brutal master, yet, strange as it may appear, the woman seems contented with her lot, and submits to her fate without a murmur. The hardships imposed upon the females are most severe and cruel. The distance of rank and consideration which exists between the black slave and his master is not greater than between the prairie warrior and his wife. Every degrading office that is imposed upon the black by the most tyrannical master, falls, among these people, to the lot of the wretched female. They, in common with other Indians, are not a prolific race; indeed, it is seldom that a woman has more than three or four children. Many of these, owing to unavoidable exposure, die young; the boys, however, are nurtured with care, and treated with great kindness by their mothers, while the girls are frequently beaten and abused unmercifully. I have never seen an idiot, or one that was naturally deformed, among them.

Of all the Indians I had before encountered, there were none who had not an extreme fondness for spirituous liquors. The prairie tribes that I have seen say the taste of such liquor is not pleasant, that it makes fools of them, and that they do not desire it. If there are exceptions to this, I think they may be set down as factitious rather than natural, the appetite having been created by occasional indulgence in the use of a little at a time.

Their diet is very simple; as I said before, from infancy to old age, their only food, with the exception of a few wild plants which they find on the prairies, is fresh meat, of which, in times of plenty, they consume enormous quantities. In common with many other tribes, they can, when necessity demands it, abstain from eating for several days without inconvenience, and they are enabled to make up at one meal the deficiency. All of them are extravagantly fond of tobacco, which they use for smoking, mixed with the dried leaves of the sumach, inhaling the smoke into their lungs, and giving it out through their nostrils. Their language is verbal and pantomimic. The former consists of a very limited number of words, some of which are common to all the prairie tribes. The latter is used and understood with great facility and accuracy by all the tribes from the Gila to the Columbia, the motions and signs to express ideas being common to all.

This pantomimic vocabulary, which is exceedingly graceful and significant, when oral communication is impracticable, constitutes the court language of the Plains; and, what was a fact of much astonishment to me, I discovered that it was nearly the same as that practiced by the mutes in one of our deaf and dumb institutions that I visited. For example, there were some five or six boys directed to take their places at the black-boards and interpret what I proposed to say. I then, by pantomimic signs, told them that

I went on a buffalo hunt, saw a herd, chased them on horseback, fired my gun and killed one, cut it up, ate some of the meat, and went to sleep—every word of which was written down upon the black-board by each boy as rapidly as the signs were made, excepting that all made the common mistake of taking the buffalo for deer.

The name of each tribe of Indians has a signification, which is represented by a sign that is well understood by them all.

The Comanche, or "Snake," is indicated by making with the hand a waving motion, in imitation of the crawling of the reptile.

The Cheyenne, or "Cut Arm," by drawing the hand across the arm to imitate cutting it with a knife.

The Arapahoes, or "Smellers," by seizing the nose with the thumb and forefinger.

The Sioux, or "Cut-throats," by drawing the hand across the throat.

The Pawnees, or "Wolves," by placing a hand on each side of the forehead, with two fingers pointing to the front, to represent the narrow, sharp ears of the wolf.

The Crows, by imitating the flapping of the bird's wings with the palms of the hands.

On approaching strangers the prairie Indians put their horses at full speed, and persons not familiar with their peculiarities and habits might interpret this as an act of hostility; but it is their custom with friends as well as enemies, and should not occasion groundless alarm.

When a party is discovered approaching thus, and are near enough to distinguish signals, all that is necessary in order to ascertain their disposition is to raise the right hand with the palm in front, and gradually push it forward and back several times. They all understand this to be a command to halt, and if they are not hostile it will at once be obeyed.

After they have stopped, the right hand is raised again as before, and slowly moved to the right and left, which signifies "I do not know you. Who are you?" They will then answer the inquiry by giving their signal. If this should not be understood, they may be asked if they are friends by raising both hands grasped in the manner of shaking hands, or by locking the two forefingers firmly while the hands are held up. If friendly, they will respond with the same signal; but if enemies, they will probably disregard the command to halt, or give the signal of anger by closing the hand, placing it against the forehead, and turning it back and forth while in that position.

No people, probably, on the face of the earth are more ambitious of martial fame, or entertain a higher appreciation for the deeds of a daring and successful warrior than the North American savages of the Plains. The attainment of such reputation is the paramount and absorbing object of their lives; all their aspirations for distinction invariably take this channel of expression. A young man is never considered worthy to occupy a seat in council until he has encountered an enemy in battle, and he who can count the greatest number of scalps is the most highly honored by his tribe. This idea is inculcated from their earliest infancy. It is not surprising, therefore, that with such weighty inducements before him, the young man who, as yet, has gained no renown as a brave or warrior, should be less discriminate in his attacks than older men who have already acquired a name. The young braves should, therefore, be closely watched when encountered on the Plains.

The prairie tribes are seldom at peace with all their neighbors, and some of the young braves of a tribe are almost always absent upon a war excursion. These forays sometimes extend into the heart of the northern states of Mexico, where the Indians have carried on successful invasions for many years. They have devastated and depopulated a great part of Sonora and Chihuahua. The objects of these forays are to steal horses and mules, and to take prisoners; and if it so happens that a war-party has been unsuccessful in the accomplishment of these ends, or has had the misfortune to lose some of its number in battle, they become reckless, and will often attack a small party with whom they are not at war, provided they hope to escape detection. The disgrace attendant upon a return to their friends without some trophies as an offset to the loss of their comrades is a powerful incentive to action, and they extend but little mercy to defenseless travelers who have the misfortune to encounter them at such a conjuncture.

While *en route* from New Mexico to Arkansas in 1849 I was encamped near the head of the Colorado River, and wishing to know the character of the country for a few miles in advance of our position, I desired an officer to go out and make the reconnoissance. I was lying sick in my bed at the time, or I should have performed the duty myself. I expected the officer would have taken an escort with him, but he omitted to do so, and started off alone. After proceeding a short distance he discovered four mounted Indians coming at full speed directly toward him, when, instead of turning his own horse toward camp, and endeavoring to make his escape (he was well mounted), or halting and assuming a defensive attitude, he deliberately rode up to them; after which the tracks indicated that they proceeded about three miles together, when the Indians most brutally killed and scalped my most unfortunate but too credulous friend, who might probably have saved his life had he not, in the kindness of his excellent heart, imagined that the savages would reciprocate his friendly advances. He was most woefully mistaken, and his life paid the forfeit of his generous and noble disposition.

I have never been able to get any positive information as to the persons who committed this murder, yet circumstances render it highly probable that they were a party of young Indians who were returning from an unsuccessful foray, and they were unable to resist the temptation of taking the scalp and horse of the lieutenant.

A small number of white men, in traveling upon the Plains, should not allow a party of strange Indians to approach them unless able to resist an attack under the most unfavorable circumstances.

It is a safe rule, when a man finds himself alone in the prairies, and sees a party of Indians approaching, not to allow them to come near him, and if they persist in so doing, to signal them to keep away. If they do not obey, and he be mounted upon a fleet horse, he should make for the nearest timber. If the Indians follow and press him too closely, he should halt, turn around, and point his gun at the foremost, which will often have the effect of turning them back, but he should never draw trigger unless he finds that his life depends upon the shot; for, as soon as his gun is discharged, his sole dependence, unless he have time to reload, must be upon the speed of his horse.

The Indians of the Plains, notwithstanding the encomiums that have been heaped upon their brethren who formerly occupied the Eastern States for their gratitude, have not, so far as I have observed, the most distant conception of that sentiment. You may confer numberless benefits upon them for years, and the more that is done for them the more they will expect. They do not seem to comprehend the motive which dictates an act of benevolence or charity, and they invariably attribute it to fear or the ex-

KEEP AWAY!

pectation of reward. When they make a present, it is with a view of getting more than its equivalent in return.

I have never yet been able to discover that the Western wild tribes possessed any of those attributes which among civilized nations are regarded as virtues adorning the human character. They have yet to be taught the first rudiments of civilization, and they are at this time as far from any knowledge of Christianity, and as worthy subjects for missionary enterprise, as the most untutored natives of the South Sea Islands.

The only way to make these merciless freebooters fear or respect the authority of our government is, when they misbehave, first of all to chastise them well by striking such a blow as will be felt for a long time, and thus show them that we are superior to them in war. They will then respect us much more than when their good-will is purchased with presents.

The opinion of a friend of mine (Jim Baker), who has passed the last twenty-five years of his life among the Indians of the Rocky Mountains, corroborates the opinions I have advanced upon this head, and although I do not endorse all of his sentiments, yet many of them are deduced from long and matured experience and critical observation. He says:

"They are the most onsartainest varmints in all creation, and I reckon tha'r not mor'n half human; for you never seed a human, arter you'd fed and treated him to the best fixins in your lodge, jist turn round and steal all your horses, or ary other thing he could lay his hands on. No, not adzackly. He would feel kinder grateful, and ask you to spread a blanket in his lodge ef you ever passed that a-way. But the Injun he don't care shucks for you, and is ready to do you a heap of mischief as soon as he quits your feed. No, Cap.," he continued, "it's not the right way to give um presents to buy peace; but ef I war governor of these yeer United States, I'll tell you what I'd do. I'd invite um all to a big feast, and make b'lieve I wanted to have a big talk; and as soon as I got um all together, I'd pitch in and sculp about half of um, and then t'other half would be mighty glad to make a peace that would stick. That's the way I'd make a treaty with the dog'ond, red-bellied varmints; and as sure as you're born, Cap., that's the only way."

I suggested to him the idea that there would be a lack of good faith and honor in such a proceeding, and that it would be much more in accordance with my notions of fair dealing to meet them openly in the field, and there endeavor to punish them if they deserve it. To this he replied:

"Tain't no use to talk about honor with them, Cap.; they hain't got no such thing in um; and they won't show fair fight, any way you can fix it. Don't they kill and sculp a white man when-ar they get the better on him? The mean varmints, they'll never behave themselves until you give um a clean out-and-out licking. They can't onderstand white folks' ways, and they won't learn um; and ef you treat um decently, they think you are afeard. You may depend on't, Cap., the only way to treat Injuns is to thrash them well at first, then the balance will sorter take to you and behave themselves."

It is highly important to every man passing through a country frequented by Indians to know some of their habits, customs, and propensities, as this will facilitate his intercourse with friendly tribes, and enable him, when he wishes to avoid a conflict, to take precautions against coming in collision with those who are hostile.

Almost every tribe has its own way of constructing its lodges, encamping, making fires, its own style of dress, by some of which peculiarities the experienced frontiersman can generally distinguish them.

The Osages, for example, make their lodges in the shape of a wagon-top, of bent rods or willows covered with skins, blankets, or the bark of trees.

The Kickapoo lodges are made in an oval form, something like a rounded haystack, of poles set in the ground, bent over, and united at top; this is covered with cloths or bark.

The Witchetaws, Wacos, Towackanies, and Tonkawas erect their hunting lodges of sticks put up in the form of the frustum of a cone and covered with brush.

All these tribes leave the frame-work of their lodges standing when they move from camp to camp, and this, of course, indicates the particular tribe that erected them.

The Delawares and Shawnees plant two upright forked poles, place a stick across them, and stretch a canvas covering over it, in the same manner as with the "*tente d'abri.*"

The Sioux, Arapahoes, Cheyennes, Utes, Snakes, Blackfeet, and Kioways, make use of the Comanche lodge, covered with dressed buffalo hides.

All the prairie Indians I have met with are the most inveterate beggars. They will flock around strangers, and, in the most importunate manner, ask for every thing they see, especially tobacco and sugar; and, if allowed, they will handle, examine, and occasionally pilfer such things as happen to take their fancy. The proper way to treat them is to give them at once such articles as are to be disposed of, and then, in a firm and decided manner, let them understand that they are to receive nothing else.

A party of Keechis once visited my camp with their principal chief, who said he had some important business to discuss, and demanded a council with the *capitan*. After consent had been given, he assembled his principal men, and, going through the usual preliminary of taking a *big smoke*, he arose, and with a great deal of ceremony commenced his pompous and flowery speech, which, like all others of a similar character, amounted to nothing, until he touched upon the real object of his visit. He said he had traveled a long distance over the prairies to see and have a talk with his white brothers; that his people were very hungry and naked. He then approached me with six small sticks, and, after shaking hands, laid one of the sticks in my hand, which he said represented sugar, another signified tobacco, and the other four, pork, flour, whisky, and blankets, all of which he assured me his people were in great need of, and must have. His talk was then concluded, and he sat down, apparently much gratified with the graceful and impressive manner with which he had executed his part of the performance.

It then devolved upon me to respond to the brilliant effort of the prairie orator, which I did in something like the following manner. After imitating his style for a short time, I closed my remarks by telling him that we were poor infantry soldiers, who were always obliged to go on foot; that we had become very tired of walking, and would like very much to ride. Furthermore, I had observed that they had among them many fine horses and mules. I then took two small sticks, and imitating as nearly as possible the manner of the chief, placed one in his hand, which I told him was nothing more nor less than a first-rate horse, and then the other, which signified a good large mule. I closed by saying that I was ready to exchange presents whenever it suited his convenience.

They looked at each other for some time without speaking, but finally got up and walked away, and I was not troubled with them again.

CHAPTER II.

COMANCHE INDIANS.

Comanche Indians.—Local Subdivisions of the Tribe.—Nomads.—Diminishing in Numbers.—Fear of visiting the Whites.—Courtship.—Polygamy.—Is-sa-keep.—Receiving Guests.—Council.—Singular Custom.—Propensity for Horse-racing.—Kickapoo Horse-race.—War Expeditions.—Method of Recruiting.—Mexican Prisoners.—Parker Family.—Treatment of Negroes.—Visit to the Fort.—Mourning Ceremonies.—Ideas of the Bible.—Opinion of the Whites.—Medicine Lodges.—Ideas of their own Importance.—Way to treat them.—Belief in the Deity.

Of all the prairie tribes, with perhaps the exception of the Dacotahs or Sioux, the Comanches are the most numerous and warlike. They have been variously estimated as numbering from 12,000 to 18,000 souls; probably the former is nearest the truth. They have three local grand divisions, namely, the Northern, Middle, and Southern, and designated by them as Tennawas, Yamparacks, and Comanches. These are subdivided into smaller bands, each having its separate chief or captain.

The division of the nation known as the "Southern Comanches" remains permanently within the limits of the territory pertaining to Texas. It consists of two bands, each of which has its principal and subordinate chiefs, and they do not of late years acknowledge the sovereignty of a common ruler and leader in their united councils nor in war. The names of their two principal chiefs were in 1854 "Senaco" and "Ketumsee." The aggregate number in the two bands at that period was about 1100 souls.

These people lead a predatory and pastoral life, roving

from place to place in search of game for their own subsistence and grass for their animals. Their range extends from the Red River to the Colorado. In the summer they are sometimes found upon the former stream, but the winters are always passed upon the waters of the Brazos and Colorado, where the grass remains fresh and green during the winter season, and the climate is mild and agreeable.

As the buffaloes have entirely abandoned their hunting grounds, and do not now extend their migrations south of Red River in this direction, and as these Indians do not venture to cross that stream in pursuit of them, they derive no sustenance from the flesh of these animals, or clothing from their skins, and they are reduced to the necessity of depending upon the deer and antelope for food and raiment. Fortunately, in this mild and genial climate they require but little clothing.

In a country like theirs, where the game is by no means abundant, the means for sustaining life are exceedingly precarious and uncertain, and the Indians who depend exclusively upon the fruits of the chase are often subjected to great privations and sufferings; and were it not for their horses and mules, which are made use of for food when nothing else can be obtained, many of them would perish from hunger. They formerly possessed great numbers of these animals, but they are rapidly diminishing, and I observed a very sensible decrease in five years.

They have lived so long near the border white settlers that they are familiar with many of their customs and habits, but, like their red kindred in other places, they unfortunately only see fit to adopt such as are detrimental to them. They are becoming addicted to the use of that bane of their race, ardent spirits, and are much more idle and licentious than before they came in contact with the pale-faces. Diseases induced by their immoral practices, with the almost continual wars in which they have been engaged, have probably contributed largely to the great aggregate of mortality among them. They themselves acknowledge that their numbers are rapidly diminishing, and that it is only a few years since they were much more populous than at present. Many of them have the discernment to foresee that the only means by which they can preserve their identity as a nation, for any great length of time, is in an immediate abandonment of their present nomadic life, and the adoption of agricultural habits.

It can not be expected that the male adults of the present generation will cast aside their national prejudices against tilling the soil (which they regard as the occupation of a slave), and at once fall into habits of industry; but may it not be hoped that the women and children can be taught the rudiments of agriculture, and the next generations derive profit therefrom?

The "Middle Comanches," as their designation implies, occupy the country lying between the other divisions of the tribe. There are two bands in this branch of the nation, called "No-co-nies" and "Ten-na-was." Their principal chiefs are named "Pah-hah-eu-ka," "Po-hah-cot-o-wit," and "Choice."

From the best information that can be obtained, they are supposed to number about 3500 souls. They spend the winters in Northwestern Texas, and in the summer move north, across the Red and Canadian Rivers, toward the Arkansas, in pursuit of the buffaloes. They migrate with the game and seasons. They are more in a state of nature than the Southern Comanches, still using the buffalo skin for a covering, and seldom visiting the white settlements.

They are on terms of peace and friendship with their neighboring brethren on either side of them, and seem to form an intermediate connecting link between them.

They interchange visits with their neighbors, and one of their sub-chiefs was present with them when they met us upon the Brazos.

They have occasionally seen the white traders, and a few of them have visited some of the outer settlements upon the Colorado, but they generally have but a very vague conception of the customs, numbers, and power of the whites. Some years since I chanced to meet with one of their chiefs at a trading-post near the Canadian. He had left his band on Red River, and come in alone to visit a Cherokee trader, and stated that he had endeavored to prevail upon some of his people to accompany him, but they all declined, upon the supposition that he was embarking upon a desperate expedition, where his life would be placed in imminent jeopardy, and they were not disposed to encounter the risks attending such a reckless adventure.

The "Northern Comanches" are much more wild than either of the others we have spoken of. Through summer and winter they range the plains upon the trails of the buffaloes. At one time their larder is overstocked and they gorge themselves to repletion, while at another time they are famishing for the aliment necessary to sustain life. All of them are alike a race of hunters, depending from day to day upon the results of the chase.

The country they inhabit extends from the Arkansas to Red River, and it is but seldom that they have met with any whites, and when I saw them in 1849 none of them had ever seen a house, with the exception of a few who had been in Mexico.

Although I have not been able to obtain sufficient data to enable me to arrive at any thing like a satisfactory estimate of the numbers of this branch of the nation, yet there is no doubt that they greatly exceed the aggregate of the other two.

COMANCHE LODGE.

The Comanches suppose their original progenitors came from the west.

Polygamy is prevalent among them, every man having as many wives as he can support.

Their courtship is as brief as it is peculiar. When he desires to marry, the suitor provides himself with horses, and such goods as he thinks will be acceptable to the father of his intended, takes them to the lodge occupied by the head of the family, and then seats himself near by to await the result of the negotiation. The father then comes out, examines what has been offered, and, if it is satisfactory, leads out his daughter and hands her over to the bridegroom, and the marriage ceremony is completed. The girl has no voice in the matter, and has no alternative but to submit to the decision of her father.

This summary method of match-making often leads to family dissension; and as young girls are often compelled to unite their fortunes with old men, this not unfrequently results in subsequent elopements with younger lovers. In such cases, the husband pursues the truants; and their former practice authorized him, in case he overtook them, to put them to death; but now they generally compromise the matter by an equivalent in horses, after which the girl becomes the property of her lover.

Ketumsee, the chief of one of the bands of Southern Comanches, a man at least sixty years old, had four wives, the eldest of whom was not over twenty years of age. They seemed very fond of the old man, and would sit by the hour combing his hair and caressing him. I showed one of them a photographic likeness of my wife, which seemed to interest her very much, and she frequently requested me to allow her to look at it afterward. She seemed to imagine that it was living, and would point to the eyes and smile, as much as to say it could see.

I upon one occasion asked her how she would like to leave Ketumsee and go home with me. She in reply pointed to the photograph, and drew her other hand across her throat, most significantly indicating that, in her judgment, my house would be any thing but a safe place for her, and as I was rather inclined to the same opinion myself, I did not feel disposed to discuss the subject any farther.

It was formerly regarded by the Comanches as an essential part of genuine hospitality that their guests should have wives assigned to them during their stay in camp. This custom, however, is now pretty much abandoned. In 1849, while *en route* to New Mexico, I met with a very large band of Northern Comanches, commanded by a venerable old chief called Is-sa-keep (Wolf's Shoulder). He requested us to encamp at a certain place, as he wished to hold a council with us. I complied with his request, and the next morning he, with about a dozen of his principal men, dressed and painted in the most fantastic manner, rode into our camp with great pomp and ceremony, dismounted at my tent, and after embracing me *à la Mexicano* (only, to use a trite phrase, "a good deal more so," as they nearly squeezed the breath out of my body), they seated themselves around the door of my tent, and intimated that they were ready for a "big talk." I informed them that we were escorting emigrants to California, and that in all probability many more would, from time to time, travel over the same road, and that our authorities would hold them responsible if these people were molested. I also informed them that our government, by treaty with Mexico, had obligated itself to put a stop to farther depredations upon the people of that country by Indians living within our territory, and that all Mexican prisoners in their hands must be turned over to our authorities forthwith, etc.

Is-sa-keep replied that the talk was very good except in the two particulars of horse-stealing and returning prisoners, which made him very sad.

After the council was concluded I mixed a glass of weak brandy toddy and offered it to the chief. He tasted the beverage and passed it to the next, and from him it went around the entire circle, all the Indians taking a sip, but at the same time making grimaces, as if it was not pleasant. The glass was handed back to me by the chief, with the remark that it was not good, as it took away their senses and made fools of them.

Shortly after this I observed my interpreter, Black Beaver, engaged in quite an animated discussion with the chief, which led me to inquire what they were talking about. At this time there were probably five hundred emigrants and soldiers collected directly around our circle, all manifesting the utmost curiosity to hear every thing that was said. Beaver, in reply to my question, then said, "He say, captain, he bring two wife for you," pointing to two girls who were sitting near by. I was a good deal embarrassed at such a proposition, made in presence of so large an assembly, but told Beaver to inform the chief that this was not in accordance with the customs of the white people; that they only had one wife at home, and were not at all disposed to marry others when abroad. This was interpreted to Is-sa-keep, and, after a brief consultation, Beaver interpreted, "He say, captain, you the strangest man he never see; every man he seen before, when he been travlin' long time, the fust thing he want, *wife.*"

Lieutenant John Buford (afterward General Buford), who was attached to my command at this time, had, just previous to our departure from Arkansas, received from his uncle in Kentucky a present of one of the finest of his large stud of thorough-bred horses, and he had taken great pains to keep him up in good running condition during our trip. He had heard of the inveterate propensity of the Comanches for horse-racing, and expected they might be disposed to try the speed of some of their own animals with his. As we were all anxious to witness the comparative racing qualities of the full-blooded stock and the Indian horses, we inquired of the chief if he was inclined to enter any of his horses against that of the lieutenant. He said he was very fond of the sport, but that, unfortunately, all of their fleetest horses were then absent on a buffalo hunt; but if, on our return, we still wished to try the experiment, he would willingly bet as many horses as we chose to risk upon the result, provided we would consent to run fourteen miles.

The race did not, therefore, come off at that time, but Beaver seemed to be fully impressed with the conviction that if it had, our thoroughbred would have been beaten.

As an evidence in favor of this supposition, he said he once accompanied a party of Kickapoos, who had purchased a very fleet race-horse from a white man in Missouri, and took him a long distance out into the Plains for the express purpose of running him against the Comanche horses. They conducted him very carefully, packing grain for him the entire distance, and took with them a large number of other horses to wager with Comanches, and they all expected confidently to make a good speculation.

They arrived at the Comanche camp, and made bets of all their horses and their blankets, and the preliminaries of the contest were satisfactorily arranged for all parties. Beaver, who was the guest of the principal chief, felt the most perfect confidence, and was disposed to venture every thing he possessed, but his host endeavored to dissuade him from betting on the race at all, telling him he would be certain to lose his property. He persisted, however, and the chief took all his bets. The race was run, and, to the astonishment and discomfiture of the Kickapoos, their horse was badly beaten. The magnanimous chief then told Beaver to take back his horses, and never again to venture in a speculation, the success of which depended upon beating the Comanches in horse-racing.

The vanquished sportsmen, with the single exception of my friend Beaver, returned home on foot, partially deprived of their clothing, and a good deal chopfallen, and, as I understand, resolved from thenceforth never to repeat the experiment.

WAR EXPEDITIONS.

When a chief desires to organize a war-party, he provides himself with a long pole, attaches a red flag to the end of it, and trims the top with eagle feathers. He then mounts his horse in his war costume, and rides around through the camp singing the war-song. Those who are disposed to join the expedition mount their horses and fall into the procession; after parading about for a time, all dismount, and the war-dance is performed. This ceremony is continued from day to day until a sufficient number of volunteers are found to accomplish the objects desired, when they set out for the theatre of their intended exploits.

As they proceed upon their expedition, it sometimes happens that the chief with whom it originated, and who invariably assumes the command, becomes discouraged at not finding an opportunity of displaying his warlike abilities, and abandons the enterprise; in which event, if others of the party desire to proceed farther, they select another leader and push on, and thus so long as any one of the party holds out.

A war-party is sometimes absent for a great length of time, and for days, weeks, and months their friends at home anxiously await their return, until suddenly, from afar, the shrill war-cry of an *avant courier* is heard proclaiming the approach of the victorious warriors. The camp is in an instant alive with excitement and commotion. Men, women, and children swarm out to meet the advancing party. Their white horses are painted and decked out in the most fantastic style, and led in advance of the triumphant procession; and, as they pass around through the village, the old women set up a most unearthly howl of exultation, after which the scalp-dance is performed with all the pomp and display their limited resources admit of, the warriors having their faces painted black.

When, on the other hand, the expedition terminates disastrously by the loss of some of the party in battle, the relatives of the deceased cut off their own hair and the tails and manes of their horses as symbols of mourning, and howl and cry for a long time.

The Comanches always have among them Mexican prisoners, whom they have captured when they were young children, and have raised and adopted into the nation. They seem readily to embrace the habits of the Indians, and intermarry with them.

I had in my employ for some considerable time a young man named Parker, who, with a sister, were captured by the Comanches on the borders of Texas when they were only six or eight years old. The Indians murdered all the family with the exception of these two children and their mother; the latter, fortunately, was absent from home at the time. They carried the children away to their prairie haunts, where they kept them for several years, until at length a Delaware trader purchased the boy and brought him to Fort Gibson, from whence he was sent home to his mother's house. She was, of course, greatly rejoiced to see him again, but deplored the loss of her daughter, and prevailed upon the young man to return into the Plains, hunt up the Comanches, and endeavor to purchase his sister from them.

He went, found the camp, and used every argument in his power to prevail upon his sister to leave the Indians and return home with him, but it was of no avail. She told him that she knew no mother except her adopted Indian parent; that her husband, children, and friends, and all else that she held dear on earth, were there, and there she was resolved to remain for the remainder of her life. He left her and returned home alone, and, if she is living, she is probably with the savages yet.

A few years since there was another white man living in Western Texas who was captured by the Comanches when a small boy, and lived with them until he was grown up. On his return to his relatives he had become so thoroughly *Comancheized* that, at times when he felt hungry, he would take his rifle, go out into his father's pasture, shoot down an ox, and, after cutting off a steak, build a fire, and cook it on a stick, leaving the remainder for the wolves; and it was some considerable time before his family could convince him of the impropriety of this improvident proceeding.

A Delaware trader, in 1850, brought into the settlements two negro girls which he had obtained from the Comanches. It appeared that they had been with a number of Seminole negroes who attempted to cross the Plains to join Wild Cat upon the Rio Grande.

The party had been intercepted by the Indians, and every one, with the exception of these two girls, put to death. They were taken to the camp, where the most inhuman barbarities were perpetrated upon them. Among other fiendish atrocities, the savages scraped through their skin into the flesh, believing that beneath the cuticle the flesh was black like the color upon the exterior. They burned them with live coals to ascertain whether fire produced the same sensations of pain as with their own people, and tried various other experiments which were attended with most acute torture. The poor girls were shockingly scarred and mutilated when I saw them.

While I was stationed at Camp Arbuckle, on the Canadian River, in 1850, a band of prairie Indians came in to see us, and, as this was probably the first time they had ever entered a white man's habitation, every thing was novel to them, and their curiosity was very much excited. The chief examined various articles of furniture, books, and pictures, but nothing seemed to attract his attention so much as an oil-cloth rug upon the floor. It was covered with bright colors, which appeared to take his fancy amazingly, and he scrutinized it very closely. He scraped it with his finger nails, and, wetting his fingers, tried to wash off the coloring; and, after he had seen all that interested him, inquired if the President had sent me all those things from Washington. My wife showed him specimens of embroidery, which pleased him so much that he paid her the compliment of proposing to exchange wives with me, and, upon my referring him to her for a decision, he informed me that he was not in the habit of trading with squaws, but if I would only say the word, he was ready to *swap* right off.

When a Comanche warrior dies, he is buried on the summit of a high hill, in a sitting posture, with his face to the east, and his buffalo robe and all his scanty wardrobe with him. His best horses and all his war implements are killed and destroyed, and the remainder of his animals have their manes and tails shaved close, and the women of the family crop their hair as a symbol of affliction and mourning. After the death the relatives and friends of the deceased assemble morning and evening outside the camp, where they cry and cut themselves with knives for half an hour or more; and this sometimes lasts for a month.

When any person dies the corpse is buried immediately. The death of a young warrior is always greatly lamented, and the mourning ceremonies continue a long time; but when an old man dies they only mourn for him a few days, upon the principle that his services were no longer useful to his people.

In 1849 I met with the widow of a prominent chief of the Southern Comanches, "Santa Ana," who had then been dead about three years; yet she still continued the mourning ceremonies, and every evening, just before sunset, she could be seen on a hill adjacent to the camp crying and howling most piteously. This woman possessed a large number of very valuable horses and mules, and she had received several very advantageous offers to renew matrimonial relations with leading men of the tribe, but she declined them all, and seemed devoted to the memory of her departed husband.

She did not associate much with the men, but pitched her lodge at a distance from all others; and I was informed that there was no man in the tribe who could excel her in hunting. She was said to have killed in one morning near Fort Chadbourn fourteen deer.

She was one of the most dignified and distinguished-looking persons we saw in the tribe.

These Indians believe that all, after death, go to a place in the spirit world where there is no scarcity of buffalo, and where their condition is supremely happy provided they have taken a plenty of scalps and stolen a goodly number of horses in this world. They also believe that the Great Spirit permits them to revisit the earth in the night-time, but requires them to return to the spirit hunting-grounds before the dawn of day.

While with the Southern Comanches I showed a Bible to Senaco, and endeavored, through the medium of a good interpreter, to make him comprehend its import. Among other things, I stated to him that it was a talk which had been communicated to our forefathers by the Great Spirit, and by them carefully handed down from generation to generation to us.

I then asked him if his people had ever heard of this book before. He answered in the negative, and added that in his opinion this talk emanated from the God of the white man, as the Comanches' God was so far distant in the sky that they could not hear him speak, and when they wished to communicate with him they were obliged to do it through the medium of the sun, which they could see and hold converse with.

They are desirous of procuring from whomsoever they meet testimonials of their good behavior, which they preserve with great care, and exhibit upon all occasions to strangers as a guarantee of future good conduct.

On meeting with a chief of the Southern Comanches in 1849, after going through the usual ceremony of embracing, and assuring me that he was the best friend the Americans ever had among the Indians, he exhibited numerous certificates from the different white men he had met with, testifying to his friendly disposition. Among these was one that he desired me to read with special attention, as he said he was of the opinion that perhaps it might not be so complimentary in its character as some of the others. It was in these words:

"The bearer of this says he is a Comanche chief, named Senaco; that he is the biggest Indian and best friend the whites ever had; in fact, that he is a first-rate fellow; but I believe he is a d—d rascal, *so look out for him.*"

I smiled on reading the paper, and, looking up, found the

chief's eyes intently fixed upon mine with an expression of the most earnest inquiry. I told him the paper was not as good as it might be, whereupon he destroyed it.

Five years after this interview I met Senaco again near the same place. He recognized me at once, and, much to my surprise, pronounced my name quite distinctly.

These Indians, like most others, are accustomed, in their diplomatic intercourse, to exchange presents, and they seem to have no idea of friendship unaccompanied by a substantial token in this form. Moreover, they measure the strength of the attachment of their friends by the magnitude of the presents they receive. In the talk which I held with Is-sa-keep, I took occasion to say that the President of the United States was the friend of his red children, and desired to live at peace with them all. He, in reply, said he was much astonished to hear this; for, judging from the few trifling presents I had made his people, he had formed the opinion that the "Big Captain" of the pale-faces held them in but little estimation.

The limited intercourse that has existed between the Comanches and the whites does not appear to have prepossessed the former much in our favor, as the following incident, which was related to me by Mr. Israel Fulsom, a very intelligent and educated Chickasaw, goes to show. Upon a certain occasion, while he was visiting them, he remarked to the chief that it was only a few years since the people of his own nation were equally as uncivilized as the Comanches, but that, through the instrumentality of the white missionaries, they had been induced to abandon their precarious hunting habits, and had learned to read and write, and to cultivate the soil, so that they were then enabled to live in the same manner as the white people, and were always supplied with abundance of food.

The chief replied that he had no doubt there were some

advantages to be derived from education, and that he had often given the subject his serious consideration, but that the pale-faces were all such arrant rascals that he was afraid to let them take up their abode with his people. Whereupon Mr. Folsom suggested to him that probably he had met with only the bad specimens of the white race, and that he himself had known very many good men among them who had conferred important benefits upon the Red Man.

The Comanche replied that possibly such might be the case, but he had always been under the impression that there were but few, if any honest white men. He said farther, that if the Chickasaws would send out one of their educated men to teach their children to read and write, they would have no objections.

Like other Indians, they submit with imperturbable stoicism and apathy to misfortunes of the most serious character, and, in the presence of strangers, manifest no surprise or curiosity at the exhibition of novelties; yet this apparent indifference is assumed, and they are, in reality, very inquisitive people. In every village may be seen small structures, consisting of a frame-work of slight poles, bent into a semi-spherical form, and covered with buffalo hides. These are called *medicine lodges*, and are used as vapor-baths. The patient is seated within the lodge, beside several heated stones, upon which water is thrown, producing a dense hot vapor, which brings on a profuse perspiration, while, at the same time, the shamans, or medicine-men, who profess to have the power of communicating with the unseen world, and of propitiating the malevolence of evil spirits, are performing various incantations, accompanied by music, on the outside. Such means are resorted to for healing all diseases; and I am also informed that their young men are obliged to undergo a regular course of steam-bathing before they are considered worthy of assuming the responsible duties of warriors. The knowledge they possess of their early history is very vague and limited, and does not extend farther back than a few generations. They say that their forefathers lived precisely as they do, and followed the buffalo; that they came from a country toward the setting sun, where they expect to return after death. They acknowledge the existence and power of a great supernatural agent, who directs and controls all things; but this power they conceive to be vested in the sun, which they appeal to on all occasions of moment.

As I remarked before, the Northern Comanches are fully impressed with the conviction that theirs is the most powerful race in existence, and in 1854 some of their chiefs sent a message to the commanding officer of one of our military posts to the effect that, as soon as the grass appeared in the spring, he intended paying him a visit, when he might expect to receive a severe whipping, and lose all his animals. Shortly afterward the post was abandoned, and our interpreter informed me that the Indians verily believed it was in consequence of the threat they had made.

The question as to what line of policy will the most speedily and effectually bring these Indians into subjection to the dictates of our authorities, and control their future movements, is one fraught with difficulties, but must sooner or later be met.

The limits of their accustomed range are rapidly contracting, and their means of subsistence undergoing a corresponding diminution. The white man is advancing with rapid strides upon all sides of them, and they are forced to give way to his encroachments. The time is not far distant when the buffaloes will become extinct, and they will then be compelled to adopt some other mode of life than the chase for a subsistence.

Excepting a portion of the Southern Comanches, they have not as yet taken the first step toward civilization, and are entire strangers to labor or husbandry. The Indians must live, and when the Plains will not afford them a maintenance, they will unquestionably seek it from their neighbors. No man will quietly submit to starvation when food is within his reach, and if he can not obtain it honestly he will steal it, or take it by force. If, therefore, we do not induce them to engage in agricultural avocations, we shall, in a few years, have before us the alternative of exterminating the race or feeding them perpetually.

That they are destined ultimately to extinction does not, in my mind, admit of a doubt, and it may be beyond the agency of human control to avert such a result. But it seems to me in accordance with the benevolent spirit of our institutions that we should endeavor to make the pathway of their exit from the sphere of human existence as smooth and easy as possible, and I know no more effectual way of accomplishing this than by teaching them to till the soil.

For the reasons before mentioned, it may at first be necessary for our government to assert its authority over them by a prompt and vigorous exercise of the military arm, and as soon as this is felt and acknowledged, the fostering hand of government should be kindly extended to them, and strong inducements offered to all who are disposed to labor, and every assistance given them upon the new sphere of action. In doing this, we discharge a debt of honor to the Red Man, and confer upon him benefits of vastly more importance than by giving him presents of money and goods, the greater part of which are oftentimes stolen by corrupt agents and unprincipled traders. The tendency of the policy I have indicated will be to assemble these people in communities where they will be more readily controlled, and I predict from it the most gratifying results.

The predatory incursions of the Northern and Middle Comanches upon the western borders of Texas and the northern states of Mexico were carried on successfully and uninterruptedly for many years. During the existence of the republic of Texas, the pioneers of that country were continually harassed by bands of these freebooters, and the result of their efforts shows how difficult it was to subdue them in war.

From 1838 to 1842, the republic was involved in continual hostilities with these Indians, and during a portion of that time they had a large force in the field, many of whom were frontier settlers, whose sinews of iron and frames of oaken firmness had undergone such a system of training that they were enabled to set at defiance the vicissitudes of the most capricious climate, and were capable of enduring almost any amount of exposure and fatigue. These men were commanded by energetic and experienced leaders, and were well qualified to fill their stations.

Thus organized, they constituted the renowned "Texas Rangers," who are to this day held up by their statesmen as examples of the most successful Indian fighters that our country has produced.

The operations of the Rangers, as with our own troops that have been stationed along the Rio Grande frontier, were generally directed against war-parties, which were well mounted, and only suffered themselves to be approached when it suited their purposes, as they could at any time make their escape to their distant homes in the north, where they were out of reach from pursuit.

In this protracted warfare it was seldom that any decisive advantages were gained over the Indians, and after expending her utmost energies in the vain attempt to chastise them into subjection, the sparsely-populated republic was finally compelled to resort to the peace policy.

One of the most prominent features in the religious creeds of the natives of this continent, and a coincidence of faith common to them all, so far as I have been able to learn, is the remarkable fact that they universally acknowledge the existence of, and pay homage to, *one great and almighty Spirit.*

They are *Theists* of the least sensual stamp; and that they have seldom, if ever, been idolaters, is a fact that is well established in the history of the race from the discovery of America. It is true that many of the tribes are in the habit of making their supplications to the great Disposer of Events through the medium of the sun, moon, or earth. This, however, is only true so far as these media are to be considered as symbolic of the real deity. They are not regarded as in themselves possessing the power of supreme divinity, but as intermediate agents through which wishes are communicated to the Creator.

In some other nations of the Old World the type has sometimes been adopted as the real and actual deity or object of worship.

"Sun-worship" seems to have been universal over the Old World. It has been found in Egypt, Chaldea, Persia, Greece, India, Scandinavia, Lapland, Britain, Germany, and many other countries. "The fire-worshipers" had been taught by their fathers to worship the sun and the fire, as emblems of the god of the world. They ceased to look beyond the emblem, and worshiped it as the real deity. In Mexico and Peru the Incas and priests claimed to be "children of the sun." But the Indians of North America have continued to look beyond the symbol to the being it represented. They have never been idolaters. They have never worshiped the emblem in the place of the true deity. And still, in their figurative language, they often speak as if they considered the sun as their god. They often call themselves "children of the sun," as well as "souls made of fire," etc. The Indian warrior and orator Tecumseh, at the conclusion of a speech, was told that his "father," the Governor of Indiana, desired him to take a chair. He rejected it with scorn. "My father!" said the indignant chief, throwing himself on the ground; "the sun is my father, and the earth is my mother, and I will repose upon her bosom!"*

In evidence of what I have stated, I remark that Du Pratz found the Indians in the Mississippi Valley worshiping a "great and most perfect Spirit, compared with whom all other things were as nothing, and by whom all things were made."

Lewis and Clarke, fifty years ago, found the Indians inhabiting the Upper Missouri possessing a religious faith which consisted exclusively in a firm belief in the existence of "*one great Spirit*" who ruled the destinies of men.

Roger Williams expressed the conviction that if any white man doubted the existence of the God of the universe, "the Indians could teach him."

The venerable missionary Heckewelder, after forty years' residence among the Delawares, said that habitual devotion to the Supreme Being was one of the most prominent traits in the mind of the Red Man.

Notwithstanding the high veneration that these people entertain for the Great Spirit, and the remarkable fact that among those I have known there is nothing in their vocabularies that enables them to give oral expression to an oath, yet, as strange as it may appear, the first expressions they learn after coming in contact with the white race are invariably those of profanity and obscenity, and this can only be accounted for from the fact that their earliest asso-

* Theology of the American Indians, National Quarterly Review, June, 1863.

ciations among the whites are with unprincipled Indian traders and immoral frontiersmen, who teach them all our vices, and none of our virtues.

Most of the Eastern tribes of Indians have, through the efforts of missionaries and philanthropists, been taught the rudiments of our revealed religion, and many of them have been worthy Christians, exercising a good influence over their red brethren. But thus far, no such efforts have ever been made to improve the moral or physical condition of the Comanches; no missionaries have, to my knowledge, ever visited them, and they have no more idea of Christianity than they have of the religion of Mohammed. We find dwelling almost at our doors as barbarous and heathenish a race as exists on the face of the earth; and while our benevolent and philanthropic citizens are making such efforts to ameliorate the condition of savages in other countries, should we not do something for the benefit of these wild men of the prairies? Those dingy noblemen of nature, the original proprietors of all that vast domain included between the shores of the Atlantic and Pacific, have been despoiled, supplanted, and robbed of their just and legitimate heritage by the avaricious and rapid encroachments of the *white man.* Numerous and powerful nations have already become exterminated by unjustifiable wars that he has waged with them, and by the effects of the vices he has introduced and inculcated; and of those that remain, but few can be found who are not contaminated by the pernicious influences of unprincipled and designing adventurers. It is not at this late day in our power to atone for all the injustice inflicted upon the *Red Men;* but it seems to me that a wise policy would dictate almost the only recompense it is now in our power to make—that of introducing among them the light of Christianity and the blessings of civilization, with their attendant benefits of agriculture and the arts.

CHAPTER III.

INDIAN WARFARE.

Indian Warfare.—French Army in Algeria.—Turkish Method of Warfare. —Tracking Indians.—Telegraphing by Smokes.—Delawares, Shawnees, and Kickapoos.—Guides in the Great Desert.—The Khebir.—Delaware's Idea of the Compass.—Black Beaver.—Jealousy of his Wife.—Comanche's Ideas of the Whites.—John Bushman.—Marriage Relations.—Jim Ned.—Great Horse-thief.—Comanche Law.—Juan Galvan.—Kickapoos good Hunters.—Respect for Law.

THE art of war, as taught and practiced among civilized nations at the present day, is no doubt well adapted to the purposes for which it was designed, viz., the operations of armies acting in populated districts, furnishing ample resources, and against an enemy who is tangible, and makes use of similar tactics and strategy. But the modern schools of military science are but illy suited to carrying on a warfare with the wild tribes of the Plains.

The vast expanse of desert territory that has been annexed to our domain within the last few years is peopled by numerous tribes of marauding and erratic savages, who are mounted upon fleet and hardy horses, making war the business and pastime of their lives, and acknowledging none of the ameliorating conventionalities of civilized warfare. Their tactics are such as to render the old system almost wholly impotent.

To act against an enemy who is here to-day and there to-morrow; who at one time stampedes a herd of mules upon the head waters of the Arkansas, and when next heard from is in the very heart of the populated districts of Mexico, laying waste haciendas, and carrying devastation, rapine, and murder in his steps; who is every where without being any where; who assembles at the moment of combat, and vanishes whenever fortune turns against him; who leaves his women and children far distant from the theatre of hostilities, and has neither towns nor magazines to defend, nor lines of retreat to cover; who derives his commissariat from the country he operates in, and is not encumbered with baggage-wagons or pack-trains; who comes into action only when it suits his purpose, and never without the advantage of numbers or position—with such an enemy the strategic science of civilized nations loses much of its importance, and finds but rarely, and only in peculiar localities, an opportunity to be put in practice.

Our little army, scattered as it has been over the vast area of our possessions, in small garrisons of one or two companies each, has seldom been in a situation to act successfully on the offensive against large numbers of these marauders, and has often been condemned to hold itself almost exclusively upon the defensive. The morale of the troops must thereby necessarily be seriously impaired, and the confidence of the savages correspondingly augmented. The system of small garrisons has a tendency to disorganize the troops in proportion as they are scattered, and renders them correspondingly inefficient. The same results have been observed by the French army in Algeria, where, in 1845, their troops were, like ours, disseminated over a vast space, and broken up into small detachments stationed in numerous intrenched posts. Upon the sudden appearance of Abd el Kader in the plain of Mitidja, they were defeated with serious losses, and were from day to day obliged to abandon these useless stations, with all the supplies they contained. A French writer, in discussing this subject, says:

"We have now abandoned the fatal idea of defending

Algeria by small intrenched posts. In studying the character of the war, the nature of the men who are to oppose us, and of the country in which we are to operate, we must be convinced of the danger of admitting any other system of fortification than that which is to receive our grand dépôts, our magazines, and to serve as places to recruit and rest our troops when exhausted by long expeditionary movements.

"These fortifications should be established in the midst of the centres of action, so as to command the principal routes, and serve as pivots to expeditionary columns.

"We owe our success to a system of war which has its proofs in twice changing our relations with the Arabs. This system consists altogether in the great mobility we have given to our troops. Instead of disseminating our soldiers with the vain hope of protecting our frontiers with a line of small posts, we have concentrated them, to have them at all times ready for emergencies, and since then the fortune of the Arabs has waned, and we have marched from victory to victory.

"This system, which has thus far succeeded, ought to succeed always, and to conduct us, God willing, to the peaceful possession of the country."

In reading a treatise upon war as it is practiced by the French in Algeria, by Colonel A. Laure, of the 2d Algerine Tirailleurs, published in Paris in 1858, I was struck with the remarkable similarity between the habits of the Arabs and those of the wandering tribes that inhabit our Western prairies. Their manner of making war is almost precisely the same, and a successful system of strategic operations for one will, in my opinion, apply to the other.

As the Turks have been more successful than the French in their military operations against the Arab tribes, it may not be altogether uninteresting to inquire by what means these inferior soldiers have accomplished the best results.

The author above mentioned, in speaking upon this subject, says:

"In these latter days the world is occupied with the organization of mounted infantry, according to the example of the Turks, where, in the most successful experiments that have been made, the mule carries the foot-soldier.

"The Turkish soldier mounts his mule, puts his provisions upon one side and his accoutrements upon the other, and, thus equipped, sets out upon long marches, traveling day and night, and only reposing occasionally in bivouac. Arrived near the place of operations (as near the break of day as possible), the Turks dismount in the most profound silence, and pass in succession the bridle of one mule through that of another in such a manner that a single man is sufficient to hold forty or fifty of them by retaining the last bridle, which secures all the others; they then examine their arms, and are ready to commence their work. The chief gives his last orders, posts his guides, and they make the attack, surprise the enemy, generally asleep, and carry the position without resistance. The operation terminated, they hasten to beat a retreat, to prevent the neighboring tribes from assembling, and thus avoid a combat.

"The Turks had only three thousand mounted men and ten thousand infantry in Algeria, yet these thirteen thousand men sufficed to conquer the same obstacles which have arrested us for twenty-six years, notwithstanding the advantage we had of an army which was successively reenforced until it amounted to a hundred thousand.

"Why not imitate the Turks, then, mount our infantry upon mules, and reduce the strength of our army?

"The response is very simple:

"The Turks are Turks—that is to say, Mussulmans—

and indigenous to the country; the Turks speak the Arabic language; the Deys of Algiers had less country to guard than we, and they care very little about retaining possession of it. They are satisfied to receive a part of its revenues. They were not permanent; their dominion was held by a thread. The Arab dwells in tents; his magazines are in caves. When he starts upon a war expedition, he folds his tent, drives far away his beasts of burden, which transport his effects, and only carries with him his horse and arms. Thus equipped, he goes every where; nothing arrests him; and often, when we believe him twenty leagues distant, he is in ambush at precisely rifle range from the flanks of his enemy.

"It may be thought the union of contingents might retard their movements, but this is not so. The Arabs, whether they number ten or a hundred thousand, move with equal facility. They go where they wish and as they wish upon a campaign; the place of rendezvous merely is indicated, and they arrive there..

"What calculations can be made against such an organization as this?

"Strategy evidently loses its advantages against such enemies; a general can only make conjectures; he marches to find the Arabs, and finds them not; then, again, when he least expects it, he suddenly encounters them.

"When the Arab despairs of success in battle, he places his sole reliance upon the speed of his horse to escape destruction; and as he is always in a country where he can make his camp beside a little water, he travels until he has placed a safe distance between himself and his enemy."

TRACKING INDIANS.

When an Indian sentinel intends to watch for an enemy approaching from the rear, he selects the highest position available, and places himself near the summit in such an attitude that his entire body shall be concealed from the observation of any one in the rear, his head only being exposed above the top of the eminence. Here he awaits with great patience so long as he thinks there is any possibility of danger, and it will be difficult for an enemy to surprise him or to elude his keen and scrutinizing vigilance. Meanwhile his horse is secured under the screen of the hill, all ready when required. Hence it will be evident that, in following Indian depredators, the utmost vigilance and caution must be exercised to conceal from them the movements of their pursuers. They are the best scouts in the world, proficient in all the artifices and stratagems available in border warfare, and when hotly pursued by a superior force, after exhausting all other means of evasion, they scatter in different directions; and if, in a broken or mountainous country, they can do no better, abandon their horses and baggage, and take refuge in the rocks, gorges, or other hiding-places. This plan has several times been resorted to by Indians in Texas when surprised, and, notwithstanding their pursuers were directly upon them, the majority made their escape, leaving behind all their animals and other property.

For overtaking a marauding party of Indians who have advanced eight or ten hours before the pursuing party are in readiness to take the trail, it is not best to push forward rapidly at first, as this will weary and break down horses. The Indians must be supposed to have at least fifty or sixty miles the start; it will, therefore, be useless to think of overtaking them without providing for a long chase. Scouts should continually be kept out in front upon the trail to reconnoitre and give preconcerted signals to the main party when the Indians are espied.

In approaching all eminences or undulations in the prairies, the commander should be careful not to allow any considerable number of his men to pass upon the summits until the country around has been carefully reconnoitred by the scouts, who will cautiously raise their eyes above the crests of the most elevated points, making a scrutinizing examination in all directions; and, while doing this, should an Indian be encountered who has been left behind as a sentinel, he must, if possible, be secured or shot, to prevent his giving the alarm to his comrades. These precautions can not be too rigidly enforced when the trail becomes "warm;" and if there be a moon, it will be better to lie by in the daytime and follow the trail at night, as the great object is to come upon the Indians when they are not anticipating an attack. Such surprises, if discreetly conducted, generally prove successful.

As soon as the Indians are discovered in their bivouac, the pursuing party should dismount, leave their horses under charge of a guard in some sequestered place, and, before advancing to the attack, the men should be instructed in signals for their different movements, such as all will easily comprehend and remember. As, for example, a pull upon the right arm may signify to face to the right, and a pull upon the left arm to face to the left; a pull upon the skirt of the coat, to halt; a gentle push on the back, to advance in ordinary time; a slap on the back, to advance in double quick time, etc., etc.

These signals, having been previously well understood and practiced, may be given by the commander to the man next to him, and from him communicated in rapid succession throughout the command.

I will suppose the party formed in one rank, with the commander on the right. He gives the signal, and the men move off cautiously in the direction indicated. The importance of not losing sight of his comrades on his right and left, and of not allowing them to get out of his reach, so as to break the chain of communication, will be apparent to all, and great care should be taken that the men do not mistake their brothers in arms for the enemy. This may be prevented by having two *pass-words*, and when there be any doubt as to the identity of two men who meet during the night operations, one of these words may be repeated by each. Above all, the men must be fully impressed with the importance of not firing a shot until the order is given by the commanding officer, and also that a rigorous personal accountability will be enforced in all cases of a violation of this rule.

If the commander gives the signal for commencing the attack by firing a pistol or gun, there will probably be no mistake, unless it happens through carelessness by the accidental discharge of fire-arms.

I can conceive of nothing more appalling, or that tends more to throw men off their guard and produce confusion, than a sudden and unexpected night-attack. Even the Indians, who pride themselves upon their coolness and self-possession, are far from being exempt from its effects; and it is not surprising that men who go to sleep with a sense of perfect security around them, and are suddenly aroused from a deep slumber by the terrific sounds of an onslaught from an enemy, should lose their presence of mind.

TELEGRAPHING BY SMOKES.

The transparency of the atmosphere upon the Plains is such that objects can be seen at great distances; a mountain, for example, presents a distinct and bold outline at fifty or sixty miles, and may occasionally be seen as far as a hundred miles.

The Indians, availing themselves of this fact, have been in the habit of practicing a system of telegraphing by means of smokes during the day and fires by night, and, I dare say, there are but few travelers who have crossed the mountains to California that have not seen these signals made and responded to from peak to peak in rapid succession.

The Indians thus make known to their friends many items of information highly important to them. If enemies or strangers make their appearance in the country, the fact is telegraphed at once, giving them time to secure their animals, and to prepare for attack, defense, or flight.

War or hunting parties, after having been absent a long time from their erratic friends at home, and not knowing where to find them, make use of the same preconcerted signals to indicate their presence.

Very dense smokes may be raised by kindling a large fire with dry wood, and piling upon it the green boughs of pine, balsam, or hemlock. This throws off a heavy cloud of black smoke which can be seen very far.

This simple method of telegraphing, so useful to the savages both in war and in peace, may, in my judgment, be used to advantage in the movements of troops co-operating in separate columns in the Indian country.

I shall not attempt at this time to present a matured system of signals, but will merely give a few suggestions tending to illustrate the advantages to be derived from the use of them.

For example, when two columns are marching through a country at such distances apart that smokes may be seen from one to the other, their respective positions may be made known to each other at any time by two smokes raised simultaneously or at certain preconcerted intervals.

Should the commander of one column desire to communicate with the other, he raises three smokes simultaneously, which, if seen by the other party, should be responded to in the same manner. They would then hold themselves in readiness for any other communications.

If an enemy is discovered in small numbers, a smoke raised twice at fifteen minutes' interval would indicate it; and if in large force, three times with the same intervals might be the signal.

Should the commander of one party desire the other to join him, this might be telegraphed by four smokes at ten minutes' interval.

Should it become necessary to change the direction of the line of march, the commander may transmit the order by means of two simultaneous smokes raised a certain number of times to indicate the particular direction; for instance, twice for north, three times for south, four times for east, and five times for west; three smokes raised twice for northeast, three times for northwest, etc., etc.

By multiplying the combinations of signals a great variety of messages might be transmitted in this manner; but, to avoid mistakes, the signals should be written down and copies furnished the commander of each separate party, and they need not necessarily be made known to other persons.

During the day an intelligent man should be detailed to keep a vigilant look-out in all directions for smokes, and he should be furnished with a watch, pencil, and paper, to make a record of the signals, with their number, and the time of the interval between them.

DELAWARES, SHAWNEES, AND KICKAPOOS.

It is highly important that parties making expeditions through an unexplored country should secure the services of the best guides and hunters, and I know of none who are superior to the Delawares and Shawnee Indians. They have been with me upon several different occasions, and I have invariably found them intelligent, brave, reliable, and in every respect well qualified to fill their positions. They are endowed with those keen and wonderful powers in woodcraft which can only be acquired by instinct, practice, and necessity, and which are possessed by no other people that I have heard of, unless it be the khebirs or guides who escort the caravans across the great desert of Sahara.

General E. Dumas, in his treatise upon the "Great Desert," published in Paris, 1856, in speaking of these guides, says:

"The khebir is always a man of intelligence, of tried probity, bravery, and skill. He knows how to determine his position from the appearance of the stars; by the experience of other journeys he has learned all about the roads, wells, and pastures; the dangers of certain passes, and the means of avoiding them; all the chiefs whose territories it is necessary to pass through; the salubrity of the different localities; the remedies against diseases; the treatment of fractures, and the antidotes to the venom of snakes and scorpions.

"In these vast solitudes, where nothing seems to indicate the route, where the wind covers up all traces of the track with sand, the khebir has a thousand ways of directing himself in the right course. In the night, when there are no stars in sight, by the simple inspection of a handful of grass, which he examines with his fingers, which he smells and tastes, he informs himself of his locale without ever being lost or wandering.

"I saw with astonishment that our conductor, although he had but one eye, and that defective, recognized perfectly the route; and Leon, the African, states that the conductor of his caravan became blind upon the journey from ophthalmia, yet by feeling the grass and sand he could tell when we were approaching an inhabited place.

"Our guide had all the qualities which make a good khebir. He was young, large, and strong; he was a master of arms; his eye commanded respect, and his speech won the heart. But if in the tent he was affable and winning, once *en route* he spoke only when it was necessary, and never smiled."

The Delawares are but a minute remnant of the great Algonquin family, whose early traditions declare them to be the parent stock from which the other numerous branches of the Algonquin tribes originated. And they are the same people whom the first white settlers found so numerous upon the banks of the Delaware.

When William Penn held his council with the Delawares upon the ground where the city of Philadelphia now stands, they were as peaceful and unwarlike in their habits as the Quakers themselves. They had been subjugated by the Five Nations, forced to take the appellation of squaws, and forego the use of arms; but after they moved West, beyond the influence of their former masters, their naturally independent spirit revived, they soon regained their lofty position as braves and warriors, and the male squaws of the Iroquois soon became formidable men and heroes, and so have continued to the present day. Their war-path has reached the shores of the Pacific Ocean on the west, Hudson's Bay on the north, and into the very heart of Mexico on the south.

They are not clannish in their dispositions like most other Indians, nor by their habits confined to any given locality, but are found as traders, trappers, or hunters among most of the Indian tribes inhabiting our continent. I even saw them living with the Mormons in Utah. They are among the Indians as the Jews among the whites, essentially wanderers.

The Shawnees have been associated with the Delawares

185 years. They intermarry and live as one people. Their present places of abode are upon the Missouri River, near Fort Leavenworth, and in the Choctaw Territory, upon the Canadian River, near Fort Arbuckle. They are familiar with many of the habits and customs of their pale-faced neighbors, and some of them speak the English language, yet many of their native characteristics tenaciously cling to them.

Upon one occasion I endeavored to teach a Delaware the use of the compass. He seemed much interested in its mechanism, and very attentively observed the oscillations of the needle. He would move away a short distance, then return, keeping his eyes continually fixed upon the needle and the uniform position into which it settled. He did not, however, seem to comprehend it in the least, but regarded the entire proceeding as a species of necromantic performance got up for his especial benefit, and I was about putting away the instrument when he motioned me to stop, and came walking toward it with a very serious but incredulous countenance, remarking, as he pointed his finger toward it, "Maybe so he tell lie sometime."

BLACK BEAVER.

In 1849 I met with a very interesting specimen of the Delaware tribe whose name was Black Beaver. He had for ten years been in the employ of the American Fur Company, and during this time had visited nearly every point of interest within the limits of our unsettled territory. He had set his traps and spread his blanket upon the head waters of the Missouri and Columbia; and his wanderings had led him south to the Colorado and Gila, and thence to the shores of the Pacific in Southern California. His life had been that of a veritable cosmopolite, filled with scenes of intense and startling interest, bold and reckless adventure.

He was with me two seasons in the capacity of guide, and I always found him perfectly reliable, brave, and competent. His reputation as a resolute, determined, and fearless warrior did not admit of question, yet I have never seen a man who wore his laurels with less vanity.

When I first made his acquaintance I was puzzled to know what to think of him. He would often, in speaking of the prairie Indians, say to me,

"Captain, if you have a fight, you mustn't count much on me, for I'ze a big coward. When the fight begins I 'spect you'll see me run under the cannon; Injun mighty 'fraid of big gun."

I expressed my surprise that he should, if what he told me was true, have gained such a reputation as a warrior; whereupon he informed me that many years previous, when he was a young man, and before he had ever been in battle, he, with about twenty white men and four Delawares, were at one of the Fur Company's trading-posts upon the Upper Missouri, engaged in trapping beaver. While there, the stockade fort was attacked by a numerous band of Blackfeet Indians, who fought bravely, and seemed determined to annihilate the little band that defended it.

After the investment had been completed, and there appeared no probability of the attacking party's abandoning their purpose, "One d—d fool Delaware" (as Black Beaver expressed it) proposed to his countrymen to make a sortie, and thereby endeavor to effect an impression upon the Blackfeet. This, Beaver said, was the last thing he would ever have thought of suggesting, and it startled him prodigiously, causing him to tremble so much that it was with difficulty he could stand.

He had, however, started from home with the fixed purpose of becoming a distinguished brave, and made a great effort to stifle his emotion. He assumed an air of determination, saying that was the very idea he was just about to propose; and, slapping his comrades upon the back, started toward the gate, telling them to follow. As soon as the gate was passed, he says, he took particular care to keep in the rear of the others, so that, in the event of a retreat, he would be able to reach the stockade first.

They had not proceeded far before a perfect shower of arrows came falling around them on all sides, but fortunately without doing them harm. Not fancying this hot reception, those in front proposed an immediate retreat, to which he most gladly acceded, and at once set off at his utmost speed, expecting to reach the fort first. But he soon discovered that his comrades were more fleet, and were rapidly passing and leaving him behind. Suddenly he stopped and called out to them, "Come back here, you cowards, you squaws; what for you run away and leave brave man to fight alone?" This taunting appeal to their courage turned them back, and, with their united efforts, they succeeded in beating off the enemy immediately around them, securing their entrance into the fort.

Beaver says when the gate was closed the captain in charge of the establishment grasped him warmly by the hand, saying, "Black Beaver, you are a brave man; you have done this day what no other man in the fort would have the courage to do, and I thank you from the bottom of my heart."

In relating the circumstance to me he laughed most heartily, thinking it a very good joke, and said after that he was regarded as a brave warrior.

The truth is, my friend Beaver was one of those few heroes who never sounded his own trumpet; yet no one that knows him ever presumed to question his courage.

At another time, while Black Beaver remained upon the head waters of the Missouri, he was left in charge of a "*cache*" consisting of a quantity of goods buried to prevent their being stolen by the Indians. During the time he was engaged upon this duty he amused himself by hunting in the vicinity, only visiting his charge once a day. As he was making one of these periodical visits, and had arrived upon the summit of a hill overlooking the locality, he suddenly discovered a large number of hostile Blackfeet occupying it, and he supposed they had appropriated all the goods. As soon as they espied him, they beckoned for him to come down and have a friendly chat with them.

Knowing that their purpose was to beguile him into their power, he replied that he did not feel in a talking humor just at that time, and started off in another direction, whereupon they hallooed after him, making use of the most insulting language and gestures, and asking him if he considered himself a man thus to run away from his friends, and intimating that, in their opinion, he was an old woman, who had better go home and take care of the children.

Beaver says this roused his indignation to such a pitch that he stopped, turned around, and replied, "Maybe so; s'pose three or four of you Injuns come up here alone, I'll show you if I'ze old womans." They did not, however, accept the challenge, and Beaver rode off.

Although the Delawares generally seem quite happy in their social relations, yet they are not altogether exempt from some of those minor discords which occasionally creep in and mar the domestic harmony of their more civilized pale-faced brethren.

I remember, upon one occasion, I had bivouacked for the night with Black Beaver, and he had been endeavoring to while away the long hours of the evening by relating to me some of the most thrilling incidents of his highly adventurous and erratic life, when at length a hiatus in the conversation gave me an opportunity of asking him if he was a married man. He hesitated for some time; then looking up and giving his forefinger a twirl, to imitate the throwing of a lasso, replied, "One time me catch 'um wife. I pay that woman, *his modder*, one hoss—one saddle—one bridle—two plug tobacco, and plenty goods. I take him home to my house—got plenty meat—plenty corn—plenty every thing. One time me go take walk, maybe so three, maybe so two hours. When I come home, that woman he say, 'Black Beaver, what for you go way long time?' I say, 'I not go nowhere; I just take one littel walk.' Then that woman he get heap mad, and say, 'No, Black Beaver, you not take no littel walk. I know what for you go way; *you go see nodder one woman.*' I say, 'Maybe not.' Then that woman she cry long time, and all e'time now she mad. You never seen 'Merican woman that a-way?"

I sympathized most deeply with my friend in his distress, and told him for his consolation that, in my opinion, the women of his nation were not peculiar in this respect; that they were pretty much alike all over the world, and I was under the impression that there were well-authenticated instances even among white women where they had subjected themselves to the same causes of complaint so feelingly depicted by him. Whereupon he very earnestly asked, "What you do for cure him? Whip him?" I replied, No; that, so far as my observation extended, I was under the impression that this was generally regarded by those who had suffered from its effects as one of those chronic and vexatious complaints which would not be benefited by the treatment he suggested, even when administered in homœopathic doses, and I believed it was now admitted by all sensible men that it was better in all such cases to let nature take its course, trusting to a merciful Providence.

At this reply his countenance assumed a dejected expression, but at length he brightened up again and triumphantly remarked, "I tell you, my friend, what I do; I ketch 'um nodder one wife when I go home."

Black Beaver had visited St. Louis and the small towns upon the Missouri frontier, and he prided himself not a little upon his acquaintance with the customs of the whites, and never seemed more happy than when an opportunity offered to display this knowledge in presence of his Indian companions. It so happened, upon one occasion, that I had a Comanche guide who bivouacked at the same fire with Beaver. On visiting them one evening according to my usual practice, I found them engaged in a very earnest and apparently not very amicable conversation. On inquiring the cause of this, Beaver answered, "I've been telling this Comanche what I seen 'mong the white folks."

I said, "Well, Beaver, what did you tell him?"

"I tell him 'bout the steam-boats, and the rail-roads, and the heap o' houses I seen in St. Louis."

"Well, sir, what does he think of that?"

"He say I'ze d—d fool."

"What else did you tell him about?"

"I tell him the world is round, but he keep all e'time say, 'Hush, you fool! do yous 'pose I'ze child. Haven't I got eyes? Can't I see the prairie? You call him round?' He say, too, 'Maybe so I tell you something you not know before. One time my grandfather he make long journey that way (pointing to the west). When he get on big mountain, he seen heap water on t'other side, jest so flat he can be, and he seen the sun go straight down on t'other side.' I then tell him all the serivers he seen, all e'time the water he run; s'pose the world flat, the water he stand still. Maybe so he not b'lieve me?"

I told him it certainly looked very much like it. I then asked him to explain to the Comanche the magnetic telegraph. He looked at me earnestly, and said,

"What you call that magnetic telegraph?"

I said, "You have heard of New York and New Orleans?"

"Oh yes," he replied.

"Very well; we have a wire connecting these two cities, which are about a thousand miles apart, and it would take a man thirty days to ride it upon a good horse. Now a man stands at one end of this wire in New York, and by touching it a few times he inquires of his friend in New Orleans what he had for breakfast. His friend in New Orleans touches the other end of the wire, and in ten minutes the answer comes back—ham and eggs. Tell him that, Beaver."

His countenance assumed a most comical expression, but he made no remark until I again requested him to repeat what I had said to the Comanche, when he observed,

"No, captain, I not tell him that, for I don't b'lieve that myself."

Upon my assuring him that such was the fact, and that I had seen it myself, he said,

"Injun not very smart; sometimes he's big fool, but he holler pretty loud; you hear him maybe half a mile; you say 'Merican man he talk thousand miles. I 'spect you try to fool me now, captain; *maybe so you lie.*"

JOHN BUSHMAN.

Previous to my departure from Fort Washita upon my Red River expedition, I employed five Delawares and Shawnees as guides and hunters. One of them, by the name of John Bushman, who could speak English and Comanche fluently, was constituted interpreter and the head man of the Indians.

I directed him to tell his comrades that I proposed to pay each of them one dollar per day during the time we should be absent. With this all seemed to be satisfied, and I supposed every thing was arranged to suit them; but it seemed that Bushman had conversed with Black Beaver upon the subject previous to leaving home, and Beaver had informed him that he had received from me two dollars and a half per day, and suggested to John that he would probably get the same compensation for his services. I was not advised of this, however, and supposed he would only expect the same pay as the other Indians, until one day, after he had acted as interpreter for me with a party of prairie Indians who had visited our camp, he came to me and said, "You not tell me yet, captain, how much you goin' give me."

I replied that I had stated to him distinctly before leaving Fort Washita that each Delaware would receive one dollar a day. He answered,

"I no understand um that-a-way, captain. Black Beaver he say maybe so give um two dollar half one day."

I told him Black Beaver was not authorized to make contracts for me; moreover, I added, a dollar a day was good pay, but in consideration of his acting as interpreter, I would allow him an additional per diem of half a dollar, which was more than he had any right to expect; that I was disposed to compensate him liberally, but that the government had no money to throw away by paying three prices for a thing.

John acquiesced in this decision, but in a very surly mood, and did not recover his usual spirits for some days. At length, however, he seemed to be content, and on our return to Fort Arbuckle, after I had settled with him, and as he was about leaving for his home, I said to him, "Well, John, you are going home now. In case I make another expedition into the Plains, would you like to accompany me?" "No," he replied, very abruptly. "And why not, pray?" "Because that government he hain't got no money to throw away."

John Bushman had acted as interpreter for me at Fort Arbuckle, when I first established that post, and he was a true specimen of the Indian type—dignified, reserved, and taciturn, self-reliant, independent, and fearless.

He was a man of eminently determinate and resolute character, with great powers of endurance, and a most acute and vigilant observer, distinguished by prominent powers of locality and sound judgment. These traits of character, with the abundant experience he had upon the Plains, made him one of the very best guides I ever met with. He never sees a place once without instantly recognizing it on seeing it the second time, notwithstanding he may approach it from a different direction; and the very moment he takes a glance over a district of country he has never seen before, he will almost invariably point out the particular localities (if there are any such) where water can be found, when to others there seems nothing to indicate it.

An incident which was related to me as occurring with one of these guides a few years since, forcibly illustrates their character. The officer having charge of the party to which he was attached sent him out to examine a trail he had met with on the prairie, for the purpose of ascertaining where it would lead to. The guide, after following it as far as he supposed he would be required to do, returned and reported that it led off into the prairie to no particular place, so far as he could discover. He was told that this was not satisfactory, and directed to take the trail again, and to follow it until he gained the required information. He accordingly went out the second time, but did not return that day, nor the next, and the party, after a time, began to be alarmed for his safety, fearing he might have been killed by the Indians. Days and weeks passed by, but still nothing was heard of the guide, until, on arriving at the first border settlement, to their astonishment, he made his appearance among them, and, approaching the commanding officer, said, "Captain, that trail which you ordered me to follow terminates here." He had, with indomitable and resolute energy, traversed alone several hundred miles of wild and desolate prairie, with nothing but his gun to depend upon for a subsistence, determined this time to carry out the instructions of his employer to the letter.

John Bushman had been married for many years, and had several children when I first met him, but his wife was getting in years, and he resolved to provide himself with a younger companion. Accordingly, he one day introduced into his household a young Mrs. Bushman, which proceeding very much exasperated the elder matron. Shortly after this innovation upon his domestic relations, I called at his cabin, and, observing the two squaws looking very demure and sad, I asked John what the trouble was. He replied, pointing to the elder, "That woman, he mad." Then, turning toward the other, he said, "That one he mad too, captain."

The day following the elder wife took her children, and left John to enjoy his honeymoon without farther molestation.

The marriage contract among the Delawares and Shawnees, it appears, is only binding so long as it suits the convenience and wishes of the parties. It can be revoked at any time when either party feels disposed; and a woman who leaves her husband is authorized by their laws to take with her all the personal property which she possessed at the date of the marriage. It can not be alienated, and her husband does not acquire the slightest claim upon it.

This law of property, I think, is a very just and wise provision, because it makes the woman somewhat independent of her husband, and, no doubt, frequently deters a tyrannical man from maltreating his wife. In the instance alluded to, Bushman's wife carried away all the horses belonging to the family, as they were her property.

JIM NED.

This somewhat remarkable specimen of humanity is a Delaware, united with a slight admixture of the African. He had a Delaware wife, and adopted the habits of that tribe, but at the same time he possessed all the social vivacity and garrulity of the negro. He was, however, exceedingly sensitive upon the subject of the African element in his composition, and resorted to a variety of expedients to conceal it from strangers, one of which was by shaving off his kinky locks, and keeping his head continually covered with a shawl "à la Turk."

When I first met Jim in 1849, he had the reputation of being one of the most expert, daring, and successful horse-thieves among the southwestern tribes. The theatre of his exploits was not confined to our territory, but his forays often extended into Mexico, and it was seldom that he returned empty-handed.

Although he was generous and hospitable in his disposition, yet he was eminently vindictive and revengeful toward those who interfered with his favorite pursuit, and it was said that several of his tribe had with their lives paid the penalty of incurring his displeasure.

My friend Black Beaver used to talk to me a great deal about this noted freebooter, but was very far from being prepossessed in his favor. They had, it seems, upon a certain occasion, a difficulty which came near resulting in a serious quarrel. Jim, no doubt thinking that his antecedents were of a character to deter any one who knew him from voluntarily placing himself in a hostile attitude toward him, remarked to Beaver, in the course of the discussion that ensued, "I suppose, sir, you've heard of one Delaware man that people call *Jim Ned?*" To which Beaver replied "that he had several times heard of the individual named."

"Very well," Jim said. "Have you not also heard that when a man incurs his displeasure, the climate becomes very sickly for him, and that he does not generally live long after it?"

Beaver was no coward, and, knowing the fact of the other's sensitive disposition, he replied, "I'ze not very rich Indian just now; I hazn't got much money, but maybe so I'ze got enough to pay for one d—d nigger, s'poze I kill him."

Jim Ned had been a great deal among the wild tribes of the Plains, and was familiar with many of their customs and peculiarities. He was with me for several weeks in 1854, and related to me several incidents in his life, which interested me not a little.

As we were sitting by our camp-fire one evening, he asked me if I knew how the prairie Indians punished an incontinent wife. I replied that I did not, unless it was by cutting off an ear, or the end of her nose. He then related to me the following incident, which came under his own observation.

Some years before, it appeared, he had been the guest of a Comanche chief, who was encamped with his band near the head waters of the Brazos. This chief was possessed of large herds of horses, that were tended and cared for by some six or eight wives of various ages, from eighteen to fifty.

During Jim's visit, one of the youngest and most attractive of these damsels was prevailed upon by a young brave to leave her lord, and elope with him upon a war expedition into Mexico. The old chief expressed much indignation toward his truant spouse and her lover, and threatened all manner of punishments on their return. Time passed by, and in the course of about two months the pair returned to the encampment. The chief soon learned that they were there, and on the following morning, just before daybreak, awoke Jim Ned, saying to him, "Get up, my friend; I want you to see a specimen of Comanche law." He was dressed in his full war costume, with his face painted in various fanciful colors, and his horse saddled at the door of his lodge. He seated himself near Jim, lighted his pipe, and, pulling several whiffs, passed it to him, after which he took his lance, mounted his horse, and rode out into the camp, and in a short time returned with his truant companion behind him.

They dismounted before the lodge, and he told the woman to sit down in a place which he designated; then, loading his rifle, he approached her, and directed her to cross her feet one above the other. When this was done, he placed the muzzle of his gun directly over them and fired, the ball passing though the centre of both feet. "Now," he said, "run away again if you like." The friends of the woman then approached and carried her off. This, Jim says, is Comanche law.

JUAN GALVAN.

While I was serving in Southern Texas, on the borders of Mexico, I became acquainted with an interesting specimen of the primitive inhabitants of that wild and sterile region.

He was a Mexican, by the name of Juan Galvan, who had passed all his life (about fifty years) upon a ranch near Lerado, on the Rio Grande.

He had often been attacked and robbed by the prairie

Indians, who, even as late as 1854, when I was there, would occasionally make raids upon the country.

Galvan was regarded as one of the best guides in the country. He understood all the mysteries of trailing and "signs" perfectly, and was often employed as guide for parties of troops sent out on scouts in pursuit of Indians. He was a brave man, and wore the scars of many battles in which he had been engaged against the savages.

He related to me several interesting adventures in his experience, which forcibly illustrated the habits and peculiarities of the Indian race.

Among others, he told me that he was, some years before, with a command of our troops in pursuit of and upon a fresh trail of Indians, when, as they entered a dense thicket of chaparral bordering an arroya, they suddenly came upon the enemy prepared to give battle.

Our men immediately made the attack, and charged into the chaparral. Galvan fired at an Indian who, a moment before, had discharged his gun at him, and his shot took effect, as he supposed, for the Indian fell upon the ground uttering the most pitiful groans. He did not stop to give him another shot, supposing he had received his death-wound, but pushed on to give battle to others.

When he had passed on about one hundred yards, however, much to his astonishment up jumped the identical savage, slapping his chest, and in a most triumphant tone crying out in Spanish, "Nada, nada, nada! Bueno, bueno, bueno!" (Nothing, nothing, nothing! Good, good, good!) and at the same time he fired his gun at him, which, it appeared, he had loaded while in the act of playing the part of the dead Indian.

At another time Galvan was out with Lieutenant Hudson and a detachment of our soldiers upon the trail of a party of Comanches, whom they overtook in an arroya.

The Indians, seeing there was no chance for escape, scattered, took cover, and commenced fighting. In a short time they espied the lieutenant, and cried out in Spanish, "Mira! mira! curahoe capitano Americano" (look! look! d—d American captain); and immediately several of them seemed determined to kill him. One approached him very close, and discharged several arrows at him, when the lieutenant ran up and seized him by the hair of the head, and attempted to cut him down with his sabre, but unfortunately the arm was so dull that he was unable to inflict much injury upon him, and the savage turned upon him with an arrow, and stabbed him so severely that he died in a few days.

KICKAPOO INDIANS.

This minute fraction of what was once a formidable tribe of Indians is now reduced to a very few warriors, a portion of whom, in 1854, lived upon the Choctaw reservation near the Witchita River.

They, like the Delawares and Shawnees, are well armed with good rifles, in the use of which they are very expert, and there are no better hunters or warriors upon the borders. They hunt altogether on horseback, and after a party of them have passed through a section of country, it is seldom that any game is left in their trace.

They are intelligent, active, and brave, and frequently visit and traffic with the prairie Indians, and have no fears of meeting these people in battle, provided the odds are not more than six to one against them.

The manner in which they execute justice upon their own people who have been guilty of infractions of their laws is shown in the following case of the murder of the Comanche agent, Colonel Stem, and another man, who were traveling together near Fort Belknap in 1853.

They were within about ten miles of the fort when they

were fired upon by two Indians, who missed them, but immediately attacked with their rifles clubbed and beat them to death.

The murderers made their escape, and no clew could be obtained of them for a long time, until at length the commanding officer of Fort Belknap received information that induced him to believe the perpetrators of the deed were Kickapoos, living near Fort Arbuckle. Accordingly, he sent an officer to that post, and the chief of the Kickapoos was called in, and told that there were good reasons for believing that some of his band had committed the act. He was then told that those persons must be given up to our authorities, and, if they attempted to escape, they must be shot down, and evidence of their identity brought to the fort.

The chief replied that their head men had been in council upon the same subject all the previous night, and that they had taken the matter into very serious consideration. The facts had been reported by a boy who was in company with the Indians when the deed was perpetrated. The murderers had made their escape, but the chief stated that his young warriors were already on their trail, and would probably overtake them, and as soon as they were apprehended they should be given up.

The chief then returned to his village, and soon afterward one of the murderers was brought in, and immediately bound, placed upon a horse, and they started with him to the fort. Before they reached there, however, he threw himself from the horse, cut his bonds with a knife he had concealed in his leggins, and attempted to flee, but he was immediately shot down through the heart by his guard, and his body carried into the fort and exhibited to the commanding officer. The chief then said that all his warriors were in pursuit of the other man, and would probably apprehend him; that he had sent them out in pairs, or twos; and that, should any of the whites meet with a single Kickapoo out by himself in any direction, they could kill him without hesitation; they would be certain to have executed the right one.

Several days elapsed without any information from the fugitive, when a runner came in and communicated the following facts. It appeared that the Indian, on leaving his village, had made his way to another camp upon the Canadian River, where he had a brother living. On entering the village, he went toward his brother's lodge, exclaiming, in a loud tone of voice, "I am the murderer of the two white men near Fort Belknap, and if any man wishes to take my life, here I am, ready to die." No one molesting him, he passed on to his brother's lodge, and seating himself, partook of supper; then, turning to his brother, said, "Here I am, my brother, a fugitive from justice. I would have gone and joined the Comanches, but I was fearful I should starve before I found them. I am hunted down like a wild beast. I am like a wounded deer, that can not get away. I had nowhere else to go but to you." He continued talking with his brother for some time, when finally the latter invited him to walk outside of the camp, where they could have a more free interchange of views. As soon as they were a short distance from the village, the brother stepped back, raised his tomahawk, and with a single blow felled the murderer to the ground, but did not kill him. He then seized him, saying, "My brother, I have repeatedly warned you of the consequences of following the path you have, and told you that it would ultimately lead you to disgrace and ruin. You have violated the laws of your tribe and of the United States, and you have thereby brought the nation into difficulty with the pale-faces, and they expect ample reparation for the deed you have committed, and it now becomes my duty to kill you." He then deliberately put him to death, and immediately went and reported the fact to the chief, who at once assembled a council of the principal men, and, after addressing them, and explaining the nature of the case, he called for a volunteer to cut off the head of the murderer, saying that the distance to the fort was too great to transport the body, and, as the commanding officer required positive evidence that the man had been killed, it became necessary that they should take the head to him. No one volunteering, he said, "As no one seems willing to do this act, I shall be obliged to do it myself;" which he accordingly did, and carried the head, with a strong escort, to Fort Arbuckle.

The foregoing incident evinces a high regard for law, and an inflexibility of spirit in the execution of its mandates seldom found among any people, and it exhibits the Kickapoo character in vivid and faithful colors.

CHAPTER IV.

PUEBLO INDIANS.

Pueblo Indians.—Early Discovery.—Situations of their Towns.—Moquis.—Coronado's Expedition.—Visit to Santa Domingo.—Laguna.—Christmas Ceremonies.—Church Services.—Bird Orchestra.—Dances.—Moqui Villages.—Peculiar Dances.—Feasting.—Origin of the Moquis.—Marriage Ceremony. — Estufas.—Pottery. — Extensive Ruins. —Large Houses. —Casas Grandes.

THREE hundred and twenty-nine years ago, and eighty-three years before the landing of the Pilgrims at Plymouth, a Franciscan missionary, named Marcus de Niza, with that spirit of self-sacrifice and devotion to the interests of his Church which characterized the monks of his order, solitary and alone traversed the vast expanse of desert country lying between the city of Mexico and the Gila River, and penetrated into the very heart of New Mexico, where he discovered a class of aborigines living in houses and towns, and far more advanced in the arts than any others that have been met with since within the limits of our possessions. These Indians cultivated cotton, and manufactured cloth from it. They also understood the art of making and coloring a very superior quality of pottery.

Their villages or towns were generally located in the most elevated and defensible positions, and regularly laid out into streets and public squares like European cities. Their houses were two, three, four, and sometimes as many as seven stories high, and occasionally pierced with loopholes for defense, but invariably the entrances were from the roofs, with no doors upon the sides. They cultivated corn, were industrious and unwarlike in their habits, and seemed to live comfortably and happy.

This same class of Indians still exists in New Mexico, and, with the exceptions of some few modifications brought about by the introduction of domestic animals and the commingling of the Catholic religion with their own primitive forms of Aztec worship, their habits, customs, and religion are almost precisely the same to-day as they were when first seen by the Spanish priest. These Indians are now called "*Pueblos*," or people who live in towns.

The most remarkable specimens of the Pueblos that I have heard of are the Moquis, who occupy seven towns or villages situated in a very inaccessible locality, about midway between the Rio del Norte and the Colorado River, and a short distance north of the Little Colorado. But very few of our people have ever visited them, and it is a most striking fact that this section, which, after Florida, was the first of our present possessions visited by Europeans, should be the last to be explored by the present generation.

The first successful attempt to explore this region was made while Nuño de Guzman was President of New Spain in 1540, and was, as I said before, intrusted to the command of Francisco Vasquez Coronado. The expedition consisted of 300 volunteers, mostly Spaniards of good families, who were induced to join the enterprise under the belief that they were to be led direct to the veritable "El Dorado."

They marched to Sonora, and thence, crossing the Gila, traveled two weeks through the desert north of that stream, until at length they reached one of the towns they were in search of, called Cibola, which they found built upon an elevated cliff, the houses having three and four stories, erected in terrace form, and the approaches to the summit of the cliff so narrow and steep as to be very difficult of access.

Nevertheless, "Coronado assailed it sword in hand, and carried it in an hour."

From thence he proceeded east to another larger town, called Tigoeux, on the Rio Grande, where he made his head-quarters during the winter of 1540–1. At this place, which some suppose to have been near Isletta, "some of the houses were seven stories in height, and rose above the rest like towers, having embrasures and loopholes."

From thence he made his expedition into the Plains, where he encountered the prairie Indians and vast herds of buffalo, and returned to Gran Quivera, on the Pecos River.

Upon the occasion of Coronado's visit to New Mexico he had a large number of sheep, and it is probable that the flocks of sheep seen among the Pueblo Indians at the present day sprang from those introduced by Coronado.

I visited one of these pueblo towns (*Santa Dominga*) in 1849. On our entrance the streets seemed to be deserted, and we were for some time unable to find any person to guide us to the residence of the governor (cacique). At length, however, we reached the house and ascended a ladder to the roof, and thence by another ladder descended through a trap-door into the principal room of the house. This method of ingress and egress must have originated from purposes of defense, as when the exterior ladder is removed there is no way of entering the establishment. Immediately on our appearance the governor set before us some meat and tortillas, and gave us an invitation "*to eat*," and the same ceremony was observed in all the houses we visited. It seemed to be a universal custom with them.

While we were conversing with the governor, who was a very dignified and sensible old Indian, we heard strange noises in the street, and, on looking out, saw four young Indians dressed in a very peculiar tight-fitting costume of

different colors, something like those we see upon the clowns in a circus. Around their heads were wreaths of wheat, and in their hands they carried gourds containing small pebbles, which they kept continually shaking.

They were going from house to house in a kind of monotonous dancing gait, at the same time crying out something in Indian which we could not understand, and as they passed along they would strike the exterior ladders of certain houses. The alcalde informed us that they were his criers, who were calling out the people to work in the field, and this ceremony, it appeared, was gone through with every day.

This pueblo was on the Rio Grande, in the settled part of the territory, and the Indians were accustomed to see Americans almost every day; yet they have preserved their national characteristics intact, and have not adopted any of the habits of the whites.

The Moqui Indians, who also live in pueblos or towns, are so remote from the settlements, and in such an inaccessible country, that but very few white men have ever visited them.

Surgeon P. G. S. Ten Broeck, United States Army, in 1851–2, paid a visit to the Pueblo of Laguna, and also to the Moqui villages, where he spent several days, having a good opportunity afforded him of witnessing their peculiar ceremonies and customs; and as his description of the remarkable idiosyncracies of this anomalous race (or rather type of a race) is highly interesting and truthful, I have taken the liberty of making some extracts from a paper furnished by him to Mr. H. R. Schoolcraft.

He attended church on Christmas at Laguna, and gives his impressions in the following words: "The church was quite a large building of stone, laid up in mud, and is surmounted by a wooden cross. It is long and narrow, and the walls are whitewashed in much the same style that the Indians paint their earthen-ware. The front is continued about ten feet above the roof, the whole overtopped by a cross, and in this wall are three arches containing as many sized bells, whose tones are by no means Orphean, and which are tolled by Indians standing on the roof, and pulling cords attached to the different clappers. (Query: where did the bells come from?)

"The Indians appear greatly delighted in jingling these bells upon all occasions; but this morning they commenced very early, and made, if possible, more noise than usual. After breakfast I entered church and found the people assembling for worship, the men in their best blankets, buckskin breeches, and moccasins, and the squaws in their gayest tilmas. Many of the latter wore blankets of red cloth thrown over the ordinary colored tilma or manta. Candles were lighted at the altar, within the limits of which were two old men performing some kind of mystic ceremony. Soon an old, ragged, dirty-looking Mexican commenced reciting the rosary of the Virgin Mary, and all who understood Spanish joined in the responses. When the rosary was finished, this same old fellow sang a long song in praise of Montezuma, which he afterward told me was written by himself, the burden of which was 'Cuando! cuando! nabro otis Montezuma, cuando!'

"This being ended, some other ceremonies which I did not understand were gone through with by the Indians; speeches were made by the governor and some of the old men, and the congregation then quietly dispersed to prepare themselves for the pastimes of the afternoon. As they passed out I noticed that a great many of them carried in their hands little baskets containing images, some of sheep and goats, others of horses, cows, and other domestic animals, and others, again, of deer and beasts of the chase, quite ingeniously wrought in mud or dough. Inquiring the reason of this, I was told that it was their custom from time immemorial that those who had been successful with herds, in agriculture, in the chase, or any other way, carry images (each of that in which he had been blessed during the past year) to the altar, there to lay them at the feet of the Great Spirit.

"But I have deferred until the last what was to me by far the most curious and interesting in this singular Christmas service—I mean the orchestra. Just over the entrance door there was a small gallery, and no sooner had the Mexican commenced his rosary than there issued from this a sound like the warbling of a multitude of birds, and it was kept up until he had ceased. There it went, through the whole house, bounding from side to side, echoing from the very rafters—fine, tiny warblings, and deep-toned, thrilling sounds. The note of the wood-thrush and the trillings of the Canary bird, were particularly distinct. What could it mean? I determined to find out, and, having worked my way up into the gallery, I there found fifteen or twenty young boys lying down upon the floor, each with a small basin two thirds full of water in front of him, and one or more short reeds perforated and split in a peculiar manner. Placing one end in the water, and blowing through the other, they imitated the notes of different birds most wonderfully. It was a curious sight; and, taken altogether, the quaintly painted church, the altar with its lighted candles and singular inmates, the kneeling Indians in their picturesque garbs, and, above all, the sounds sent down by the bird orchestra, formed a scene not easily forgotten. I believe I was more pleased with this simple and natural music than I have ever been with the swelling organs and opera-singers who adorn the galleries of our churches at home. About four o'clock this afternoon a party of seven men and as many squaws appeared in the yard in front of the church, accompanied by an old man bearing a *tombe*, and commenced one of their dances.

"The *tombe* is a peculiar drum, used by all the Indians in this country at their festivals. It is made of a hollow log about two and a half feet long, and fifteen inches in diameter. A dried hide, from which the hair has been removed, is stretched over either end, and to one side a short pole is lashed, to support the instrument when played upon. A drum-stick, like those used for the bass drum, but with a longer handle, is employed in playing, and with this they pound away with great energy, producing a dull roar, which is audible at a considerable distance, and is almost deafening to one unaccustomed to it, if approached too near. The dancers were accompanied by a band of elderly men, who immediately commenced singing in time with the *bum-bum* of the tombe. All the dancers appeared in their best attire, the men and squaws wearing large sashes, most fancifully worked and dyed, and also eagle and turkey feathers in their hair and hanging down their backs, and from the waist of each was suspended a skin of the silver-gray fox. The men's legs were naked from the knee down, and painted red. Their hair hung loose upon their shoulders, and both men and women had their hands painted with white clay in such a way as to resemble open-work gloves. The women had on beautifully-worked mantas, and were barefooted, with the exception of a little piece tied about the heel, which looked like that part of an embroidered slipper. They all wore their hair combed over their faces in a manner that rendered it utterly impossible to recognize any of them. Every man carried in his hand a gourd partly filled with little pebbles, which he shook in exact time with the music. They dance a kind of hop-step, and the figure is something like the countermarch, the couple leading up toward the church, and then turning, filed back again. The women keep their elbows close to their sides, and their heels pressed firmly together, and do not raise the feet, but shuffle along with a kind of rolling motion, moving their arms, from the elbows down, with time to the step. At times each man dances around his squaw, while she turns herself about, as if her heels formed a pivot on which she moved. Dancers, tombe, and singers keep most excellent time, and there is no discord among the gourds. After dancing a short time in front of the church, they went into the Plaza and continued till dark, when they separated."

These dances were continued on the 26th, 27th, and 28th of December, in the same manner as on Christmas.

On the 31st of March, 1852, the doctor visited the Moquis at their villages. He says of them, "Between eleven and twelve to-day we arrived at the first towns of Moqui. All the inhabitants turned out, crowding the streets and house-tops to have a view of the white men. All the old men pressed forward to shake hands with us, and we were at once feasted upon guavas and a leg of mutton broiled on coals. After the feast we smoked with them, and they then said that we should move our camp in, and that they would give us a room and plenty of wood for the men, and sell us corn for the animals; accordingly, our command was moved into town.

"The three villages here are situated on a strong bluff about 300 feet high, and from 30 to 150 feet wide, which is approached by a trail passable for horses at only one point. This is very steep, and an hour's work in throwing down stones, with which it is in many places built up, could render it utterly inaccessible to horsemen. At all other points they have constructed footpaths, steps, etc., by which they pass up and down. The side of the rock is not perfectly perpendicular, but, after a sheer descent of 60 or 70 feet, there are ledges from five to eight yards wide, on which they have established their sheep-folds. The bluff is about 800 yards long, and the towns are some 180 yards apart.

"The houses are built of stone, laid in mud (which must have been brought from the plain below, as there is not a particle of soil upon the rock), and in the same form as the other pueblos. They are whitewashed inside with white clay. Hanging by strings from the rafters I saw some curious and rather horrible little Aztec images, made of wood or clay, and decorated with paint and feathers, which the guide told me were '*saints*;' but I have seen the children playing with them in the most irreverent manner."

Speaking of the dances of the Moquis, the doctor says: "The dance of to-day has been a most singular one, and differs from any I have seen among the other Pueblo Indians, the dresses of the performers being more quaint and rich. There were twenty men and as many women, ranged in two files. The dresses of the men were similar to those before described, except that they wear on their heads large pasteboard towers, painted typically, and curiously decorated with feathers, and each man has his face entirely covered with a visor made of small willows with the bark peeled off, and dyed a deep brown. The women all have their hair put up in the manner peculiar to virgins; and immediately in the centre, where the hair is parted, a long, straight eagle's feather is fixed. But by far the most beautiful part of their dress is a tilma of some three and a half feet square, which is thrown over the shoulders, fastened in front, and, hanging down behind, reaches half way below the knee. This tilma is pure white. Its materials I should suppose to be cotton or wool. Its texture is very fine, and it has one or more wide borders of beautiful colors, exceedingly well wrought in and of curious patterns. The women also wear visors of willow sticks, which are colored a bright yellow, and arranged in parallel rows like Pandean pipes. On each side of the files is placed a small boy, who dances or canters up and down the line, and is most accurately modeled after the popular representation of his satanic majesty's imps. With the exception of a very short-fringed tunic reaching just below the hip-joint, and a broad sash fastened around the waist, the boy is entirely naked. The whole body is painted black, relieved by white rings placed at regular intervals over the whole person. The appearance of these little imps as they gamboled along the line of dancers was most amusing. They had neither a tombe accompaniment nor a band of singers; but the dancers furnished their own music, and a most strange sound it was, resembling very much the noise, on a large scale, of a swarm of blue-bottle-flies in an empty hogshead. The dance was a most monotonous one, the dancers remaining in the same place, and alternately lifting their feet in time to the song and the gourds. The only change of position was an occasional 'about face.'

"When they first came in, two old men, who acted as masters of ceremonies, went along the whole line, and, with a powder held between the thumb and fore finger, anointed each dancer on the shoulder. After dancing a while in the mode above described, the ranks were opened, and, rugs and blankets being spread upon the ground, the virgins squatted on them, while the men kept up a kind of murmuring dance in front. Every third or fourth female had at this time a large hollow gourd placed before her, on which rested a grooved piece of wood, shaped like an old-fashioned wash-board, and by drawing the dry shoulder-blade of a sheep rapidly across this, a sound was produced similar to that of a watchman's rattle. After performing the same dance on each side of the Plaza, they left, to return again in fifteen minutes; and thus they kept it up from sunrise till dark, when the dancing ceased.

"As appendages to the feast, they had clowns who served as messengers and waiters, and also to amuse the spectators while the dancers were away. The first batch consisted of six or eight young men in breech-clouts, having some comical daubs of paint on their faces and persons, with wigs made of black sheepskins. Some wore rams' horns on their heads, and were amusing themselves by attempts at dancing, singing, and running races, when they were attacked by a huge grizzly bear (or rather a fellow in the skin of one), which, after a long pursuit and many hard fights, they brought to bay and killed. They then immediately opened him, and took from out of his body a quantity of guavas, green corn, etc., which his bearship had undoubtedly appropriated from the refreshments provided for the clowns. But no sooner had they disposed of Bruin than a new trouble came upon them in the shape of two ugly little imps, who, prowling about, took every opportunity to annoy them; and when, by dint of great perseverance, they succeeded in freeing themselves from these misshapen brats, in rushed eight or ten most horrible-looking figures (in masks), all armed with whips, which they did not for a moment hesitate to apply most liberally to any of the poor clowns who were so unlucky as to fall into their clutches. They even tied some hand and foot, and laid them out in the Plaza.

"It seemed they were of the same race as the imps, and came to avenge the treatment they had received at the hands of the clowns, for the 'limbs of Satan' returned almost immediately, and took an active part in their capture, and in superintending the flaggellating operations. Such horrible masks I never saw before; noses six inches long, mouths from ear to ear, and great goggle eyes as big as half a hen's egg, hanging by a string partly out of the socket.

"The simple Indians appeared highly delighted with these performances, and I must avow having had many a hearty laugh at their whimsicalities.

"While the dances were going on, large baskets filled with guavas of different forms and colors, roasted corn, bread, meat, and other eatables, were distributed by the virgins among the spectators. The old governor tells me this evening that it is contrary to their usages to permit the females to dance, and that those whom I supposed to be young virgins were in fact young men, dressed for the occasion. This is a custom peculiar to the Moquis, I think, for in all other pueblos I visited the women dance.

"The government of these people is hereditary, but does not necessarily descend to the sons of the incumbent; for if the people prefer any other blood relation, he is chosen.

"The population of the seven villages I should estimate at 8000, of which one half is found in the first three. They say that of late years wars and diseases have greatly decreased their numbers. They spoke of fevers and disease, which I supposed to be phthisis and pertussis. They observe no particular burial rites. They believe in the existence of a Great Father, who lives where the sun rises, and a Great Mother, who lives where the sun sets. The first is the author of all the evils that befall them, as war, pestilence, famine, etc.; and the Great Mother is the very reverse of this, and from her are derived the blessings they enjoy. In the course of the 'talk,' the principal governor made a speech, in which he said, 'Now we all know that it is good the Americans have come among us, for our Great Father, who lives where the sun rises, is pacified; and our Great Mother, who lives where the sun sets, is smiling, and, in token of her approbation, sends fertilizing showers (it was snowing at the time), which will enrich our fields, and enable us to raise the harvest whereby we subsist.'

"Of their origin they give the following account:

"Many, many years ago, their Great Mother brought from her home in the west nine races of men, in the following forms: first, the deer race; second, the sand race; third, the water race; fourth, the bear race; fifth, the hare race; sixth, the prairie-wolf race; seventh, the rattlesnake race; eighth, the tobacco-plant race; ninth, the seed-grass race. Having placed them on the spot where their villages now stand, she transformed them into men, who built the present pueblos, and the distinction of races is still kept up. One told me he was of the sand race, another the deer, etc. They are firm believers in metempsychosis, and say that when they die they will resolve into their original forms, and become bears, deer, etc. The chief governor is of the deer race.

"Shortly after the pueblos were built, the Great Mother came in person, and brought them all the domestic animals they now have, which are principally sheep and goats, and a few very large donkeys. The sacred fire is kept continually burning by the old men, and all I could glean from them was that some great misfortune would befall their people if they allowed it to be extinguished. They know nothing of Montezuma, and have never had any Spanish or other missionaries among them. All the seeds they possess were brought from where the morning star rises. They plant in May or June, and harvest in October or November. They do not plow or irrigate, but put their seeds in the sand, and depend upon the rains for water. They raise corn, melons, pumpkins, beans, and onions; also a cotton of which I procured a specimen, and a species of mongrel tobacco. They have also a few peach-trees, and are the only Pueblo Indians who raise cotton. They have no small grain of any kind. They say they have known the Spaniards ever since they can remember. About twenty years ago, a party of some fifteen Americans, the first they ever saw, came over the mountains and took the Zuni trail. Six years afterward, another party, with four females, passed through.

"Their mode of marriage might well be introduced into the United States, with the Bloomer costume. Here, instead of the swain asking the hand of the fair one, she selects the young man who is to her fancy, and then her father proposes the match to the sire of the lucky youth. This proposition is never refused. The preliminaries being arranged, the young man, on his part, furnishes two pairs of moccasins, two fine blankets, two mattresses, and two sashes used at the feast; while the maiden, for her share, provides an abundance of eatables, when the marriage is celebrated by feasting and dancing.

"Polygamy is unknown among them; but at any time, if either of the parties become dissatisfied, they can divorce themselves, and marry others if they please. In case there are children, they are taken care of by the respective grandparents. They are simple, happy, and most hospitable people. The sin of intoxication is unknown among them, as they have no kind of fermented liquors. When a stranger visits one of their houses, the first act is to set food before him, and nothing is done 'till he has eaten.'

"In every village are one or more edifices under ground, and you descend a ladder to get into them. They answer to our village groceries, being a place of general resort for the male population. I went into one of them. In the centre was a small square box of stone, in which was a fire of guava bushes, and around this a few old men were smoking. All around the room were Indians naked to the 'breech-clout;' some were engaged in sewing, and others spinning and knitting.

"On a bench in the background sat a warrior most extravagantly painted, who was undoubtedly undergoing some ordeal, as I was not allowed to approach him. They knit, weave, and spin, as in the other pueblos, and, besides, make fabrics of cotton.

"The villages of the Moquis are seven in number, and more nearly correspond to the seven cities of Cibola than any which have yet been discovered. They are situated in the same valley—they are upon a bluff. Oraivaz, called Musquins by the Mexicans, is almost due west from the bluff, and about thirty miles distant. There is another town at twenty miles west by south, and two more about south-southwest, and some eight or ten miles distant from the first three. Of these, the two at the southern extremity of the bluff are the largest, containing probably 2000 inhabitants; Oraivaz is the second in size. They all speak the same language except Harno, the most northern town of the three, which has a language and some customs peculiar to itself.

"It seems a very singular fact that, being within 150 yards of the middle town, Harno should have for so long a period its own language and customs. The other Moquis say the inhabitants of this town have a great advantage over them, as they perfectly understand the common language, and none but the people of Harno understand their dialect. The women are the prettiest squaws I have yet seen, and are very industrious. Their manner of dressing the hair is very pretty. While virgins, it is done up on each side of the head in two inverse rolls, which bear some resemblance to the horns of the mountain sheep. After marriage they wear it in two large knots on each side of the face. These people make the same kind of pottery as the Zuñians and Lagunians."

Notwithstanding the country west of the Rio del Norte

presents so barren and forbidding an aspect that it is only here and there along the immediate borders of the few water-courses that the soil will yield any returns to the husbandman, yet this country was once much more populous than at present. The numerous ruins of houses and towns scattered all over the country most incontestably establish this fact; moreover, the character of these ruins goes to show that the people who erected them were more advanced in architecture than the Pueblo's, or any other Indians now existing in that country.

Captain Sitgreaves, in his expedition from Zuni to the Colorado, passed for nine miles through a continuous succession of these ruins, in a locality where there was no water for many miles, which induced him to believe that the disintegration of the rocks from the surrounding heights had filled up the beds of the streams, and rendered the situation of this ancient city uninhabitable.

Captain J. H. Simpson, United States Engineers, who in 1849 was attached to an expedition made into the Navahoe country, in Northwest New Mexico, describes the ruins of several enormous houses he met with, which were built of stone, in a style of architecture and masonry far better than that we find in the pueblos that are now occupied. Some of these houses contained from 100 to 160 rooms, each upon the ground floors, all, excepting the estufas, of small dimensions, and not exceeding twelve by eight feet in area; the doors only about three feet by two, and the windows some twelve inches square, with no chimneys. They all had the large underground council-rooms, or estufas, like those in the pueblos of the present day, and this would seem to indicate that they were built by a race of people having similar habits; yet the Pueblo Indians do not pretend to know any thing about their origin. All that can be gleaned from them upon the subject is, that they are "*casas grandes*" (big houses), which is very apparent. What appears very mysterious to me in regard to it is that the beams, rafters, and floors in some of these ruins should have remained for so great a length of time as sound and perfect as they were when put in, in some instances even exhibiting the print of the dull (probably) stone axe used in cutting them.

If the origin of these ruins was of a date anterior to the discovery of New Mexico by the Spaniards, I can only account for the preservation of the wood-work from the fact of the extreme purity and dryness of the atmosphere.

K*

CHAPTER V.

RED RIVER EXPEDITION.

Red River Expedition. — Order.—Early Efforts to explore it.—Navigable Portion. — Copper Ores. — New Ore. — Dr. Hitchcock's Opinion.—Great Gypsum Belt.—Cause of bad Taste in the Water.—Witchita Mountains. —Extent of Choctaw Reservation.—Beautiful Country. —Visit of Witchetaws. —Buffaloes. —Comanche Trails.—Buffalo Chase.—Panther killed.— Unaccountable Appearance of Water. — South Winds. —Encamping.— Head of North Fork.—Visit to Canadian River. —Mirage.—Head of Salt Fork.—*Laño-Estacado.*—Prairie Dog Town.—Leaving the Train.—Bad Water.—Suffering from the Effects of bad Water.—Reach the Head of the main Fork of Red River.—Beautiful Scenery.—Bears.—Remarkable Cañon.

ON the 5th of March, 1852, I received the following order:

(SPECIAL ORDERS, NO. 33.)

"*Adjutant General's Office, Washington, March* 5, 1862.

"Captain R. B. Marcy, 5th Infantry, with his company as an escort, will proceed, without unnecessary delay, to make an examination of the Red River and the country bordering upon it, from the mouth of Cache Creek to its sources, according to the special instructions with which he will be furnished.

* * * * * * *

"Brevet Captain G. B. McClellan, Corps of Engineers, is assigned duty with this expedition. * * * *

"By command of Major General Scott.

"(Signed) R. JONES, *Adjutant General.*"

As some of the most interesting events connected with this expedition may possess sufficient attraction for many who feel an interest in such matters to compensate them for the perusal, I have determined to give them a passing notice here.

I had spent the greater portion of the three previous years in exploring the country lying upon the Canadian River of the Arkansas, and upon the head waters of the Trinity, Brazos, and Colorado Rivers of Texas.

During this time my attention had frequently been called to the remarkable fact that a great portion of one of the largest and most important rivers in the United States had remained up to that late period wholly unexplored and unknown. The only information we had upon the subject was derived from Indians, and was, of course, very indefinite and unsatisfactory; in a word, the country embraced within the basin of Upper Red River had always been to us a "*terra incognita*."

Several enterprising travelers had at different periods attempted to explore this river, but as yet none had succeeded in finding its head waters.

At a very early period officers were sent out by the French government to explore Red River, but their examinations appear to have extended no farther than the vicinity of the present town of Natchitoches, Louisiana. On the 3d of May, 1806, three years after the cession to the United States, by the First Consul of the French Republic, of that vast territory then known as Louisiana, a small party known as the Exploring Expedition of Red River, consisting of Captain Sparks, Mr. Freeman, Lieutenant Humphry, and Dr. Curtis, with seventeen private soldiers, embarked at St. Catharine's Landing, near Natchez, Mississippi, and started to ascend Red River to its sources.

This party encountered many difficulties and obstructions in the navigation of the river, among the numerous bayous in the vicinity of the great raft, but finally overcame them all, and found themselves above this formidable obstacle.

They were, however, here met by a large force of Spanish troops, the commander of which forced them to turn back and abandon the enterprise.

Another expedition was fitted out in 1806 by our government, and placed under the command of that enterprising young traveler, Lieutenant Pike, who was ordered to ascend the Arkansas River to its sources, thence to strike across the country to the head of the Red River, and descend that stream to Natchitoches. After encountering many privations and intense sufferings in the deep snows of the lofty mountains about the head waters of the Arkansas, Lieutenant Pike arrived finally upon a stream running to the east, which he took to be Red River, but which subsequently proved to be the Rio Grande. Here he was taken by the Governor of New Mexico and sent home by way of Chihuahua and San Antonio, thus putting a stop to his explorations.

General Wilkinson, under whose orders Lieutenant Pike was serving at the time, states, in a letter to him after his return, as follows: "The principal object of your expedition up the Arkansas was to discover the true position of the sources of Red River. This was not accomplished." Lieutenant Pike, however, from the most accurate information he could obtain, gives the geographical position of the sources of Red River as in latitude 33° N., and longitude 104° W. Again, in 1819–20, Colonel Long, of the United States Topographical Engineers, on his return from an exploration of the Missouri River and the country lying between that stream and the head of the Arkansas, undertook to descend the Red River from its sources. The colonel, in speaking of this in his interesting report, says: "We arrived at a creek having a westerly course, which we took to be a tributary of Red River. Having traveled down its valley about two hundred miles, we fell in with a party of Indians, of the nation of 'Kaskias,' or 'Bad Hearts,' who gave us to understand that the stream along which we were traveling was Red River. We accordingly continued our march down the river several hundred miles farther, when, to our no small disappointment, we discovered it was the Canadian of the Arkansas, instead of Red River, that we had been exploring.

"Our horses being nearly worn out with the fatigue of our long journey, which they had to perform barefooted, and the season being too far advanced to admit of our retracing our steps and going back again in quest of the source of Red River, with the possibility of exploring it before the commencement of winter, it was deemed advisable to give over the enterprise for the present and make our way to the settlements on the Arkansas. We were led to the commission of this mistake in consequence of our not having been able to procure a good guide acquainted with that part of the country. Our only dependence in this respect was upon Pike's map, which assigns to the head waters of Red River the apparent locality of those of the Canadian."

Dr. James, who accompanied Colonel Long, in his journal of the expedition, says: "Several persons have recently arrived at St. Louis, in Missouri, from Santa Fé, and, among others, the brother of Captain Shreeves, who gives information of a large and frequented road, which runs nearly due east from that place, and strikes one of the branches of the Canadian; that, at a considerable distance south of this point, in the high plain, is the principal source of Red River.

"His account confirms an opinion we had previously formed, namely, that the branch of the Canadian explored by Major Long's party in August, 1820, has its sources near those of some stream which descends toward the west into the Rio del Norte, and, consequently, that some other region must contain the head of Red River." He continues:

"From a careful comparison of all the information we have been able to collect, we are satisfied that the stream on which we encamped on the 31st of August is the Rio Raijo of Humboldt, long mistaken for the sources of Red River of Natchitoches. In a region of red clay and sand, where all the streams become nearly the color of arterial blood, it is not surprising that several rivers should have received the same name; nor is it surprising that so accurate a topographer as the Baron Humboldt, having learned that a red river rises forty or fifty miles east of Santa Fé, and runs to the east, should conjecture it might be the source of Red River of Natchitoches.

"This conjecture (for it is no more) we believed to have been adopted by our geographers, who have with much confidence made their delineations and their accounts to correspond with it."

Hence it will be seen that up to this time there was no record of any traveler having reached the sources of Red River, and that the country upon the head waters of that stream had heretofore been unexplored. The Mexicans, and Indians on the borders of Mexico, are in the habit of calling any river, the waters of which have a red appearance, "Rio Colorado," or Red River, and they have applied this name to the Canadian in common with several others; and as many of the prairie Indians often visit the Mexicans, and some even speak the Spanish language, it is a natural consequence that they should adopt the same nomenclature for rivers, places, etc. Thus, if a traveler in New Mexico were to inquire for the head of Red River, he would most undoubtedly be directed to the Canadian, and the same would also be the case in the adjacent Indian country. These facts will account for the mistake into which Baron Humboldt was led, and it will also account for the error into which Colonel Long and Lieutenant Pike have fallen in regard to the sources of the stream which we call Red River.

Dr. Gregg, in his "Commerce of the Prairies," tells us that on his way down the south bank of the Canadian his Comanche guide, Manuel (who, by-the-by, traveled six hundred miles with me upon the Plains, and whom I always found reliable), pointed out to him breaks or bluffs upon a stream to the south of the Canadian, near what we ascertained to be the true position of the head of the north branch of Red River, and where it approaches within twenty-five miles of the Canadian. These bluffs he said were upon the "Rio Negro," which the doctor supposed to be the Witchita River; but, after having examined that section of country, I am satisfied that the north branch of Red River must have been alluded to by the guide, as the Witchita rises farther to the east. It therefore seems probable that "Rio Negro" is the name which the Mexicans have applied to Red River of Louisiana.

Having organized my party, and laid in a supply of provisions for our expedition at Fort Belknap, on the Brazos River, in Texas, we, on the 1st day of May, left that post, and on the 9th we reached the mouth of Cache Creek, the point at which we were ordered to commence our examinations.

This point was at that time about two hundred miles, by the meanderings of the river, above the remotest white settlements where steam-boats had yet reached. I am confident, however, that at a high stage there will be sufficient depth of water to allow small steamers to ascend the river about fifty miles above Cache Creek.

At a low stage of water the river becomes very shallow, and can then be forded at almost any point. At the mouth of Cache Creek the Red River was about two hundred yards wide and four feet deep, with a current of three miles per hour.

Cache Creek takes its rise in the Witchita chain of mountains. It is, at the mouth, one hundred and fifty feet wide and three feet deep, flowing rapidly over a hard clay and gravel bed, between high, abrupt banks, through a valley about a mile wide of rich alluvium, and bordered by timber, which is the best I met with west of the Cross Timbers, and well adapted for building purposes. The soil in the valley is admirably suited for the culture of all kinds of grain; and an analysis of the subsoil by Professor Shephard, of Amherst College, showed that it possessed strong and enduring constituents.

Just before we reached Cache Creek we passed a small stream, where we picked up several pieces of copper ore lying upon the surface, where the rains had washed away the turf.

The analysis of these specimens by Professor Shephard is alluded to in his report as follows: "The most interesting of the copper ores submitted by Captain Marcy was a specimen from the main or South Fork of Red River, near the Witchita Mountains.

"It is a black, compact ore, strongly resembling the black oxide of copper from the Lake Superior mines, for which substance I at first mistook it. It was partially coated by a thin layer of the rare and beautiful atacamite.

"This is the first instance in which this species has been detected in North America. On subjecting the black ore to a close investigation, it proves to be a substance hitherto undescribed, and it affords me much pleasure to name it, in honor of the very enterprising and successful explorer to whom mineralogy is indebted for the discovery, *Marcylite.* In small fragments it melts in the heat of a candle, to the flame of which it imparts a rich blue and green color. This is especially striking when a blowpipe is employed. The slightest heat of the instrument suffices for the fusion of the ore. The chloride of copper is volatilized, and spreads over the charcoal support, from which the splendid green color rises also. Analysis gave the following as the composition of the ore:

Copper	54.30
Oxygen and Chlorine	36.20
Water	9.50
	100.00,

with traces of Silica.

"The above is undoubtedly a very valuable ore for copper, as it is very rich in metal, and easy of reduction in the furnace."

We discovered traces of copper ore in several other localities on Red River, and also upon the Big Witchita, in 1854, but it generally occurred in small detached fragments, from the size of a pea to that of a hen's egg. With one exception, however, we saw no veins of the ore.

While upon this subject, I take occasion to relate a circumstance that occurred while I was stationed at Camp Arbuckle, on the Canadian River, during the autumn of 1850.

My old Delaware guide, Black Beaver, one day came to me, and, taking me aside, very mysteriously and cautiously pulled out from his pocket several large pieces of green carbonate of copper, at the same time saying, "Maybe so money." I assured him that it was copper, and asked him if it was abundant where he found it. He said there was "*a heap.*" And upon my inquiring whether he was willing to show me the locality, he said, "Bob Jones (a rich Chickasaw) he say, s'poze find um copper mine, give um four hundred dollars." I informed him that I was willing to pay the same amount, provided the ore was sufficiently abundant, and an arrangement was made with him to go with me the following morning to the place where he obtained the specimens. I made my arrangements, accordingly, for an early departure; but Beaver did not make his appearance; and, after my patience was exhausted in waiting, I rode over to his house, where I found him looking very sulky, and having apparently made no preparations for the trip. I asked him if he was ready to go. He replied, "I s'pect maybe so I not go, captain." "Why not?" I inquired. He said, "Delaware law, s'poze show um 'Merican man mine, kill um." I then endeavored to convince him that there was no danger of any one knowing where we proposed to go; but he had fully determined not to have any thing farther to do with it, and I could not persuade him to change his resolution.

I however succeeded subsequently in discovering the locality without his agency, and found a considerable quantity of detached pieces of the ore, some of which were as large as a man's head. It was lying upon the surface of the ground; but we found no vein. I believe, however, as we traced the surface ore for at least three hundred yards in a direct line, that excavations might discover a vein beneath this line.

We afterward sent a wagon, and transported a load of this ore to Fort Smith, and it was sent thence to New Orleans and Liverpool, where it was smelted by a Welch mining company, and the proceeds paid all the expenses of the transportation. Farther than this, nothing was ever done.

Doctor Edward Hitchcock, in speaking of the prospects for copper in the country upon Red River, says:

"How much copper may be expected in such a region as that on Red River I have no means of judging, because I know of no analogous formation; but as we have proof that it is an aqueous deposit, and that igneous agency has been active not far off (this is a strongly-marked characteristic upon the Big Witchita), it would not be strange if the vicinity of the Witchita Mountains should prove a prolific locality."

From the geological formation of the Witchita Mountains, and the character of the quartz and the black sand which we observed there, we were induced to believe that gold might be found, but Dr. Hitchcock did not appear to regard this as of much consequence. He says: "But, though your discovery of gold (we found only one small specimen) will probably excite more attention, I feel that the great gypsum deposits of the West which you have brought to light will be of far more consequence to the country."

In several of my exploring expeditions I had passed through the great gypsum belt alluded to by the doctor, in an easterly and westerly direction, at six different points of latitude, from the Canadian River on the north to the Rio Grande on the south, and have observed it extending in a course nearly northeast and southwest over the entire distance. It is from 50 to 100 miles wide, and about 350 miles in length, and is embraced within the meridians 99 and 104½ of west longitude, and the 32d and the 36th parallels of north latitude.

In many places I have observed all the varieties of gypsum, from the common plaster of Paris of commerce, to pure selenite, and among specimens of the latter were some pieces three feet by four in surface, and two inches in thickness, and as perfectly transparent as any crown glass I ever saw. Placing one of these specimens upon the page of a book, at a short distance off, it was impossible to tell that any thing covered it, so perfectly plain did the letters show beneath the plate.

It is to be regretted that I could not have brought home some of these beautiful specimens, but my means of transportation were too limited to allow it.

Wherever I have encountered this mineral I have invariably found the water bitter and unpalatable, which arises from the decomposition of the rock, as an analysis of the water has shown that the taste depends upon the presence of three salts in nearly equal proportions, two of which, sulphate of magnesia or Epsom salts, and chloride of sodium, are very sapid.

Dr. Hitchcock remarked upon the formation: "I do not wonder that you were deeply impressed with the vast extent of this deposit."

Professor D. D. Owen, in his late valuable report of a geological survey of Wisconsin, Iowa, etc. (1852), describes a gypseous deposit twenty to thirty feet thick, and occupying an area from two to three square miles; and he says that "for thickness and extent this is by far the most important bed of plaster-stone known west of the Appalachian chain, if not in the United States." The distinguished professor did not of course know, when he wrote this, that there was in the United States another deposit of this mineral several thousand times as large as the one mentioned by him.

The only other gypsum formations in the world known to geologists which compare with this in magnitude are those described by Mr. Darwin in his admirable work on the geology of South America, and are situated along the western slope of the Cordilleras, and in Patagonia and Chili. Some of these beds occur of the enormous thickness of six thousand feet, and others are eleven hundred miles in surface extent.

Dr. Hitchcock adds: "The specimens of this gypsum put into my hands correspond with your descriptions. One of them, of snowy whiteness, and compact, it seems to me might answer for delicate gypseous alabaster, so extensively wrought in other lands for monumental purposes. The selenite was regarded among the ancients as the most delicate variety of alabaster, and was employed by the wealthy, and in palaces for windows, under the name of *Phengites.* It has the curious property of enabling a person within the house to see all that passes abroad, while those abroad can not see what is passing within; hence Nero employed it in his palace. If the splendid plates which you describe occur in any quantity, it may hereafter be of commercial value, as it certainly will be of mineralogical interest."

One of the most prominent features of the country in the Red River basin is the Witchita chain of mountains. The following quotations from my journal, written upon the ground, will give my impressions as I passed through them.

"The chain is about fifty miles in length, and from five to fifteen miles wide, running about south 60° west. These mountains, and those at the head of the Brazos River, are the only elevations of any considerable magnitude in all that vast expanse of territory included between the Red and the Pecos Rivers. Rising, as they do, in the midst of a vast naked prairie, they present a most striking and anomalous feature in the scenery of that otherwise monotonous landscape.

"Their conformation is generally of a coarse, soft, flesh-colored granite, the peaks conical, occasionally terminating in sharp points, standing at intervals of from one fourth to one mile apart. Red River passes directly through the western extremity of the chain.

"The more we have seen of the country about these mountains, the more pleased we have been with it. Indeed, I have never visited any country that, in my opinion, possessed greater natural local advantages for agriculture than this. Bounteous Nature seems here to have strewed her favors with a lavish hand, and to have held out every inducement for civilized man to occupy it. The numerous tributaries of Cache Creek, flowing from granite fountains, and winding, like net-work, in every direction through the valleys in the mountains — with the advantages of good timber, soil, and grass, the pure, elastic, and delicious climate, with a bracing atmosphere — all unite in presenting rare inducements to the husbandman. It would only be necessary for our practical farmers to visit this locality; they could not be otherwise than pleased with it. And were it not for the fact that the greater part of the most desirable lands lie east of the 100th meridian of longitude, and within the limits of that vast territory ceded by our government to the Choctaws in 1831, it would be purchased and settled by our citizens in a very few years. As it is now situated, far beyond the limits of the settlements, and directly within the range of the Comanches, it is of no use to the Choctaws themselves, as they seldom venture among the prairie tribes, and do not even know the character of this part of their own territory. They have a superabundance of fertile lands bordering upon the Red and Canadian Rivers, near the white settlements of Texas and Arkansas, and they prefer occupying those to going farther out. They have thrown aside their primitive habits in a great degree, and abandoned the precarious and uncertain life of the hunter for the more quiet avocation of the husbandman. They look upon the wild Indian in much the same light as we do, and do not go among them; indeed, there is but little in common with them and the wild Indians."*

* The lands included within the Choctaw reservation, which are not occupied or made use of by them, are embraced within the 97th and 100th degrees of west longitude, and are bounded upon the north and south by the Canadian and Red Rivers, being about one hundred and eighty miles in

The remarks which follow were made while we were encamped at an old Witchetaw village near the eastern extremity of the mountains.

"Our camp is upon a branch of Cache Creek, about a mile above the village last occupied by the Witchetaws, before they left the mountains. Here they lived and planted corn for several years, and they exhibited much taste and judgment in selecting this site for their town. It is situated upon an elevated plateau, directly along the south bank of the creek, and commands an extended view of the country to the north, south, and east. From its commanding position it is well secured against surprise, and is, by nature, one of the most defensible places I have seen.

"The landscape here presented to the eye has a most charming diversity of scenery, consisting of mountains, woodlands, glades, water-courses, and prairies, all laid out and arranged in such peculiar order as to produce a most delightful effect upon the senses.

"This must have been a favorite spot for the Indians, and why they have abandoned it I can not imagine, unless it was through fear of the Comanches.

"The soil here, in point of fertility, surpasses any thing we have before seen, and the vegetation in the old corn-fields, consisting of rank weeds twelve feet high, was so dense that it was difficult to force a horse through it.

"The timber is sufficiently abundant for all purposes of the agriculturist, embracing over-cup (oak), post-oak, black walnut, pecan, hackberry, ash, black or Spanish oak, elm, and China. We found here the wild passion-flower, and a beautiful variety of the sensitive plant, which we had not before met with.

length by fifty in width, and constituting an aggregate of about nine thousand square miles of valuable and productive lands, or one thousand square miles more than the State of Massachusetts.

"The creek, just above the village, flows directly at the base of a perpendicular wall of porphyritic trap, 300 feet high, and studded with dwarf cedars, which, taking shallow root in the crevices of the formation, receive their meagre sustenance from the scanty decomposition of the rocks.

"This interesting escarpment has a columnar structure, with parallel flutings traversing the face in a vertical direction from top to bottom, and has the appearance of being the vertical section of a round hill that has been cleft asunder, and one half removed.

"All the sides of this hill, except that upon the creek, are smooth, with gentle and easy slopes, covered with grass up to the very verge of the acclivity. On riding up the smooth ascent of this eminence, and suddenly coming upon the edge of the giddy precipice, one involuntarily recoils with a shudder at the appearance of this strange freak of Nature. Large veins of quartz traversed this formation, and, upon examination, it was found to be cellular, like sponge or honey-comb, with the cells filled with liquid naphtha, about the consistency of tar, and having a strong resinous odor. (It has since occurred to me that this might have been the petroleum now so extensively known in commerce.)

"On the 27th of May, shortly after we had pitched our tents upon Otter Creek, a large party of Indians made their appearance on the opposite bank, and requested us to cut a tree for them to cross upon, as they wished to have a 'talk with the capitan.' Accordingly, we cut down a tall tree, which fell across the stream, and they came over, and encamped near us.

"They proved to be a hunting party of Witchetaws, about 150 in number, and were commanded by an old chief, 'Canaje-Hexie.' They had with them a large number of horses and mules, heavily laden with jerked buffalo meat, and ten wild horses which they had lassoed upon the prairie. They said they had been in search of us for several days; having learned we were coming up Red River, they were desirous of knowing what our business was in this part of their country. I replied to them that I was going to the head of Red River for the purpose of visiting the Indians, cultivating their friendship, and delivering to them 'a talk' from the Great Captain of all the whites, who, in token of his kindly feelings, had sent some presents to be distributed among such of his Red children as were friends to Americans; and as many of them continue to regard Texas as a separate and independent republic, I endeavored to impress upon them the fact that the inhabitants of that state were of the same nation as the whites in other parts of the United States. I also told them that all the prairie tribes would be held responsible for the depredations committed against the people of Texas, as well as elsewhere in our territories. I made inquiries concerning the country through which we still had to pass in our journey.

"They said we would find one more stream of good water about two days' travel from here; that we should then leave the mountains, and after that find no more fresh water to the sources of the river. The chief represented the river from where it leaves the mountains as flowing over an elevated, flat prairie country, totally destitute of water, wood, or grass, and the only substitute for fuel that could be had was the buffalo 'chips.' They remarked in the course of the interview that some few of their old men had been to the head of the river, and that the journey could be made in eighteen days by rapid riding; but the accounts given by those who had made the journey were of such a character as to deter others from attempting it. They said we need have no apprehension of encountering

Indians, as none ever visited that section. I inquired of them if there were not holes in the earth where the water remained after rains. They said no; that the soil was of so porous a nature that it soaked up the water as soon as it fell. I then endeavored to hire one of their old men to accompany me as guide; but they said they were afraid to go into the country, as there was no water, and they were fearful they would perish before they could return. The chief said, in conclusion, that perhaps I might not credit their statements, but that I would have abundant evidence of the truth of their assertions if I ventured much farther with my command. This account of the country ahead of us was truly discouraging, and we had any thing but an agreeable prospect before us. As the Indians, from their own statements, had traveled a great distance to see us, I distributed some presents among them, with a few rations of pork and flour, for which we received their acknowledgments in their customary style—by begging for every thing else they saw.

"About 25 miles below this the main river had forked, and we had taken the north branch.

"After passing the mountains, we arrived at a point where the branch we were upon again divided into two nearly equal branches.

"The water in the south branch (which I called the 'Salt Fork') is bitter and nauseating. The water in the north branch, which we ascended, was not sweet, but could be drank. It was at the confluence 105 feet wide, three feet deep, with a rapid current.

"*June* 1. One of the Delawares caught two bear cubs in the mountains to-day, one of which he brought in his arms to camp. He seems perfectly contented, and we shall take the young brute along with us.

"Our course here leaves the mountains, and we launch

out into the prairie before us, which appears to be an uninterrupted level plain as far as the eye can penetrate. I can not leave these mountains without a feeling of sincere regret. The beautiful and majestic scenery throughout the whole extent of the chain, with the charming glades lying between them, clothed with luxuriant sward up to the very bases of the rugged sides, besides the many springs of delicious water bursting forth from the solid walls of granite, and bounding along over the débris at the base, forcibly remind me of my own native hills, and the idea of leaving these for the desert plains gives rise to an involuntary feeling of sadness similar to that I experienced on leaving home.

"Our course led us up along the North Fork over a very monotonous country, with nothing of special interest until, on the 4th of June, as I was riding with one of the Delawares in advance of the train, we suddenly (as we rose upon an eminence) came in sight of four buffalo cows, with their calves, very quietly grazing in a valley below us. We at once put spurs to our horses, and, with our rifles in readiness, set off at a brisk gallop in pursuit, but, unfortunately, the animals had 'the wind' of us, and instantly bounded away over the prairie at full speed. We followed about three miles, but they had so much the start that we could not overtake them without giving our horses more labor than we cared about, and so abandoned the chase.

"Our greyhounds caught two deer in fair chase upon the open prairie, and they had several races in pursuit of antelopes, but had not as yet been able to come up with them. We occasionally saw a few wild turkeys, but they were not as abundant here as we found them below. There were several varieties of birds around our camp, among which we observed the white owl, meadow lark (which I have seen every where I have traveled), mocking-bird, kingbird, swallow, quail, etc.

"We passed the trail of a large party of Comanches on the 6th, going south with their families and lodges. The Comanches, during the past year, have not been friendly with the Delawares and Shawnees, and although there have as yet been no organized demonstrations of hostilities, they have secretly killed several men, and, in consequence, our hunters entertain a feeling of revenge toward them. They, however, go out alone every day on their hunts, six or eight miles from the command, and seem to have no fears of the Comanches. They are liable to encounter them at any moment, and, being poorly mounted, they could not escape by running; their only alternative in such an event would be to act on the defensive. I have cautioned them several times, but they say they are not afraid to meet any of the prairie Indians provided the odds are not greater than six to one. They are well armed with good rifles, the use of which they understand perfectly, and are very determined and brave fellows.

"*June* 7. Taking two of the Indians this morning, I went out for the purpose of making an examination of the surrounding country, and ascertaining whether good water could be found upon our route for our next encampment. We had gone about three miles in a westerly direction, when we struck a fresh buffalo track leading north; thinking we might overtake him, we followed up the trace until we came near the summit of an eminence upon the prairie, when I sent one of the Indians (John Bull) to the top of the hill, which was about one fourth of a mile distant, to look for the animal. He had no sooner arrived at the point indicated than we saw him make a signal for us to join him by riding round rapidly several times in a circle, and immediately put off at full speed over the hills. We set out at the same instant upon a smart gallop, and on reaching the crest of the hill discovered the terrified animal fleeing at a most furious pace, with John Bull in hot pursuit about 500 yards behind him. As we followed on down the prairie we had a fine view of the chase. The Delaware was mounted upon one of our most fractious and spirited horses, that had never seen a buffalo before, and, on coming near the animal, he seemed perfectly frantic with fear, making several desperate surges to the right and left, any one of which must have inevitably unseated his rider had he not been a most expert and skillful horseman. During the time the horse was plunging and making such efforts to escape, John, while he controlled him with masterly adroitness, seized an opportunity and gave the buffalo the contents of his rifle, breaking one of his fore legs, and somewhat retarding his speed; he still kept on, however, making good running, and it required all the strength of our horses to bring us alongside of him. Before we came up, our most excellent hunter, John Bull, had recharged his rifle and placed another ball directly back of the shoulder; but so tenacious of life is this animal, that it was not until the other Delaware and myself gave him four additional shots that we brought him to the ground.

"On our return we observed a pack of wolves, in company with a multitude of ravens, making merry over the carcass of the buffalo we had killed in the morning.

"In the evening, shortly after we had turned out our animals to graze, and had made every thing snug and comfortable about us, ourselves reclining very quietly after the fatigue of the day's march, one of the hunters came into camp and informed us that a panther had crossed the creek but a short distance above, and was coming toward us. This piece of intelligence, as may be supposed, created no little excitement in our quiet circle. Every body was up in an instant, seizing muskets, rifles, or any other weapon that came to hand, and, followed by all the dogs in camp, a very general rush was made toward the spot indicated by the Delaware. On reaching the place, we found where the animal, in stepping from the creek, had left water upon his track, which was not yet dry, showing that he had passed within a short time. We pointed out the track to several of the dogs, and endeavored, by every means which our ingenuity could suggest, to inspire them with some small degree of that enthusiasm which had animated us. We coaxed, cheered, and scolded, put their noses into the track, clapped our hands, pointed in the direction of the trail, hissed, and made use of divers other canine arguments to convince them that there was something of importance on hand, but it was all to no purpose. They did not seem to enter into the spirit of the chase, or to regard the occasion as one in which there was much glory to be derived from following in the footsteps of their illustrious predecessor. On the contrary, the zeal which they manifested in starting out from camp suddenly abated as soon as their olfactories came in contact with the track, and it was with very great difficulty that we could prevent them from running away. At this moment, however, our old bear-dog came up, and no sooner had he caught a sniff of the atmosphere than, suddenly coming to a stop and raising his head into the air, he sent forth one prolonged note, and started off in full cry upon the trail. He led off boldly into the timber, followed by the other dogs, which had now recovered confidence, with the men at their heels, cheering them on and shouting most vociferously, each one anxious to get the first glimpse of the panther. They soon roused him from his lair, and, after making a few circuits around the grove, he took to a tree.

"I was so fortunate as to reach the spot a little in advance of the party, and gave him a shot which brought him to the ground. The dogs then closed in with him, and others of the party, coming up directly afterward, fired several shots which took effect, and he was dead. He proved to be a fine specimen of the North American cougar, measuring eight and a half feet from the nose to the end of his tail.

"We encamped one evening upon a small creek which, with the exception of some pools of standing water, was dry. In the course of an hour, however, some of the men, who had been up the creek, came running back into camp greatly excited, and crying, "Here comes a plenty of water, boys!" And, sure enough, in a few minutes, to our astonishment and delight (as we were doubtful about having a supply), a perfect torrent came rushing down the dry bed of the rivulet, filling it to the tops of its banks, and continued running, turbid, and covered with drift and froth, as long as we remained. Our Delawares looked upon this as a special favor from the Great Spirit, and a favorable augury to the success of our enterprise. To us it was a most mysterious and inexplicable phenomenon, as there had been no rain for three days, with a cloudless sky. If the stream had been of much magnitude, we should have supposed that the water came from a distance, where there had been rains, but it did not rise over three or four miles from where we encamped. I have always since regretted that I did not follow up the stream to its source, as I might have discovered from whence the water came.

"Upon the Plains south of the Canadian, where I have traveled during the summer months, a strong breeze has usually sprung up about eight o'clock in the morning, and lasted until after night, reaching its maximum intensity about three o'clock in the afternoon. This breeze comes from the south, and generally rises and subsides with as much regularity as the sea-breeze upon the Atlantic coast, which fact has given rise to the opinion that it emanates from the Gulf of Mexico. However this may be, these cool and bracing winds temper the atmosphere, heated to intensity by the almost vertical rays of the sun, rendering it comfortable and pleasant even in midsummer.

"*June* 11. We crossed Sweetwater Creek at three o'clock this morning, and traveled eight miles in a westerly course, when we crossed two fresh Indian trails, which, from the circumstance of there being no trace of lodge-poles, our guide pronounced to have been made by war-parties; and he says that he has, during the day, seen four Indians upon a hill in the distance, but they turned on seeing him, and galloped off. The fact of their not being disposed to communicate with us looks suspicious, and they may have hostile intentions toward us; but, with our customary precautions, I think we shall be ready to receive them, either as friends or enemies.

"Our usual method of encamping is, where we can find the curve of a creek (which has generally been the case), to place ourselves in the concavity, with the wagons and tents extending around in a semicircle, uniting at each extremity of the curve of the creek, so as to inclose a sufficient space for the command; thus we are protected on one side by the creek, and upon the other by the line of wagons and tents. Immediately after reaching our camping-ground, all the animals are turned out to graze, under charge of the teamsters, who are armed, and remain constantly with them, keeping them as near the command as the supply of grass will permit. We generally commence the day's march about three o'clock in the morning, and are ready to encamp by eleven o'clock; this gives ample time for the animals to graze before night, when they are driven into camp. The horses and mules are picketed within the inclosure, while the oxen are tied up to the wagons; sentinels are then posted upon each side of the encampment, and kept constantly walking in such directions that they may have the animals continually in view.

"Many have supposed that cattle in a journey upon the Plains would perform better and keep in better condition by allowing them to graze in the morning, before starting upon the day's march, which would involve the necessity of traveling during the heat of the day. These persons are of opinion that animals will only feed at particular hours of the day, and that the remainder of the day must be allotted them for rest and sleep, and that, unless these rules are adhered to, they will not thrive. This opinion, however, is, I think, erroneous; and I also think that cattle will adapt themselves to any circumstances, so far as regards their working hours and their hours of rest. If they have been accustomed to labor at particular hours of the day, and the order of things is at once reversed, the working hours being changed into hours of rest, they may not do as well for a few days, but they soon become accustomed to the change, and eat and rest as well as before.

"By starting at an early hour in the morning during the summer months, the day's march is over before it becomes very warm; whereas (as I have observed), if the animals are allowed to graze before starting, the march must continue during the middle of the day, when the animals (particularly oxen) will suffer much from the heat of the sun, and, so far as my experience goes, will not keep in as good condition as when the other plan is pursued. I have adopted this course, and our oxen have continued to improve upon it. Another and important advantage to be derived from this is found in the fact that the animals, being tied up at night, are not liable to be lost or stolen."

We continued on up the North Fork of Red River until the 16th of June, when we reached the sources of this stream. The following is an extract from my journal of that day:

"*June* 16. Striking our tents at three o'clock this morning, we followed up the south bank of the river, which runs in a westerly course for eight miles, when it suddenly turns to the southwest, and here the elevated bluffs which we have had in view for several days past approach the river upon each side, until there is but a narrow gorge or cañon for the passage of the stream. These bluffs are composed of calcareous sandstone and clay, rising precipitously from the banks of the stream to the height of three hundred feet, when they suddenly terminate in the almost perfectly level plain of the 'Llano estacado.' Here the river branches out into numerous ramifications, all running into the deep gorges of the plain. Taking the largest, we continued up it, riding directly in the bed of the stream for about five miles, when we reached the source of this branch of the river, and, by ascending upon the table lands above, we could see the heads of the other branches which we had passed a few miles below.

"The latitude at this place, as determined by several observations of Polaris, is 35° 35′ 3″, and the longitude 101° 55′. These results make our position only about twenty-five miles from the Canadian River; and as I am anxious to determine how our observations conform to those we made in ascending that stream in 1849, I propose taking ten men, and leaving the main body of the command to guard our oxen and stores, to make a trip in a due north course to the Canadian. This will serve to show the connection between that stream and a certain known point upon the head of the north branch of Red River, and is, in my opinion, a geographical item which it is important to establish and confirm by actual observation, particularly as the Canadian has by several travelers been mistaken for Red River.

"At our encampment of this evening is the last running water we have found in ascending this branch of Red River.

We are near the junction of the last branch of any magnitude that enters the river from the north, and about three miles from the point where it debouches from the plains, in a grove of large cottonwood-trees upon the south bank of the river. Under the roots of one of the largest of these trees, which stands near the river, and below all others in the grove, we buried a bottle containing the following memorandum:

"'On the 16th day of June, 1852, an exploring expedition, composed of Captain R. B. Marcy, Captain G. B. McClellan, Lieutenant J. Updegraff, and Dr. G. C. Shumard, with fifty-five men of Company "D," 5th Infantry, encamped here, having this day traced the north branch of Red River to its sources. Accompanying the expedition were Captain J. H. Strain, of Fort Washita, and Mr. J. R. Suydam, of New York city.'

"On the 17th, accompanied by eleven of our party, I started in a northerly direction to go in search of the Canadian River, leaving the main party encamped on Red River.

"Our route led us immediately out upon the elevated plateau of the Staked Plain, where the eye rested upon no object of relief within the scope of vision, and our Delaware guide, John Bushman, whom I had informed that we expected to reach the Canadian that day, expressed great incredulity as to the reliance to be placed upon our astronomical conclusions. He asked me, 'How you know maybe so Canadian twenty-five miles?' I informed him that this was determined by observations upon the moon and stars. The expression of his countenance indicated that he regarded us either as 'big medicine men' or fools, and when we reached the summit of the plain before mentioned, he turned to me and said, 'Maybe no Canadian there' (pointing to the east). It certainly did not look much like it; but, after traveling about fifteen miles, our eyes were suddenly gladdened by the appearance of a valley before us, which I at once recognized as that of the Canadian, and, after traveling about ten miles farther, we found ourselves upon that stream.

"This was a matter of much gratification to us, as it confirmed the accuracy of our calculations regarding the geographical position of the sources of the North Fork of Red River. John Bushman was evidently greatly astonished at the precision of the estimates, and was now prepared to believe in our powers to almost any extent. He came to me that evening and said, 'I want you, captain, to look at stars agin, and tell me where Comanches gone;' and I could not persuade him that we were incapable of determining the exact location of every Indian camp in the country by simply looking at the stars with a telescope.

"The point where we struck the Canadian is at the mouth of a small stream called Sandy Creek, upon the map of the road I made from Fort Smith to Santa Fé in 1849. This, being near longitude 101° 45′, and latitude 35° 58′, makes our calculations for this and the head of Red River approximate very closely.

"On the 20th of June we turned south toward the Salt Fork, and, after going twelve miles, skirting the border of the Staked Plain from whence issued the numerous tributaries of the North Fork, we reached the valley of a very beautiful stream, twenty feet wide and six inches deep, running rapidly over a gravelly bed, through a valley about a mile wide, of sandy soil, with large cottonwood-trees along the banks. I have called this 'McClellan's Creek,' in compliment to my friend Captain McClellan, who I believe to be the first white man that ever set eyes upon it.

"We were happy, on arriving here, to find the water perfectly pure and palatable; and we regard ourselves as most

THE MIRAGE.

singularly fortunate in having favorable weather. The rains of the last two days have made the atmosphere delightfully cool, and afford us water in many places where we had no reason to expect it at this season of the year.

"During the middle of the day, when the earth and the adjacent strata of the air had become heated by the almost vertical rays of the sun, we observed, as usual, upon the 'Llano estacado,' an incessant tremulous motion in the lower strata of the atmosphere, accompanied by a most singular and illusive mirage. This phenomenon, which so bitterly deluded the French army in Egypt, and has been observed in many other places, is here seen in perfection.

"The very extraordinary refraction of the atmosphere upon these elevated plateaus causes objects in the distance to be distorted into the most wild and fantastic forms, and often exaggerated to many times their true size. A raven, for instance, would present the appearance of a man walking erect, and an antelope often be mistaken for a horse or buffalo. In passing along over this thirsty and extended plain in a warm day, the eye of a stranger is suddenly gladdened by the appearance of a beautiful lake, with green and shady groves directly upon the opposite bank. His heart beats with joy at the prospect of speedily luxuriating in the cool and delicious element before him, and he urges his horse forward, thinking it very strange that he does not reach the oasis. At one time he imagines that he has made a sensible diminution in the distance, and goes on with renewed vigor and cheerfulness; then again he fancies that the object recedes before him, and he becomes discouraged and disheartened; and thus he rides for miles and miles, and still he finds himself no nearer the goal than when he first saw it; when, perhaps, some sudden change in the atmosphere would dissipate the illusion, and disclose to him the fact that he had been following a mirage.

"On the 22d we struck the principal branch of the Salt Fork near where it debouches from the Staked Plain, and directly at the source is an elevated hill, with abrupt sides, terminating in a level summit, somewhat in the form of a truncated cone.

"We were much gratified in finding the water at the head of this branch, as in the North Fork, sweet and wholesome. This settles the question that these branches of Red River do not take their rise in salt plains, as has been very generally supposed. On the contrary, the water at their sources, in the eastern borders of the Staked Plain, is as pure as can be desired; and this character continues upon all the confluents until they enter the gypsum formation, when they become impregnated with salts that impart a new character to the water, which continues to its junction with the Mississippi.

"Upon the rocky bluffs bordering the river we found silicified wood in great quantities strewed about over a distance of two miles. The petrifaction was most perfect, exhibiting all the fibres, knots, and bark as plainly as in the native state, and was quite like cottonwood.

"Near the place where we pitched our tents on the 22d was an old Indian encampment, where John Bushman discovered that a battle had been fought within the two preceding months. The evidences of this were apparent from the remains of a large fire upon which the victorious party had burned the lodges and other effects of the vanquished. Pieces of the lodge poles, and a quantity of fused glass beads, with small pieces of iron and other articles pertaining to their domestic economy, which had partially escaped the conflagration, were found scattered about the camp.

"On the 24th we left the Salt Fork, and, striking south over very rough and undulating prairies, we, on the 27th, came in sight of the valley of the Ke-che-a-qui-ho-no, or the principal branch of Red River. Directly in front of us we could see the high table lands of the Llano estacado towering up some eight hundred feet above the surrounding country, and bordered by precipitous escarpments, capped with a stratum of snow-white gypsum, which glistened in the sun's rays like burnished silver.

"Our route from the Salt Fork led us through an almost continuous dog town, which has probably suggested the

PRAIRIE DOG TOWN.

name the Comanches have applied to the main branch of the Red River of Ke-che-a-qui-ho-no, or 'Prairie-Dog-Town River.'

"The river where we struck it was nine hundred yards wide, flowing over a sandy bed, with but little water in the channel, and the valley was inclosed on each side by rugged hills and deep gorges.

"On the 28th, after marching eight miles, we reached the

base of the elevated cliffs that border the Llano estacado, which spreads out to the south and west like the steppes of Central Asia in an apparently illimitable desert.

"I supposed, from the appearance of the country in the distance, that I should be able to find a passage for our wagons along at the foot of these cliffs; but, on closer examination, we found the ground so much cut up by abrupt ridges and deep gullies that it was impracticable to take our train any farther up this branch of the river. Accordingly, I determined to leave it here, and, with a small escort of ten men, to push on and endeavor to reach the sources of the river.

"Taking provisions for six days, packed on mules, we started on the 29th, and were obliged to follow directly in the bed of the river, as the banks on both sides were so rough as to render it very difficult to travel over them.

"In one of the deep ravines which we encountered on the south side of the river we discovered a grotto inclosed with gypsum rocks, which appeared to have been worn out by the action of water, forming an arched passway. The sides were perfectly smooth, and composed of strata of three distinct bright colors, green, pink, and white, arranged in such order as to give it an appearance of singular beauty.

"We found a small rill of water issuing from this cavern, and on tracing it up discovered a spring of very cold water bursting out from the solid rock. The day was very warm (the thermometer standing at twelve o'clock M. at 104° Fahrenheit in the shade), and the reflection of the sun's rays from the white sand in the bed of the river made it exceedingly oppressive. We were much exhausted and very thirsty, and we all took huge draughts of this water; but, as soon as the cold sensation passed away, we discovered that the water was highly charged with salts, and very bitter and unpalatable. Indeed, the water in the river and in all the tributaries we passed was of the same character. We bivouacked that night at a small pool of bitter water, and our intense thirst caused us to drink it freely, but, instead of allaying, it only served to increase it.

"At daylight on the 30th we were in the saddle again, and set out at a brisk pace, hoping to find some good water during the day.

"The lofty escarpments which bounded the valley on each side rose precipitously from near the water's edge to the enormous altitude of from five to eight hundred feet, and in many places there was not room for a horse to pass between the foot of the acclivity and the water.

"It was altogether impossible to travel upon either bank of the river, and the only place where a horse could pass was directly along the defile of the river bed. We found frequent small rivulets flowing into the river through the deep glens on each side, but the water in them all was impregnated with the nauseating salts. A very good imitation of this compound may be made by dissolving a teaspoonful of Epsom salts in a tumbler of sweet water.

"Our noon halt was upon the river, and we sent our Delawares out in all directions to search for fresh water, but they all returned unsuccessful. At this time we had become so much affected by the frequent and unavoidable use of the water that we experienced constant burning pains in the stomach, attended with loss of appetite, and the most vehement and feverish thirst. We endeavored to disguise the taste of the water by making coffee with it, but it retained the same disagreeable properties in that form that it had in the natural state.

"At four in the evening we again pushed forward up the river, praying most devoutly that we might reach the end of the gypsum formation before night, and that the river, which was still of very considerable magnitude, would branch out and soon come to a termination.

"Four miles from our halting-place we passed a large affluent coming in from the north, above which there was a very perceptible diminution in the main stream; and in going a few miles farther, we passed several more, causing a still greater contraction in its dimensions. All these affluents were similar in character to the parent stream, bordered with lofty and precipitous bluffs, with gypsum veins running through them similar to those upon the main river.

"Toward evening we arrived at a point where the river divided into two forks of about equal dimensions. We followed the left, which appeared somewhat the largest, and here found the bluffs receding several hundred yards from the banks upon each side, leaving a very beautiful and quiet little nook, wholly unlike the stern grandeur of the rugged defile through which we had been passing. This glen was covered with a rich carpet of verdure, and embowered with the foliage of the graceful china and aspen, and its rural and witching loveliness gladdened our hearts and refreshed our eyes, long fatigued with gazing upon frowning crags and deep, shady ravines.

"After traveling twenty-five miles we encamped upon the main river, which had now become reduced to one hundred feet in width, and flowed rapidly over a sandy bed.

"Although we were suffering most acutely from the effects of the nauseating and repulsive water in the river, yet we were still under the painful necessity of using it. Several of the men had been taken with violent cramps in the stomach and vomiting, yet they did not murmur; on the contrary, they were cheerful, and indulged in frequent jokes at the expense of those who were sick. The principal topic of conversation with them seemed to be a discussion of the relative merits of the different kinds of fancy iced drinks which could be procured in the cities, and the prices that could be obtained for some of them if they were within reach of our party. Indeed, it seems to me that we were not entirely exempt from the agitation of a similar subject; and, from the drift of the argument, I have no doubt that a moderate quantity of Croton water, cooled with Boston ice, would have met with a very ready market in our little mess. Indeed, if I mistake not, one of the gentlemen offered as high as two thousand dollars for a single bucket of the pure element; but, unfortunately for him, this was one of those rare occasions in which money was not sufficiently potent to obtain the object desired.

"We spread our blankets, and endeavored to obliterate the sensation of thirst in sleep; but, so far as I was concerned, my slumbers were continually disturbed by dreams, in which I fancied myself swallowing huge draughts of ice-water.

"We saddled up at a very early hour on the 1st of July, and pushed forward up the river for several miles, when we passed a large affluent putting in from the north. A few miles farther brought us to another; and, in the course of the forenoon, several tributaries had been passed, which reduced the main stream into a narrow channel of only twenty feet wide; and here its bed, which had every where below been sandy, suddenly changed to rock; the water, which before had been turbid, flowing clear and rapidly over it, and, to our great delight, it was entirely free from salts.

"After undergoing the most intense sufferings from drinking the disgusting fluid below here, we indulged freely in the pure and delicious element as we ascended along the narrow dell through which the stream found its way.

"After following up for two miles the tortuous meanderings of the gorge, we reached a point where it became so much obstructed with huge piles of rock that we were obliged to leave our animals, and clamber up the remainder of the distance on foot.

"The gigantic escarpments of sandstone, rising to the giddy height of 800 feet upon each side, gradually closed in as we ascended, until they were only a few yards apart, and finally united overhead, leaving a long, narrow corridor beneath, at the base of which the head spring of the principal or main branch of Red River takes its rise. This spring bursts out from its cavernous reservoir, and, leaping down over the huge masses of rock below, here commences its long journey to unite with other tributaries in making the Mississippi the noblest river in the universe. Directly at the spring we found three small cottonwood-trees, one of which was blazed, and the fact of our having visited the place, with the date, marked upon it.

"On beholding this minute rivulet as it wends its tortuous course down the steep descent of the cañon, it is difficult to realize that it forms the germ of one of the largest and most important rivers in America, floating steamers upon its bosom for nearly 2000 miles, and depositing an alluvion along its borders which renders its valley unsurpassed for fertility.

"We took many copious draughts of the cool and refreshing water in the spring, and thereby considered ourselves, with the pleasure we received from the beautiful and majestic scenery around us, amply remunerated for all our fatigue and privations. The magnificence of the views that presented themselves to our eyes as we approached the head of the river exceeded any thing I had ever beheld. It is impossible for me to describe the sensations that came over me, and the exquisite pleasure I experienced as I gazed upon these grand and novel pictures.

"These stupendous escarpments of solid rock, rising precipitously from the bed of the river to such a height as, for a great portion of the day, to exclude the rays of the sun, were worn away, by the lapse of time and the action of the water and the weather, into the most fantastic forms, that required but little effort of the imagination to convert into works of art, and all united in forming one of the grandest and most picturesque scenes that can be imagined. We all, with one accord, stopped and gazed with wonder and admiration upon a panorama which was now for the first time exhibited to the eyes of civilized man. Occasionally might be seen a good representation of the towering walls of a castle of the feudal ages, with its giddy battlements pierced with loopholes, and its projecting watch-towers standing out in bold relief upon the azure ground of the pure and transparent sky above. In other places, our fancy would metamorphose the escarpments into a bastion front, as perfectly modeled and constructed as if it had been a production of the genius of Vauban, with redoubts and salient angles all arranged in due order. Then, again, our fancy pictured a colossal specimen of sculpture, representing the human figure, with all the features of the face distinctly defined. This, standing upon its lofty pedestal, overlooks the valley, as if it had been designed and executed by the Almighty Artist as the presiding genius of these dismal solitudes.

"All here was crude Nature, as it sprung into existence at the fiat of the Almighty Architect of the universe, still retaining its primeval type, its unreclaimed sublimity and wildness, and it forcibly inspired me with that veneration and awe which are so justly due to the high antiquity of Nature's handiworks, and which seem to increase as we consider the solemn and important lesson that is taught us in reflecting upon their permanence when contrasted with our own fleeting and momentary existence.

"We clambered up to the summit of the escarpment, over the head of the spring, and here found ourselves upon the level plain of the Llano estacado.

"The approximate geographical position of this point, as determined by courses and distances from the place where we left the train, is in latitude 34° 42′ north, and longitude 103° 7′ 11″ west; and its elevation above the sea, by careful barometric observations, is 2450 feet.

"The moment we passed the gypsum formation (about three miles from the head of the river) the water became pure and sweet.

"We were undoubtedly the first white men who had ever visited the locality, and, from the great difficulty of its access, I doubt if any others will go there very soon.

"Near the head of the river we saw numerous fresh bear tracks, and several of the animals themselves, two of which we killed, but they generally made their escape into the rocky defiles, where we were unable to follow them.

"One of our Delawares (John Bull) had quite an exciting brush with a large bear, but did not succeed in getting alongside of him, as he was mounted upon the same fractious horse which he rode in the buffalo chase, and he became perfectly furious and unmanageable the moment he saw the bear. This is often the case, and there is nothing that frightens a horse so much as one of these animals.

"We returned to our camp where we left the train, at the foot of the defile or cañon through which the river passed, on the 3d of July, the distance to the head of the river being sixty-five miles."

I could not determine in my own mind whether this remarkable defile had been formed, after a long lapse of time, by the continued action of the current, or had been produced by some great convulsion of Nature, or whether both causes had contributed to its formation, some paroxysmal convulsion having first given birth to an extensive fissure, and the ceaseless erosion of the water having afterward reduced it to its present condition; but the following remarks of the late Dr. Hitchcock upon the subject are quite conclusive.

"Your account of the remarkable *cañons* of Red River, where it comes out from the borders of the 'Llano estacado,' as given in your lecture before the American Geographical and Statistical Society, has been read by me with great interest. For several years past I have been engaged in studying analogous phenomena to this, which seems to me a neglected part of geology. The cañons of our southwestern regions are among the most remarkable examples of erosions on the globe, and the one on Red River seems to me to be on a more gigantic scale than any of which I have found a description. You seem in doubt whether this gorge was worn away by the river, or is the result of some paroxysmal convulsion. You will allow me to say that I have scarcely any doubt that the stream itself has done the work. The fact that when a tributary stream enters the main river it passes through a tributary cañon, seems to me to show conclusively that these gorges were produced by erosion, and not by fractures; for how strange would it be if fractures should take those ramifications and curvatures which a river and its tributaries present. And, moreover, I find cases where I can prove, from other considerations, that streams of water (existing and ancient rivers) have eaten out gorges quite as difficult to excavate as any of the cañons of the West; so that, if we must admit that rivers have done a work equally great in one case, all presumption is removed against their doing the same in other cases. I have a great number of facts, which I hope to be able, if life be spared, to present to the public on this subject, and I am very glad to add the cañons of Red River to the number."

CHAPTER VI.

Turning homeward.—Peculiar Basin.—Another Panther killed.—Witchita Mountains.—Mount Scott.—Buffalo Chase.—Witchetaw Villages.—Fine Soil.—Reported Massacre.—Mexican Prisoners.—Accused of Horse-stealing.—Arrival at Fort Arbuckle.—Anxiety of Friends.—Review of Characteristics of the Country passed over.—Ranges of the Indians.

ON the 4th of July we turned our faces homeward, and traveled along down the "Ke-che-a-qui-ho-no." Our first camp was made at a very peculiar pond of water. It is almost round, about 250 feet in diameter, with the water 30 feet deep, and perfectly transparent and sweet. The surface of the water is some 20 feet below the top of the bank, the sides of which are nearly perpendicular; and the surrounding country, for several miles, rises to the height of from 100 to 200 feet. As this pond seems to be supplied by springs, and has no visible outlet, it occurred to me that there might be a subterraneous communication which carried off the surplus water and the earth from the depression of the reservoir.

On approaching this pond previous to our encamping, one of the officers and myself, who were in advance of the command, espied a huge panther very leisurely walking away in an opposite direction; and as, in hunters' parlance, we "had the wind of him," it enabled me to ride sufficiently near to give him a shot before he discovered us. He made a tremendous leap into the air, and, running a short distance, fell dead, shot directly through the heart.

We continued down the river, over an arid, sandy country, almost entirely destitute of timber or good water, until

HEAD OF KE-CHE-A-QUI-HO-NO.

the 15th, when we again entered the Witchita Mountains, and skirted along the southeastern base for two days.

The soil here is of excellent quality, and sustains a heavy vegetation. In addition to the advantages of rich soil, good timber, and water, which every where abound near these mountains, may be added the great salubrity of the climate. The atmosphere in these elevated regions is cool, elastic, and bracing, and the breezes which sweep across the Plains temper the heat of the sun, and render the atmosphere, even in midsummer, cool and comfortable.

The particular district embracing the Witchita Mountains has for many years been occupied and (with much justice, it seems to me) claimed by the Witchetaw Indians, who have a tradition that their original progenitor issued from the rocks of these mountains, and that the Great Spirit gave him and his posterity the country in the vicinity for a heritage, and here they continued to live and plant corn for a long time.

Notwithstanding this claim of the Witchetaws, which the fact of occupancy and possession has guaranteed to them, yet the whole of this beautiful country, as far as the 100th degree of west longitude, is included in the grant made by the United States to the Choctaws, who thereby possess the greater part of the lands upon Upper Red River that are really valuable.

The Witchetaws are an insignificant tribe in point of numbers, not having more than about 500 souls in the nation, and are not, of course, prepared to substantiate or enforce their title to this country; and, indeed, I very much doubt if they have any claims upon the consideration or generosity of our government, being the most notorious and inveterate horse-thieves upon the borders, as the early frontier settlers of Texas can testify; and they are only held in restraint now by fear of the troops near them. They have always been extremely jealous of the motives of the white people who have wished to penetrate to the interior of their country, and have, upon several occasions, driven off parties who attempted to examine the country about the Witchita Mountains.

The Choctaws and Chickasaws do not occupy more than one fourth of their reservation, and the remaining three fourths is of sufficient dimensions to form a new Territory, which is far better adapted to agriculture than any other of our Territories.

On the 18th we passed through the mountains and encamped upon the bank of a stream on the north side. Our position here was directly at the base of the most elevated peak in the Witchita chain, which, in honor of our distinguished lieutenant general, I named "Mount Scott." Towering as it does above all surrounding eminences, this peak presents a very imposing feature in the landscape, and a conspicuous landmark for many miles around. The altitude above the base, as determined with the sextant, is 1135 feet.

To the north of Mount Scott lies one of the most beautiful valleys I ever saw. It is about three miles wide, inclosed between two ranges of mountains, and through it winds a lovely stream of pure water about fifty yards wide, the lively current of which rushes wildly down over an almost continuous succession of rapids and rocky defiles. It is fringed with gigantic pecan, over-cup, white ash, elm, and hackberry trees. About the base of the mountains we found the post-oak, and toward their summits the red cedar grows.

While encamped at this place, I took my rifle, and, mounting a small Indian pony belonging to my servant, started up the creek for the purpose of hunting deer. I had only gone about two miles, when I suddenly discovered a buffalo bull cropping the grass under some oaks near the creek. No sooner, however, did I see him, than, raising his head, and giving one look in the direction from which I was approaching, he set off at a spanking gallop over the prairie. I applied the rowels most vigorously to the diminutive beast I bestrode, and endeavored, by making a cut-off over the hills, to get within rifle range, but the utmost efforts of the pony were unequal to the task, and all I could do was to give him a running salute as he passed at 200 yards distance.

On the 19th, as we were passing along a small tributary of the Witchita called Rush Creek, we suddenly came in sight of several squaws, who were collecting the tall grass which grows along the banks of the creek. They no sooner espied us than they jumped upon their horses, and were about making off. Some of them, however, stopped at the command of our interpreter, while one or two galloped away in the direction of their village to give notice of our approach. They proved to be Witchetaws and Wacos, and, informing us that their villages were about four miles in advance, invited us to pay them a visit. We passed through the villages, which lay directly in our route, and encamped about half a mile below them, in the valley of Rush Creek.

Immediately on our arrival we were accosted by a large crowd of men, who were anxious to learn where we had been, and whether we had met with any Comanches; and as it was very seldom that any whites had ever visited them before, they seemed very glad to see us, probably anticipating presents.

There were two villages here, occupied by the two tribes just mentioned. They were situated in the rich and fertile valley of Rush Creek, where they cultivated corn, peas, beans, pumpkins, and melons. They had no agricultural implements except a small hoe, with which they prepared the ground for the reception of the seed, and performed all other work in the cultivation of the crop. The prolific nature of the soil gave them bountiful returns, and were it not for their improvident natures, they might, with little labor, have sufficient for the whole year. But, like other Indians, they only cared for the present, and, from the time the corn was fit for roasting, they were continually eating and feasting until it was consumed.

The village of the Witchetaws had 42 lodges, each containing two families of about ten persons. These lodges are made by erecting a frame-work of poles, placed in a circle in the ground with the tops united in an oval form, and bound together with numerous withes or wattles, the whole nicely thatched with grass; and, when completed, it makes a very commodious and comfortable domicil. The interior arrangements are such that every person has a bunk, raised from the ground and covered with buffalo hides, forming a couch which is far from being uncomfortable. When seated around their fires in the centre of the lodges, they have an air of domestic happiness about them which I did not expect to find.

The lodges are about 25 feet in diameter at the base, 25 feet high, and in the distance have very much the appearance of a group of haystacks. With the exception of a few families that live upon the Canadian, the whole Witchetaw nation is concentrated at this place; their numbers do not exceed 500 souls. They have, during the early settlement of Texas, given more trouble to the people upon the northern borders of that state than any other Indians. They have no regard for truth, will steal, and are wholly unworthy of confidence, and their vicious propensities are now only kept in check from fear.

Living, as they do, between the white settlements and the prairie tribes, they are at the mercy of both; they seem to be conscious of this fact, and express a desire to be on terms of friendship with all their neighbors. At my urgent request they presented us with several bushels of green corn, which was very acceptable, as we had seen no vegetables for several months.

The Wacos live about a mile from the Witchetaws, in a village constructed like the other. There are 20 lodges in this village, and about 200 souls. Their habits and customs are similar to the Witchetaws, with whom they frequently intermarry, and are upon the best and most friendly terms.

Both of these tribes subsist for a great portion of the year upon buffalo and deer, and wear the buffalo robes like the Comanches. They also use the bow and arrow for killing game; some of them, however, are provided with rifles, and are good shots. They have a large stock of horses and mules, many of which are the small Spanish breed with the Mexican brand upon them, and have probably been obtained from the prairie tribes; while others are large, well-formed animals, and have undoubtedly been stolen from the border whites.

We learned from these Indians, much to our surprise, that a report had been made to the commanding officer of Fort Arbuckle, by a Keechi Indian, to the effect that our whole party had been overpowered and massacred by the Comanches near the head of Red River.

The account given by the Indian was so circumstantial and minute in every particular, showing a perfect knowledge of all our movements, with our numbers and equipments, that the information was evidently communicated by persons who had been near us, and observed our movements. This accounted for the fact of the Indians avoiding us upon all occasions.

They probably regarded us as out on a hostile expedition, and may have supposed that the report of our massacre would deter other troops from following us.

The old chief To-se-quash informed us that Pah-hah-eu-ka's band of "Middle Comanches," in consequence of some of their people having been killed near one of our military posts in Texas, were greatly exasperated, and would fight the whites whenever they met them.

The following morning I sent for the chiefs of the two villages, for the purpose of endeavoring to persuade them to surrender to us two Mexican prisoners in their possession, one a man about forty years of age, and the other a boy of fifteen.

The man had been with the Indians since he was a child, and said he did not wish to leave them; that he had become as great a rascal as any of them (to which I gave full credence), and should not feel at home any where else.

It appeared, however, that the boy had only been with them a few months. He stated that he was kidnapped by the Kioways from his home near Chihuahua; that, in consequence of their brutal treatment, he escaped, and made his way to the Witchita Mountains, where a Witchetaw hunter found him in nearly a famished state, and brought him to this place. He said he had been kindly treated by the Witchetaws, but was anxious to leave them and go with us. He appeared to be very intelligent, and could read and write in his own language.

In a talk with the chiefs, I told them that the American people were now on terms of friendship with the Mexicans, and that by treaty we had obligated ourselves to return to them all prisoners in the hands of Indians in our territory, and to prevent farther depredations being committed upon them; that the principal chief of the whites (the President) would not regard any tribe of Indians as friends who acted in violation of this treaty; that he confidently hoped and expected all the tribes who were friendly to our people would comply strictly with the requirements of the treaty, and give up all prisoners in their possession. I then requested them to release to me the boy, and told them if they did this I should make them some presents of articles that had been sent out by the President for such of his Red children as were his friends. They hesitated for a long time, stating that the boy belonged to a Waco, and he loved him so much that it was doubtful if he could be persuaded to part with him. Whereupon I told them that if they released the boy quietly, I should reward them; but otherwise I had determined to take him from them by force, and if compelled to resort to this course, should give them nothing in return. This appeared to have the desired effect, and they said if I would make the family into which he had been adopted a few presents, in addition to what I had promised them, they would release him. I accordingly distributed the presents, and took possession of the boy. Upon turning him over to us they divested him of the few rags of covering that hung about his person, and reluctantly gave him to us; and he made his exit from the Witchetaw nation in the same costume in which he entered the world. We soon had him comfortably clothed, and he was much delighted with the change.

While we were out on the Plains we had found two Indian horses, and had them in our possession on our arrival at the Witchetaw villages.

One of the officers of our party had, previous to our departure from Fort Belknap, lost a very fine horse, and he had discovered subsequently that some of To-se-quash's band had stolen it. I mentioned the circumstance to the chief, and required him either to return the horse or give another in place of it. At first he denied that his people had taken the horse; but, upon our showing conclusively that such was the case, he acknowledged the act, but said that we had stolen two of their horses, and when those were returned he would restore ours. It appeared that some of their hunters had lost two horses which we had found, and, although we did not look upon the two cases as being exactly parallel, yet we returned one of their horses, and gave the other to the lieutenant.

About daylight on the 28th the party marched into Fort Arbuckle, where we found our friends much astonished and delighted at our sudden reappearance among them, when they had supposed us all massacred by the Comanches.

The report had been generally believed by the officers, and the commanding officer at Fort Arbuckle had made an official report of the circumstances to the War Department. We immediately dispatched letters to our friends, informing them of our safety, and, after making the necessary arrangements for returning the escort to Fort Belknap, I set out for Washington.

On reaching home, I learned that my father's family had been so fully convinced of the truth of the absurd rumors in regard to us that they had all put on mourning attire, and a funeral sermon had been preached upon the occasion. Besides this, I had the novel satisfaction of reading in the papers several quite complimentary obituary articles upon the death of Captain Marcy.

In a comprehensive review of the physical characteristics of the particular section of Red River which is comprised within the limits of the district assigned to the attention of the expedition, it will not perhaps be considered irrelevant to make a few general observations upon the more prominent features of the country bordering upon this stream, from its confluence with the Mississippi to its sources. It will be observed, by reference to a map of the country embracing the basin of this river, that in ascending from the mouth, its general direction as high as Fulton,

Arkansas, is nearly north and south; that here it suddenly changes its course, and maintains a direction almost due east and west to its sources. One of the first peculiarities which strikes the mind on a survey of the topography of this extensive district of country is the general uniformity of its surface: with the exception of the Witchita range, no extensive chains of lofty mountains diversify the perspective, and but few elevated hills rise up to relieve the monotony of the prospect. Another distinguishing feature of this river is, that the country on its upper waters differs in every respect from that in the vicinity of its mouth. The valley is found to comprise two great geographical sections, each having physical characteristics entirely distinct from the other. The main branch of the river, from the point where it debouches out of the Staked Plain, flows through an arid prairie country almost entirely destitute of trees, over a broad bed of light and shifting sands, for a distance, measured upon its sinuosities, of some 500 miles. This country, for the most part, is subject to periodical seasons of drought, which preclude the possibility of cultivation except by means of artificial irrigation. It then enters a country covered with forest-trees of gigantic dimensions, growing upon an alluvial soil of the most pre-eminent fertility, which sustains a very diversified sylva, and affords to the planter the most bountiful returns of all the products suited to this latitude. On entering this section of the river we find that the borders contract, and the water, for a great portion of the year, washes both banks, at a high stage, carrying away the loose alluvium from one side and depositing it upon the other in such a manner as to produce constant changes in the channel, and to render the navigation difficult. This character prevails through the remainder of its course to the Delta of the Mississippi, and throughout this section it is subject to heavy inundations, which often flood the bottoms to such a degree as to produce very serious consequences to the planters, destroying their crops, and, upon subsiding, occasionally leaving a deposit of white sand over the surface, rendering it thenceforth entirely barren and worthless.

Below the great raft a chain of lakes continues to skirt the river for more than 100 miles: these are supposed to have been formed in the ancient channels and low grounds of former streams, whose discharge had gradually been obstructed by an embankment formed of the sedimentary matter brought down the river from above.

These lakes are from five to fifty miles in length, from a quarter to three miles wide, and are filled and emptied alternately as the floods in Red River rise and fall; they serve as reservoirs, which, in the inundations of the banks of the river, receive a great quantity of water, and, as it subsides, empty their contents gradually, thereby tending to impede the rapid discharge of the floods upon the Delta. Like all rivers of great length which drain a large extent of country, Red River is subjected to periodical seasons of high and low water. The floods occur at very uniform epochs, but the quantity and elevation of the water, as well as its continuance at a high stage, vary constantly.

During the winter the water often remains high for several months, but the heavy rise which has almost invariably been observed during the month of June often subsides in a very few days.

The estimated distance, by the meanderings of the stream, from the mouth to Preston, Texas, is 1600 miles, and from this point to the sources of the main branch 500 more, making the entire length of the river 2100 miles.

On emerging from the timbered lands upon Red River into the Great Plains, we pass through a strip of forest called the Cross Timbers. This extensive belt of woodland, which forms one of the most prominent and anomalous features upon the face of the country, is from five to thirty miles wide, and extends from the Arkansas River in a southwesterly direction to the Brazos, some 400 miles.

At six different points where I have passed through it, I have found it characterized by the same peculiarities; the trees, consisting principally of post-oak and black-jack, standing at such intervals that wagons can without difficulty pass between them in any direction. The soil is thin, sandy, and poorly watered. This forms a boundary-line, dividing the country suited to agriculture from the great prairies, which for the most part are arid and destitute of timber. It seems to have been designed as a natural barrier between civilized man and the savage, as upon the east side there are numerous spring-brooks flowing over a highly prolific soil, with a superabundance of the best of timber, and an exuberant vegetation, teeming with the delightful perfume of flowers of the most brilliant hues; here and there interspersed with verdant glades and small prairies, affording inexhaustible grazing, and the most beautiful natural meadows that can be imagined; while on the other side commence those barren and desolate wastes, where but few small streams greet the eye of the traveler, and these are soon swallowed up by the thirsty sands over which they flow. Here but little woodland is found, except on the immediate borders of the water-courses.

From the point where Red River leaves the timbered lands, the entire face of the country, as if by the wand of a magician, suddenly changes its character. The bluffs now approach nearer the river, and the alluvial bottoms, which below here have been exceedingly rich and productive, contract, and do not support that dense and rank vegetation which characterizes the lower portion of the valley. The undergrowth of cane-brakes and vines disappears, and is no more seen throughout the entire extent of the valley. The lands adjacent gradually rise, and exhibit broad and elevated swells of surface, with spacious valleys intervening, and the soil continues to become more and more sterile as we ascend, until we reach the 101st degree of latitude. From this point, with but few exceptions, there is no more arable land.

The Comanches and Kiowas resort in great numbers to the waters of the North Fork of Red River. Vestiges of their camps were every where observed along the whole course of the valley; and the numerous stumps of trees which had been cut down by them at different periods indicated that this had been a favorite resort for them during many years.

In several places we found camps that had only been abandoned a few days, and some where the fires were still burning. From the great extent of surface over which the grass was cropped at some of these places, and from the multitude of tracks, it was evident that these Indians were supplied with an immense number of horses; and they had been, without doubt, attracted here by the superior quality of the grass, and the abundance of the sweet cottonwood, upon the bark of which they feed their horses in the winter season.

Should the government authorities ever have occasion to communicate with these Indians, many of them can be found here during the autumn and winter months. In the summer season they travel north in pursuit of the buffalo, generally ranging between the North Fork of the Canadian and the Arkansas River.

The elevated table lands in which Red River, Brazos, and Colorado take their rise, extend from the Canadian River in a southerly course to near the Rio Grande, some four hundred miles, between the 32d and 37th parallels of latitude. In places it is nearly two hundred miles wide, and is embraced within the 101st and 104th meridians of longitude. Its elevation above the sea is two thousand four hundred and fifty feet at the head of Red River. It is very level, smooth, and firm, and spreads out in every direction as far as the eye can reach, without a tree, shrub, or any other herbage to intercept the vision. The traveler, in passing over it, sees nothing but one vast, dreary, and monotonous waste of barren solitude. It is an ocean of desert prairie, where the voice of man is seldom heard, and where no living being permanently resides. The almost total absence of water causes all animals to shun it; even the Indians do not venture to cross it except at two or three points, where they find a few small ponds of water. I was told in New Mexico that, many years since, the Mexicans marked out a route with stakes across this plain, where they found water; and hence the name by which it is known throughout Mexico, of "El Llano estacado," or the "Staked Plain."

P

CHAPTER VII.

INDIAN RESERVATIONS.

Arrival at Fort Belknap.—Troubles of the Small Tribes of Texas.—Jose Maria.—Council.—Major Neighbors.—Wolf Dance.—Comanche Visit to the Tonkawas.—Admiration for the Major's Wardrobe.—Enlists in a War Expedition.—Little Witchita River.—Big Witchita River.—Perilous Position of Major Neighbors.—Head of Big Witchita.—Bad Water.—Reach Brazos River.—Head of the Brazos.—Abundance of Game.—Ketumsee.—Clear Fork of the Brazos.—Council.—Location of the Reservations.—Summary.—Double Mountain Fork.—Mesquit Tree.—Mesquit Gum.—Civilizing Comanches.

In 1853, the Legislature of Texas passed an act authorizing the general government to have selected and surveyed, from any vacant lands within the limits of the state, reservations amounting to twelve leagues, for the exclusive use of the Indians inhabiting that Territory.

I was, in 1854, selected by the War Department to go out into the unsettled parts of the state, and, in conjunction with Major Neighbors, special agent for those Indians, to locate and survey these reservations.

I had already explored a great portion of Northern and Western Texas, and was perfectly familiar with the character of the country upon Red River, Trinity, some sections of the Brazos, and Colorado; but up to that time there was no record of any white man having explored the Brazos or the Big Witchita Rivers to their sources. As these streams were included within the limits of Texas, and as I deemed it desirable to locate the Indians as far as possible away from the white settlements, I determined to explore the streams alluded to. Accordingly, after procuring a suitable escort and outfit, I proceeded to Fort Belknap, on the Brazos River, where I was joined by Major Neighbors, with several Delawares for guides, interpreters, and hunters.

The Indian tribes in Texas at that time were the Southern Comanches, Witchetaws, Wacos, Towackanies, Ionies, Anahdakas, Caddos, Tonkawas, and Keechis.

These Indians, with the exception of the Comanches, constituted minute remnants of what were once formidable tribes, but now the aggregate of their slender numbers would hardly reach 2500 souls.

The borderers of Texas have often made war upon them without the slightest provocation, and have, time and time again, robbed them of their fields, and forced them to abandon their agricultural improvements, and remove farther and farther away as the white settlers encroached upon them. They have been robbed, murdered, and starved, until they have been reduced to mere skeletons of nominal tribes, which, when we went among them, were so much disheartened and discouraged that they were perfectly willing to submit to any change that held out to them the least guarantee of security.

These tribes are disposed to live in peace and harmony with the whites, and all they ask is to be allowed to cultivate their little patches of ground without farther molestation.

They all possess a greater or less number of horses, and many of their young men follow the chase, while the old men, women, and children stay at home, and raise corn, beans, peas, watermelons, squashes, etc.

They have, as a general rule, kept their races pure and unadulterated from admixture with the whites, yet it is said that many of their women are far from being chaste.

Soon after our arrival at Fort Belknap, Major Neighbors and myself called the chiefs of the small tribes together, and held a council with them concerning the settlement upon the new reservations.

The Ionies and Anahdakas were represented by their chief Jose Maria, who has the blood of both tribes in his veins. He was a fine specimen of his race, about sixty years of age, with an erect, elastic carriage, and a dignified and commanding demeanor.

A young and very intelligent chief, named Tiner, who commands that portion of his tribe living upon the Brazos River, appeared for the Caddos.

The Witchetaws and Wacos were represented in the person of an old chief, called Ock-a-quash, a full-blooded Witchetaw, who contends with another chief, "*Oche-rash*," for the precedency of rank.

A subordinate chief or captain, called *Utsiocks*, was the representative of the Towackanies.

Major Neighbors and myself, after the council was convened, informed the Indians that we had been sent out by the United States authorities to locate reservations for them, and that the government expected, as soon as this was done, they would go upon the lands, and there make their permanent abodes.

Jose Maria stated that he and his people were perfectly well aware that their Great Father (the President) had abundant power to send them wherever he chose; but, if it was convenient, he would prefer having their lands assigned to them below Fort Belknap, upon the Brazos. That, if this favor was granted him, as soon as the lands were surveyed and marked out, he should be ready to take possession of them with his followers. He appeared to have the welfare of his tribe at heart, and wished to get the best location of lands possible for them. He says his people have a tradition that they originally emanated from the hot springs of Arkansas; that from them they moved to Red

River, in the vicinity of Natchitoches, where they resided many years, but were driven by the whites from that section of country to the Brazos, where they had lived ever since. That they had been driven from their homes several times by the whites since they came upon the Brazos, and that they now cherished the hope that their troubles were ended, and that they would in future have permanent homes for their families. He added that he would prefer to be settled as near the fort as possible, in order that he might receive protection against the incursions of the prairie tribes. That heretofore he had had his enemies, the pale-faces, on one side of him, and those lawless robbers, the Comanches, on the other; but that, of the two evils, he rather preferred being near the former, as they generally allowed him to eat a portion of what he raised, but that the Comanches took every thing; and although the whites had heretofore been equally prone to make war upon them, yet, if they must die, they should prefer to make their entrance into the spirit land with full bellies, and for this reason he would, if it was agreeable to us, take his chances on the Brazos, near the fort.

These views were concurred in by Tiner and Ock-a-quash. The chief of the Towackanies said they were not authorized to enter into any definite arrangements for their people, but would go home and lay the proposition before them, when they would decide whether they would remain where they were in the Choctaw nation, or remove into Texas.

The Tonkawas were not represented in the council, and, indeed, they were generally regarded as renegades and aliens from all social intercourse with the other tribes. They were more like the Digger Indians of the Rocky Mountains than any others I have met with, never attempting to cultivate the soil or build houses. They lived in temporary bark or brush tenements, affording but little protection from the weather, and derived a miserable, meagre subsistence from fish, small animals, reptiles, roots, or any thing else that afforded the least nutriment. They were the most ragged, filthy, and destitute Indians I have seen; and their ideas of comfort and their manner of living are but one grade above those of the brutes. Indeed, the following incident, which was related to me by my friend and associate, Major Neighbors, would rather favor the hypothesis that in their own judgment, at least, there may be some remote consanguinity between them and a very ignoble quadruped.

It appears that, during the existence of the Republic of Texas, the major was appointed agent for the Tonkawas, and went out into the Plains and took up his abode with them. After about a year he succeeded in gaining their confidence, and ingratiated himself into especial good standing and favor with the principal chief, who manifested every disposition to oblige him whenever an opportunity offered.

These Indians, in common with all the aborigines of this continent, were eminently superstitious, believing in the agency of invisible spirits in controlling the every-day affairs of life, and in the efficacy of "medicine-bags" and charms in healing diseases, etc. They also, like the other tribes, had their national dances for different important occasions, and among these ceremonies was one which seemed to me very curious, and entirely different from any other I had heard of. It was called the "*Wolf Dance*," and was intended to commemorate the history of their origin and creation. Their traditions have handed down to them the idea that the original progenitor of the Tonkawas was brought into this world through the agency of the wolves.

ORIGIN OF THE TONKAWAS.

The dance is always conducted with the utmost solemnity and secrecy, and with all the pomp and ceremony their limited means allows; and it was only by the most urgent entreaty, and the exercise of all his influence with the chief, that he was permitted to become a spectator upon the important occasion, and then upon the express condition that it should be kept secret from the other Indians.

Before the performance commenced he was clandestinely introduced into a large dance-lodge, where he was secreted by the chief in such a position that he could observe what was going on without himself being seen.

Soon after this, about fifty warriors, all dressed in wolf skins from head to feet, so as to represent the animal very perfectly, made their entrance upon all-fours in single file, and passed around the lodge, howling, growling, and making other demonstrations peculiar to that carnivorous quadruped.

After this had continued for some time, they began to put down their noses and sniff the earth in every direction, until at length one of them suddenly stopped, uttered a shrill cry, and commenced scratching the ground at a particular spot. The others immediately gathered around, and all set to work scratching up the earth with their hands, imitating the motions of the wolf in so doing; and, in a few minutes, greatly to the astonishment of the major, they exhumed from the spot a genuine live Tonkawa, who had previously been interred for the performance.

As soon as they had unearthed this strange biped, they ran around, scenting his person and examining him throughout with the greatest apparent delight and curiosity. The advent of this curious and novel creature was an occasion of no ordinary moment to them, and a council of venerable and sage old wolves was at once assembled to determine what disposition should be made of him.

The Tonkawa addressed them as follows: "You have taken me from the spirit land where I was contented and happy, and brought me into this world where I am a stranger, and I know not what I shall do for subsistence and clothing. It is better you should place me back where you found me, otherwise I shall freeze or starve."

After mature deliberation the council declined returning him to the earth, and advised him to gain a livelihood as the wolves did; to go out into the wilderness, and rob, kill, and steal wherever opportunity presented. They then placed a bow and arrows in his hands, and told him with these he must furnish himself with food and clothing; that he could wander about from place to place like the wolves, but that he must never build a house or cultivate the soil; that if he did he would surely die.

This injunction, the chief informed the major, had always been strictly adhered to by the Tonkawas.

The Tonkawas, in point of numbers when compared with the Comanches, are a very insignificant tribe; and the latter, whenever they come in contact, always exercise a most arbitrary and domineering control over them. As an instance of this, while my friend Neighbors was quartered with them, a war-party of forty Comanches, led by the chief Mo-ko-cho-pe, came into camp, and, riding up to the chief's lodge, ordered him, in a most abrupt and dictatorial manner, to take charge of their horses and prepare supper for them, as they proposed spending the night there. Every thing they directed was promptly done, even to furnishing them with forty of their most attractive girls, which, according to the customs of some of the tribes at that period, was regarded as essential to perfect hospitality.

In the mean time the major was endeavoring to place himself on as favorable a footing as possible with the chief, telling him who he was, and that the authorities of the republic desired to establish and preserve peaceable relations with all the prairie tribes, but more especially with the Comanches.

The chief did not exactly respond to these friendly sentiments; on the contrary, he said he believed the whites were generally great rascals; nevertheless, he acknowledged that my friend appeared to be an exception to the rule, and that he was rather inclined to like him than otherwise; and he even condescended to express considerable admiration for the new coat he wore. The major, understanding the import of the compliment, at once pulled off the garment and gave it to him. Another Indian then came up and gave his especial approbation to the cut of his vest, another considered his pants very becoming, while others thought his cravat, boots, and stockings were very comfortable. All of these articles were taken off and distributed as they were mentioned, until at length the agent of the Lone-star republic found himself divested of all his apparel, with the exception of his linen shirt, out of a wardrobe which he had but recently procured from Austin.

The figure which the warriors cut with his garments must have been ludicrous in the extreme; and the major said that, notwithstanding he was almost in a state of nature himself, yet, when he saw one of these people, with only a satin vest, or a coat, pants, or cravat, strutting about with all the pride of a city exquisite, he was unable to preserve his dignity, and laughed most heartily.

After they had stripped him of every thing they could get, they applauded his liberality in the highest terms, and acknowledged that he was a first-rate fellow; indeed, they thought he was almost good enough to be a Comanche; and, as an evidence of their good opinion, they were willing he should join them in the horse-stealing expedition upon which they were then bound; and, as an incentive to his ambition, they promised, in the event of his good behavior, that they would give him a Comanche wife, and adopt him into the tribe on their return.

He knew the effect of declining this flattering offer would be to incur their displeasure, and set out with them, determined to make his escape the first opportunity that offered.

After traveling several days they arrived at a Mexican ranch, where there were large herds of cattle, and, as they were quite hungry, the major, at the request of the chief, applied to the proprietor for some beef, and promised him payment through the Indian Bureau on his return to Austin. The old man, however, declined letting his beef go unless the money was paid upon the spot. When this was reported to Mo-ko-cho-pe, he went to the Mexican himself, and told him that if he delivered to them two beeves within half an hour's time it might be well with him, but if the beeves were not turned over at the time named he would burn his ranch and destroy all his cattle.

This had the desired effect, and the beef was delivered very soon.

A few days after this the major made his escape from the Indians and returned to Austin, where he was enabled to replenish his wardrobe.

After concluding our "talk" with the Indians at Fort Belknap, we set forward to explore the country upon the Big Witchita and the head waters of the Brazos. This region was then a "terra incognita," and has not been occupied by white men since.

The following extracts from my journal, giving my impressions of the country as I passed over it, will probably convey a more accurate idea of this section than can be given in any other way.

"On the 15th of July we left Fort Belknap, and traveled back on the Preston road for fourteen miles to the '*Cotton-*

wood Spring,' upon the large prairie east of that post. Here we encamped, and at an early hour the following morning left the road, striking out into the prairie with a course a few degrees west of north toward the Little Witchita River, passing over a rolling country covered with groves of mesquit-trees, and intersected by several spring-branches (tributaries to 'Salt Creek'), flowing through valleys clothed with a dense coating of verdure, and teeming with a multitude of beautiful flowers of brilliant hues, the aroma from which filled the atmosphere with a most delicate and fragrant perfume.

"We made our camp at a fine large spring near the head of one of the branches of the west fork of the Trinity.

"Our course the next day was northwest for six miles, crossing several small tributaries of the Trinity, all of which were wooded with mesquit, and occasionally a grove of post-oak was seen, with here and there a cottonwood or willow tree along the banks.

"The water in all these branches is clear and palatable, and may be relied on throughout the season.

"The geological features of this section are characterized by a predominance of dark sandstone, which in many places crops out or is laid bare by the action of water, and is covered with detached fragments of volcanic scoria.

"We are encamped to-night upon a confluent of the 'Little Witchita,' which is here bordered by high, abrupt, rocky bluffs. The water stands in pools along the bed of the stream, and, although by no means good, it is drinkable.

"Our course on the morning of the 18th was nearly west, gradually deflecting to the southward, for the purpose of avoiding the numerous branches of the Witchita, but we soon discovered they would take us too far out of our course, and turned north, crossing them at right angles.

"Our march this morning led us along a gradual slope of beautiful and picturesque country, interspersed with mesquit glades and prairie lawns, for about eight miles, when we found ourselves, on reaching the crest of the ascent, upon the summit level of three streams, the 'Brazos,' 'Trinity,' and the 'Little Witchita.' Here a most beautiful panorama was opened out to our view. On our left, in the distance, could be seen the lofty cliffs bordering the Brazos, while in front of us, toward the sources of the Little Witchita, were numerous conical mounds, whose regular and symmetrical outlines were exhibited with remarkable truth and distinctness on a background of transparent blue sky. On our right, several tributaries of the Little Witchita, embellished with light fringes of trees, flowed in graceful sinuosities among green flowering meadows, through a basin of surpassing beauty and loveliness as far to the east as the eye could reach—all contributing enticing features to the romantic scenery, and producing a most pleasing effect upon the senses.

"We continued the same course on the 19th, crossing several more of the Witchita tributaries, which caused us considerable detention in excavating banks and constructing bridges to cross our train.

"The soil in the valleys of all these streams is a rich mellow alluvion of a highly productive character, and, were it not for the scarcity of timber which begins to be apparent, this would undoubtedly prove a desirable farming locality.

"The adjacent uplands are broken and rolling, but the soil possesses the elements of fertility. Upon the summit of the bluffs, at the head of the streams we are now passing, nothing can be seen toward the west but one unbroken expanse of prairie, spreading out beyond till it is lost in the dim distance.

"In previous communications to the War Department, I

have spoken of the great deficiency of building timber where I have traveled west of the '*Cross Timbers.*' It may be added here that the same facts are observed in this section; and although mesquit is found sufficient for fuel, yet there is a great scarcity of timber suitable for building purposes. There are, however, many quarries of stone, which might answer as a substitute.

"If this country is ever densely populated by agriculturists, a new era in husbandry must be instituted. Nature seems to demand this. Instead of clearing up timbered lands for the plow, as in the Eastern States, it will be necessary to cultivate timber; indeed, this has already been commenced in some Western prairies with successful results.

"We find an abundance of game throughout this section, and our hunters are enabled to keep the entire command supplied with fresh meat, so that we have had no occasion to make use of our beef cattle.

"Our noon halt to-day was upon the summit of a hill, where we found a spring of cool, wholesome water, surrounded with a luxuriant crop of grass, which afforded our cattle the very best pasturage.

"After noon we continued on for about eight miles over mesquit glades, when we arrived in a broad lowland valley, through which meanders a stream about twenty feet wide and two feet deep. This proved to be the main trunk of the Little Witchita. Its banks are about ten feet high, very abrupt, and skirted with elm and cottonwood. The water has a slightly brackish taste, but is palatable.

"We remained in camp on the 20th, making preparations to leave the train and escort at this place, while Major Neighbors and myself proposed to make an excursion toward Red River. As we should, under any circumstances, be obliged to return this way, and could move much more rapidly with pack mules than with our wagons, and as we did not anticipate meeting hostile Indians in this direction, we determined to take with us only our Delawares and three soldiers. Accordingly, on the following morning, we started at an early hour in a course nearly due east down the valley of the creek upon which we had encamped, and, after descending fifteen miles, arrived at a point where another large tributary from the north united with the main branch. Directly at the confluence our Indians discovered a swarm of bees, that had taken up their abode in a dry limb of a gigantic old cottonwood-tree. We were anxious to get the honey, but a small hatchet was the only substitute for an axe in our possession; and as chopping down the tree with this was out of the question, I was upon the point of leaving the industrious little insects in quiet possession of the fruits of their labors, when one of the Delawares resorted to the ingenious expedient of climbing a small tree standing near the cottonwood, and, on reaching the top, swung himself within reach of the limb that contained the desired treasure. He was soon seated upon it, and, fastening to it a lariat which was thrown to him, we seized the other end, and with our united efforts broke off the part containing the honey, which afforded us all a bountiful feast. We then resumed our journey down the stream, and traveled thirteen miles before we encamped.

"The character of the country along the valley is similar to that at our last camp. The soil is exceedingly rich, producing a heavy crop of grass, but the valley is subject to inundation, and no woodland is seen except directly along the banks of the stream.

"The valley varies from half a mile to two miles in width, and is shut in by rolling uplands, entirely void of any timber save mesquit.

"There are timbered lands below this point, but they are

mostly disposed of by the state, and are not now vacant; we did not, therefore, deem it advisable to proceed any farther in this direction, and on the morning of the following day turned north toward the Big Witchita River, not expecting to find any more tributaries to the Little Witchita, but, after traveling about five miles, we crossed another nearly as large as the main branch. This proved to be the most northerly confluent. It was twelve feet wide, the banks high, and lined with large pecan-trees, and, as we have seen none of this timber upon the other branches, it occurred to us that it might appropriately be named the 'Pecan Fork.' The water during this dry season stands in pools along the bed of the creek, but it is free from salts and palatable.

"There is more timber along this branch than upon the others, but away from the stream no woodland is seen, and the soil here does not appear to be as prolific as upon the other branches.

"Leaving the valley of the 'Pecan Fork,' we continued on in a north course over a very elevated prairie for seven miles, which brought us upon the crest of the ridge dividing the waters of the 'Little' from those of the 'Big Witchita,' from whence we descended by a smooth and regular grade for eight miles, and entered the valley of the latter stream, making our noon halt in a grove of hackberry-trees, near a pool of muddy water.

"After dinner we crossed the valley, which was here about three miles wide, and found ourselves standing upon the bank of the Big Witchita, and, ascending about four miles, discovered a large spring of cold pure water bursting out from the bank near the river, and here made our bivouac for the night.

"After a long and tiresome march, through an atmosphere heated almost to suffocation by the intense rays of a southern sun, it is difficult for one who has not experienced the sensation to conceive the exquisite pleasure imparted by a drink of cold water, particularly after being deprived of it for a long time. Such was the case with us upon this occasion, and every one now seemed perfectly happy and contented with himself and all the world.

"The 'Big Witchita' River at this point is 130 yards wide and three feet deep, with a current of about three miles per hour. The water is of a reddish cast, and rather turbid, but does not contain so much sedimentary matter as the water of the Little Witchita. It is so excessively bitter and nauseating to the taste that it can only be drunk in cases of the greatest extremity, and is similar to the water of Red River.

"We are at this place about twenty-five miles above the mouth of the river (one of our Delawares having visited this locality before and estimated the distance), yet the river is wider here than at its confluence with Red River.

"It never rises above its banks, which are from ten to twenty feet high, and although its general direction is nearly east and west, it frequently flows toward all points of the compass within a short distance. Its course is very tortuous, running from one side to the other of a valley about four miles wide, bounded upon both sides by lofty bluffs. The soil in the valley is a dark red and exceedingly rich alluvion, covered with the very best grass; unfortunately, however, the almost total absence of woodland, and the very great scarcity of good water, will render this section unsuited to the purposes of agriculture.

"With the exception of a scanty skirt of cottonwood-trees along the course of the river (and even this, in many places, entirely disappears), there is no timber in this part of the valley. These considerations influenced us in rejecting this as a locality suited to the wants of the Indians, except for purposes of hunting.

"On the morning of the 23d we reluctantly took our departure from the cold spring, crossed the river, and ascended a large tributary which entered from the northwest, about four miles above our camp of last night. This stream is about thirty yards wide and two feet deep, and flows with a lively current over a stratum of rock and gravel, between high banks bordered with cottonwood and hackberry trees. The water is bitter, but not so unpalatable as that in the principal branch. It is clear, and probably issues from the gypsum formation.

"We observed several places where the beavers had left evidences of their industry, and in one spot they had quite recently cut down several large trees. This suggested to us the name we have applied to this pretty stream, 'Beaver Creek.'

"We made our noon halt upon it, about twelve miles above its mouth, and partook of a sumptuous dinner of fish and soft-shell turtle, with which the stream abounds.

"We have been exceedingly annoyed for a few days past with horse-flies. They are enormously large, and their savage attacks upon our animals cause them much acute suffering. A dark blue variety that I saw was nearly, if not quite as large as a small humming-bird, and they no sooner light upon an animal than the blood follows copiously.

"We left the creek in the evening and traveled back to the Big Witchita, making our camp upon the north bank, near some pools of fresh water in a ravine.

"In the morning we turned south, and directed our course for camp, where we arrived about twelve o'clock, found every thing quiet, and our animals in fine condition for our onward march.

"An early departure was made on the following morning, and we marched twelve miles along the south bank of the creek, making our camp at some pools of muddy water.

As we ascend this stream, the timber along the banks diminishes in size and quantity, and at this place the few trees that are seen do not average more than fifteen feet in height.

"We are now near the sources of the principal branch of the Little Witchita, and as our course from hence will probably lead us along the ridge dividing the Brazos from the Big Witchita, the waters of both of which are wholly unfit for use, we sent our Indians out, soon after we encamped, to search for good water in advance. They returned in the evening and reported a supply fifteen miles distant.

"We resumed our march the next day, in a course a little south of west, along the high prairie 'divide,' making our night halt upon the summit of a very elevated bluff bordering the valley of the Big Witchita, and about 400 yards distant from a small spring of water in a deep ravine.

"In our course to-day we passed near a very prominent mound, standing upon the crest of the dividing ridge where it has the greatest elevation. From its anomalous conformation and peculiar outline, it presents an eminently conspicuous landmark, and can be distinguished for many miles in all directions.

"At the base of this mound we discovered some rich specimens of the blue carbonate of copper, and near this we also observed a vein of iron ore, fifteen feet in thickness, of exceedingly rich quality.

"The dwarf red cedar first shows itself upon the bluffs of the Big Witchita, in the vicinity of our camp, and, with the exception of a few mesquit-trees, it is the only wood in this section.

"On the morning of the 27th we again sent our Delawares in advance to search for water, as we were fearful, if we proceeded on with our ox-teams without taking this precaution, we might be obliged to encamp without that most necessary element. As the country in this direction is becoming so exceedingly arid, we have resolved, after going as far as we find water sufficient for all our animals, to leave the train with a majority of the escort, and push rapidly on, with a few mounted men and pack animals, to the sources of the river. Our Indians returned in the evening with their horses much jaded, and reported that they could find no good water within a distance of twenty-five miles, save one small spring, only affording sufficient for a few men.

"We therefore, on the following morning, found a suitable place to encamp our train, about ten miles south of the Big Witchita, upon a small tributary of the Brazos, where the water was good, and the grass and fuel abundant. On visiting this spot, Major Neighbors at once recognized it as the place where, a long time since, he had remained for several weeks the guest of a former chief of the Southern Comanches (Mo-ko-cho-pe). He had good reasons for retaining a vivid recollection of the locality, as during his stay here his life was placed in imminent jeopardy. A war-party of Northern Indians, on their return from a foray into Mexico, in passing along the borders of Texas had lost one of their number in a skirmish with some of the frontiermen, and, on their arrival at Mo-ko-cho-pe's camp, learning that my friend Neighbors was there, they at once determined that he should be the victim to atone for the death of their comrade. They accordingly insisted upon his being given up to them, and enforced their arguments with threats of vengeance upon their hosts in the event of a refusal to comply with their demands.

"Mo-ko-cho-pe replied to them that Major Neighbors was his friend and guest, and that if he did not protect him he should be guilty of a flagrant breach of hospitality; that he would never give his sanction to such an outrage, and if they persisted in carrying out their designs, they would first have to kill him, as he was resolved to protect him at all hazards. When the council was over, Mo-ko-cho-pe informed the major of the result, and advised him to remain constantly with him during the stay of the warriors. He complied implicitly with this advice, and was not sorry when the war-party took its departure for home.

"On the following morning, after giving directions to Lieutenant Pearce for moving the camp, Major Neighbors, the doctor, and myself, accompanied by five Indians and four soldiers, all well mounted, with pack mules loaded with the few supplies that were absolutely necessary for a twelve days' trip, including four five-gallon India-rubber water-sacks, set out with the firm resolve to see the head of the Big Witchita and Brazos Rivers before our return.

"Although our numbers were small, and we were about to penetrate into the heart of a country infested by Indians of the most lawless propensities, yet the scarcity of water compelled us to adopt this course in order to proceed any farther in this direction.

"Our course for the first ten miles was nearly west, along upon the crest of the lofty cliffs bordering the valley of the Witchita, when we turned to the north, and descended by a very tortuous course the precipitous sides of the bluffs, at the base of which we struck the trail of a party of Indians traveling to the north with five stolen horses. They had passed about ten days previous, and were moving slowly, all of which was evident from the fact that the whites never visit this section, and that five of the horses whose tracks we saw were shod.

"Continuing on up the valley for fifteen miles, we had the good fortune to discover a small spring of cold pure water near the bank of the river, and here we bivouacked for the night.

"We had taken the precaution in the morning to fill

our India-rubber sacks with water, but, after traveling a few hours exposed to the hot rays of the sun, the taste of the water became so rank and disagreeable that we could not drink it. I had, however, previous to leaving New York city, purchased for my own use a canteen made of the gutta-percha, and I was happy to find that this did not impart any disagreeable properties to water, even after remaining for several days exposed to the sun's rays in an atmosphere heated to a temperature of 102° in the shade.

"I take this occasion to remark that, in my opinion, the gutta-percha is far preferable as a material for water vessels to the India-rubber, and I have no hesitation in recommending for use in a southern climate the water-tanks and canteens made of this material.

"The India-rubber, after it has been manufactured for a few months, besides communicating an unwholesome taste to water, becomes adhesive, and destroys the fabric upon which it is spread, whereas the gutta-percha, after five months' exposure in the climate of Texas, did not adhere in the least, and was unimpaired by use.

"An accident occurred this evening which gave us no little alarm. While we were bathing in the river we heard the cry of fire, and, running back to camp, discovered the grass burning furiously, and, in spite of the vigorous efforts of the Indians, already in close proximity to our equipage. We dashed in, and were fortunate enough to secure most of the articles before the flames reached them.

"As we are now just entering the country where gypsum is the predominating rock, and as we had satisfied ourselves in our former travels that the chances for finding good water in a section where this mineral abounds are but few, we pushed forward as rapidly as possible up the river, crossing several small streams, all of which we tasted, but found the character of the water similar to that in the main river.

After traveling twenty-seven miles we found the river reduced to a width of only thirty yards. We continued on for ten miles farther, hoping every turn would disclose to us a fresh-water tributary, but we were disappointed, and encamped upon a small affluent of bitter water, which we were obliged to make use of. Several of the party have been attacked with diarrhœa and cramps in the bowels from drinking the water, and it causes all to feel more or less uncomfortable.

"The portion of the valley over which we have been passing for the last forty miles is barren and sandy, and the only woodland is upon the bluffs, which are covered with dwarf cedar, with an occasional lonely cottonwood or mesquit in the valley. Here and there may be seen a small patch of wild rye or gramma grass, but the principal herbage in the valley is a coarse variety of grass unsuited to the palates of our animals.

"On the following morning we left our salt-water bivouac at an early hour, and traveled rapidly on through the rough and intricate labyrinth of cedar bluffs which are closing in near the river bank, and rendering it necessary to pass over them in threading the narrow defile of the valley. A few miles brought us to a point where the river separated into several branches, all having their origin in the valley before us. Taking the principal one of these, we followed it up for several miles through the lofty bluffs bounding the valley, until we reached its source upon the plateau above. We found ourselves here about two hundred and fifty feet above the bed of the stream, and, on turning toward the valley from whence we had just emerged, a most beautiful and extensive picture greeted our eyes —the different confluents of the Witchita dividing as they neared their sources into numerous ramifications, all of which we were enabled from our lofty observatory to trace in their tortuous meanderings to the very heads, and beyond these could be discerned the dim outline of a range of mountains, which stretched away to the south toward the Brazos. All united in forming a landscape pleasing to the eye; but this is the only feature in the country which has left an agreeable impression upon my memory, and I bade adieu to its desolate and inhospitable borders without the least feeling of regret, for it is, in almost every respect, the most uninteresting and forbidding land I have ever visited. A barren and parsimonious soil, affording little but weeds and coarse unwholesome grass, with an intermixture of cacti of most uncomely and grotesque shapes, studded with a formidable armor of thorns which defies the approach of man or beast, added to the fact already alluded to of the scarcity of wood or good water, would seem to render it probable that this section was not designed by the Creator for occupation, and I question if the next century will see it populated by civilized man. Even the Indians shun this country, and there were no evidences of their camps along the valley, so that the bears (which are numerous here) are left in undisturbed possession. On leaving the Witchita, we traveled south toward the Brazos for six miles through mesquit groves, when we were rejoiced to find a miniature spring of fresh water dripping slowly out from under a rock near the crest of the ridge dividing the waters of the Witchita from those of the Brazos. After suffering intensely from thirst for two days, it may be imagined that it made our hearts glad to taste the pure element once more.

"As there was no reservoir to retain the water as it issued from the rocks, we went to work with our knives and tin cups, and in a few minutes each of us had excavated a small hole in the hard clay, which soon filled, and gave us a most refreshing draught. I am not prepared to say that it was equal to Croton water cooled with Rockland ice (being of a deep brown color, and thick with sediment), yet I doubt if the good people of Gotham ever enjoyed their boasted and justly renowned beverage more than we did this. It was free from salts—that was sufficient for us—and we did ample justice to its merits, as numerous cupsful, which disappeared in rapid succession down our parched and feverish throats, abundantly evinced.

"Our course from the spring was nearly parallel with the chain of mountains now distinctly visible, apparently about fifteen miles to our right. The direction of the chain seems to be nearly north and south, and extends off, as far as the eye can reach, toward the Brazos. Our route lay in the direction of one of the most prominent peaks of the chain, which was a very perfect cone, and apparently symmetrical upon all sides. Many of the other peaks, however, were truncated and irregular. Twelve miles' travel brought us to a branch of the Brazos, fifty feet wide and two feet deep, with a rapid current flowing over a bed of quicksand, and the water, as usual, bitter and unpalatable.

"On the 1st of August we continued on toward the conical peak of the mountains for twelve miles, when we struck another branch of the Brazos, which was spread out over a broad bed of loose sand that absorbs most of the water. We followed up the north bank of this for a few miles, when we encountered still another tributary, of an entirely different appearance. It was shut in by high, abrupt clay banks, the water clear, deep, and covered with water grasses, very much like one of our northern spring-brooks, and I felt the utmost confidence that we should find the water fresh, but it proved to be, if possible, worse than that in the other branches.

"It is thirty yards wide, from two to fifteen feet deep, and runs through a valley about two miles wide, with no trees upon its banks.

"It was literally alive with a multitude of large cat and buffalo fish, several of which we caught and cooked for our dinner, and can vouch for their good flavor.

"After dinner we crossed the stream, which we called 'Catfish Fork,' and in eight miles passed the Round Mountain, making our camp in the mountains five miles beyond.

"We find many spring-brooks issuing from the sides of the mountains, but, unfortunately, the formation here is gypsum, and all the streams are bitter.

"On the following morning we made our way with difficulty over the rugged mountainous region for several miles, when we reached the base of a high peak, which we determined to ascend. Accordingly, leaving our horses in charge of the men, we clambered up the precipitous sides of the eminence, and, on attaining the summit, found ourselves in a position overlooking the surrounding country for a great extent in all directions.

"The principal trunk of the Brazos, which was about two miles to the south, could be traced in its course through the mountains to the west to its very source, and beyond this, after passing a plain of several miles in extent, could be seen another group of mountains much more elevated than those we are now traversing. They seem to be about forty miles distant, and present much the appearance of some of the most elevated spurs in the Witchita range, and fully as elevated.

"The outline of the crest of this group is more deeply serrated and irregular, and the apices of the peaks more acute than those of the range we are now standing upon, having every appearance of upheaval and volcanic origin. If this conclusion is correct, they are probably composed of primitive rocks, and, from their geographical position and the direction of the group, both of which are nearly in the direct line connecting the two primitive ranges of the

Guadalupe and Witchita, it has occurred to me that this might be an intermediate outcrop of the same continuous chain. I was surprised to find these lofty mountains at the sources of the Brazos, as I had before supposed the entire face of the country lying between the Pecos and Red Rivers to be one continuous and unbroken plain, and that the Brazos, like the Red and Colorado Rivers, had its origin in the table lands of the Llano estacado. On facing to the east, and looking back over the country we had been traversing, it seemed to be an almost perfectly smooth and level surface, without a hill or valley, through which we could trace the several tributaries of the Brazos, as they flowed on in graceful curves, until they finally united in one common receptacle, generally known as the main or 'Salt Fork.' This we followed with our eyes for many miles, when it gradually disappeared in the murky atmosphere in the distance.

"After feasting our eyes for some time upon this rare and magnificent scenery, we reluctantly turned our steps down the mountain, and rode forward to the river.

"It was a broad, shallow stream, very similar to the other branches I have described, about forty yards wide, with a bed of light quicksand, and the water very saline to the taste. We were subsequently told by the Comanches that above this point, upon the plain between the two ranges of mountains, this stream passes over a field of salt (chloride of sodium), and that above that the water is palatable.

"After traveling ten miles south from the Brazos we left the gypsum formation, and at length discovered a pool of fresh water. We were all much rejoiced at our good fortune, and bivouacked for the night, determined to solace ourselves at this oasis for the privations of the past three days.

"The water was free from salts, but heavily charged

with sediment, and we were obliged to boil it for some time, and remove from the surface a very considerable percentage of thick vegetable matter before it was fit for use.

"For two days past we have seen an extensive fire on the prairie to the southwest, and supposed it was made by some of Pah-hah-eu-ka's band, who, our Delawares say, are ranging somewhere in this vicinity; but we subsequently learned from the Comanches that a war-party of one hundred and fifty northern Comanches, Kioways, Arapahoes, Cheyennes, and Sioux passed here about this time on their way to join another party of one hundred of their people who had passed farther west, with the intention of rendezvousing at the crossing of the Rio Grande, below the Presidio del Norte, from whence they proposed to penetrate Mexico, indiscriminately putting to death men, women, and children, laying waste haciendas, driving off animals, and doing all the mischief in their power.

"Thus they proposed to avenge the death of nearly a hundred of their comrades who last winter were entrapped by the Mexicans in a mountain pass near Durango, and met with a just punishment for their many unprovoked atrocities.

"They have been in the habit of visiting the different towns in northern Mexico for the ostensible purpose of traffic, and professing, at the same time, the most devoted friendship, and often even making treaties of amity and peace, wherein they pledge themselves forever to regard their dupes as brothers, and to refrain in future from committing depredations upon them, while, pending the negotiations, they are looking around to see where they can operate to the best advantage, when suddenly they disappear from the neighborhood, driving off animals, and killing all who oppose their designs.

"These outrages had been repeated so often that the

Mexicans, upon the occasion we have alluded to, resolved to turn the tables upon them. They accordingly met the Indians with much apparent friendship, and invited them to hold a council, for the purpose of discussing the preliminaries of a treaty of peace.

"The council was convened in a valley of the mountains, the only approaches to which were through certain passes that could easily be defended by a few men. These they had taken the precaution to guard with a good number of soldiers, who, as soon as the council commenced its deliberations, fell upon the astonished Comanches, and put nearly all of them to death. The few that escaped wandered back to their homes in the north, where they told the sad tale of their disaster, and there was mourning for a long time. A feeling of indignation was aroused, with an insatiable thirst for revenge, which resulted in fitting out the large party I have spoken of. What would have been our fate had we encountered them it is impossible to tell; we were, however, perfectly contented to return home without seeing them.

"The foregoing facts were detailed to us by several of the Comanches, and corroborated by the Delawares, and I have no doubt are strictly correct.

"I have not learned the result of this expedition, but the presumption would be that a party of this magnitude, composed of the choice spirits of several different warlike tribes, all burning with a thirst for revenge, and animated by a spirit of rivalry and desire for distinction, which such an alliance would undoubtedly engender, would not return without making an effort to accomplish their designs, and I fear the Mexicans have suffered a terrible retribution.

"I was very desirous of extending our explorations to the mountains beyond the head of the Brazos, but my associate, Major Neighbors, was unwilling to go farther in that direction, as he had already suffered much from drinking the gypsum water; as, moreover, one of the soldiers had become very much debilitated from the same cause, I reluctantly abandoned the project, and contented myself with merely seeing from a distance the position of some of the sources of the river, without visiting the localities 'in propria persona.' I am enabled, however, from the view I obtained upon the summit of the mountain, and from the courses I noted down, with compass in hand, at several different points on our route, to trace the streams with considerable accuracy, and to approximate to the distances.

"The next morning we directed our course toward the eastern extremity of a low mountain, nearly south from our last camp, which I recognized as the same I had seen in 1849, from the point where the Dona Ana road strikes a stream which has heretofore been known as the double mountain fork of the Brazos. My Delaware guide (Black Beaver) upon that occasion correctly informed me that this mountain was near the South Fork of the Brazos.

"On reaching the South Fork we found it similar in character to the branch we passed yesterday, and about the same magnitude. Immediately after crossing it we ascended the mountain, which was here composed of sandstone and gypsum, and covered with cedar bushes.

"Upon the summit was an extensive plateau very much resembling the Llano estacado, and it is highly probable this may be a spur of that plain.

"Toward the east from this elevation nothing could be seen but one continuous mesquit flat, dotted here and there with small patches of open prairie, while in the opposite direction, in a due west course, we discerned the elevated mountains beyond the head of the Brazos. Two peaks presented themselves to the view from this position, the outline of which was similar to the figure on the following page.

"After leading our horses down the mountain, or pla-

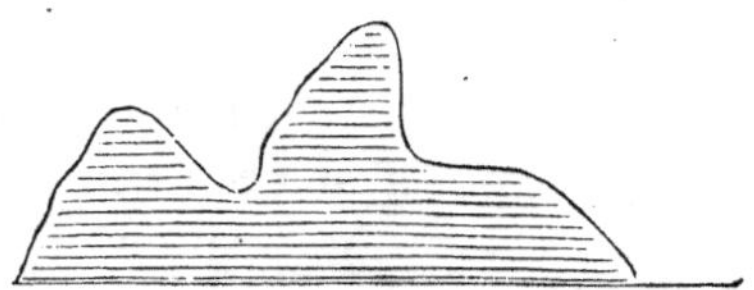

teau, we turned our faces toward the train and traveled until ten o'clock at night, encamping at a pool of despicable water, with which we manufactured a cup of salt coffee, and with a venison steak, cooked by friend Neighbors in his best camp style (which, 'by-the-by,' would not bring discredit upon a professional cuisiniére), we managed to make a supper.

"On the following morning we saddled up early and rode rapidly forward, hoping to find some good water for our breakfast. Eighteen miles brought us to some pools of water in the bed of a creek, where we breakfasted, and continued on down the bank of the stream for eight miles, when we encountered a terrific thunder-shower, which called into requisition all our gutta-percha and India-rubber habiliments, and those of the party who were not provided with them were thoroughly drenched.

"The country through which we are now passing is gently undulating and covered with mesquit-trees. The soil is very rich, producing several varieties of gramma and mesquit grasses, and begins to be watered with streams of fresh water.

"The deer and turkeys are plenty in this section, and our hunters have no difficulty in supplying us with fresh meat. We now and then see an antelope; I have, however, met with very few during the entire trip, and they seem to have almost disappeared since I was in this country in 1849.

"We encamped upon the creek, where we found a supply of good running water, and the following morning passed another larger stream flowing from the south. We here left the main creek and turned to the left, ascending a small spring-branch for twelve miles, finding water along the entire distance.

"This stream runs south 20° west, and takes its rise upon the south side of the ridge dividing the Clear Fork from the Salt Fork of the Brazos. It will always afford a sufficiency of good water for the largest trains in the dryest seasons, and I have no doubt that the large creek entering from the south, before mentioned, would supply water for many miles farther in the direction of its course. Had we known these facts before leaving the main body of the escort, we would have had no difficulty in bringing the train much nearer the sources of the Brazos.

"Passing the sources of the spring-creek, in the evening we traveled fifteen miles over mesquit uplands, and encamped at a spring of good water. Our course the next morning was north 20° east for fifteen miles, which carried us to the borders of a valley inclosed with a barrier of lofty and rugged hills, which shut out the bleak northers that in the winter sweep across these prairies.

"From the crest of these hills the valley below presented a carpet of verdant grasses, besprinkled with a profusion of flowers of the most vivid hues, through the midst of which meandered one of the most beautiful streams of pure water I have seen in this country.

"We entered this charming valley, and on reaching the banks of the creek discovered that a large party of Kickapoos, with their usual good taste, had occupied this locality for a hunting camp. The skeletons of their lodges (fifty-six in number) were still standing, and, judging from the piles of deer's hair which we observed in several places, and the bones scattered over the ground in all directions, they must have made a successful hunt while here. Our

Indians pronounced it four weeks since the camp had been occupied.

"Passing the creek, we continued on for ten miles, when we again struck the main trunk of the Brazos, and, ascending five miles, our eyes were once more gladdened by the sight of the encampment of the escort.

"We joined our comrades, and, after the privations we had necessarily been subjected to during our excursion, enjoyed exceedingly the few luxuries our remaining stores afforded.

"The weather during our absence had been very hot (the thermometer sometimes at 102° Fahrenheit in the shade), we had been obliged to ride during almost the entire day for the whole journey, yet the trip had not been without its attractions, and we trust the information we have obtained concerning this hitherto unknown region will be of sufficient importance to compensate us for our trouble.

"Those of us who had suffered from the effects of the gypsum water were relieved as soon as we left that mineral. Even the soldier who had been so very ill was almost entirely restored on our arrival at the main camp.

"In conversing with the Comanches afterward upon this subject, they said they always avoided this country as much as possible; that whenever they had visited it they had invariably been afflicted with diarrhœa, and several of their children had died from the effects of it.

"On the morning of the 7th we struck our camp and crossed the river with our train, descending upon the south side to the old Kickapoo camp, where we remained on the day following, and examined the creek to its confluence with the Brazos.

"The valley is about a mile wide, the soil productive and well watered, but, with the exception of mesquit and a few hackberry-trees, there is no timber, which we regard as an insuperable objection to selecting this as a reserve for the Indians. There are, however, many quarries of the very best building stone in the valley, which might serve a white population in lieu of timber, and this may yet become a superior farming locality. The deep prolific soil would unquestionably produce bountiful returns of any grain suited to this latitude, and would, for a long term of years, require no fertilizing auxiliaries.

"Our course on the following day was southeast, over a mesquit country for twelve miles, making our camp on a small tributary of the Brazos, where we found an abundance of good living water.

"Our course the next day was the same, over a very undulating and, in places, broken country, traversed by several small spring-branches of good water, between which we passed through groves of mesquit, but possessing little other interest until we reached a large creek running toward the Brazos, which winds through a broad valley inclosed with hills upon either side, and has more timber upon its borders than any we have seen above. The water is good, and the high banks have sufficient capacity to contain it all at the highest stage. This valley would be a good position for an Indian reserve, but it is disposed of and not now vacant.

"Quite a sensation was created in our camp during the afternoon by several strangers whom we saw in the distance crossing the valley and coming toward us. On their arrival they proved to be a Comanche chief (Ketumsee), with two of his wives, who had come to pay us a visit. He stated that they had received a message from us some time since requesting the chiefs of the Southern Comanches to meet us, and that he had for several days endeavored to prevail upon some of the principal men to accompany him, but they all made objections, and he finally determined to set out alone in search of us. He had been traveling fast for six days, and had only struck our trail the day previous, and he was apparently very glad to overtake us. We gave him a cordial welcome, and told him we would make him as comfortable as possible while he chose to remain our guest. He is a tall, fine-looking man, about fifty-five years of age, with an open, intelligent countenance, and assures us (which of course we are expected to believe) that he is the best friend to the whites in the Comanche nation. He acknowledges that there are others who profess friendship, but are not necessarily sincere. Taking his word for it, he is not one of that stamp. He stated that his own band, with but few exceptions, are disposed to avail themselves of the present opportunity to change their wandering life, and learn to live like their more civilized brethren. He also says that they are as yet perfectly ignorant of every thing relating to agriculture, and it will be necessary for their Great Father to send them farmers to teach them before they can attempt it.

"Ketumsee brought with him a letter from the commanding officer at Fort Chadbourn, in which he communicated to us the melancholy intelligence of the death of Captain Van Beuren, and expressing his opinion that some members of Ketumsee's band were implicated in the outrage.

"In reply to our interrogatories upon this subject, he, with much apparent frankness and sincerity, gave us his version of the matter, which was, in substance, as follows:

"He asserts that nearly all the depredations which are committed by the Indians in Texas can be traced directly to the Northern tribes. That all the depredating parties are organized among these Indians, but that occasionally one of them passes his camp, when they talk to his young men, and endeavor to persuade them to join the expedition. That he has always given them good advice, entreating them to refrain from making war upon the whites, and showing them that they have nothing to gain by so doing. They are perfectly aware that we are much more powerful than themselves, and that they will be held to a strict account for any atrocities they may commit. He says his counsels are generally listened to and adopted by his warriors, but that now and then an impetuous young man, more anxious than others for distinction, will not take his advice or obey his commands, and goes off with a war-party. Such, he says, might have been the case in the recent affair alluded to, and one of his band may have been engaged therein, but he did not think that he should be held responsible for such acts, after he had done all in his power to prevent them. He states farther, that those of his people who make war upon the whites must take the consequences to themselves, as they will receive no countenance or protection from him. Whether he is sincere or not in what he has stated we have no means of determining, but his manner certainly impressed us with confidence in his good faith.

"On the morning of the 11th we left our camp before daylight, and traveled ten miles in the same course as the day previous, which carried us into the valley of a fine stream of running water, with several varieties of timber upon its borders. The soil in the valley is arable in the highest degree, and the natural resources of the locality fulfill all the conditions necessary for making good farms. This section is appropriated, and not available for the Indians.

"On the following morning we breakfasted at the very unfashionable hour of one o'clock, and were *en route* an hour afterward in a southwest course toward the high ridge dividing the main Brazos from the Clear Fork, and at ten o'clock crossed the road leading to Dona Ana, encamping near the Fort Belknap and Phantom Hill road, at a point ten miles east of the crossing of the Clear Fork.

"It was our intention to have intersected this road twenty miles farther west, but our guide was in this instance at fault, and although I repeatedly expressed my opinion that our course was leading us too far east, the Delawares believed they were right, and we suffered them to proceed.

"As they have generally been very correct in their judgment regarding courses and localities, this error must be regarded as an exception to the general rule. They, like all their brethren with whom I have been associated, are more perfect in the art of woodcraft than any people I have ever known. They are full of expedients for all emergencies, and their great experience upon the prairies renders their services highly valuable.

"Soon after crossing the California road, which I had traveled in 1849, we entered a section covered with large mesquit-trees, beneath which were innumerable large sunflowers, spreading over the entire country as far as we could see, and giving it a brilliant yellow hue.

"These continued as far as the crossing of the Clear Fork of the Brazos, upon the Phantom Hill road, which point we reached the next day about ten o'clock A.M.

"A change takes place in the physiognomy of the country in passing from the main or Salt Fork to the beautiful Clear Fork of the Brazos, which seems almost magical.

"We here find, within the small space of a day's travel, all that is rude, barren, and uninteresting in nature, in close proximity to that which is most pleasing and beautiful in pastoral scenery.

"Nature here evinces, in this sudden transition, a caprice that I have rarely observed in contiguous localities. Indeed, I doubt if two streams can be found in widely separated districts that present a greater contrast.

"The waters of the former stream are red, heavily loaded with earthy matter, exceedingly bitter to the taste, and flow sluggishly over a bed of quicksand, through a valley almost destitute of timber, while the waters of the latter flow rapidly over a bed of limestone and gravel of dazzling whiteness, which exhibits their purity and limpidity in such a manner that the smallest objects are distinctly visible at the depth of fifteen feet, while the banks are clothed with a variety of trees of gigantic dimensions, covered in many places with parasitical dependences, which overshadow the stream, and are reflected from the surface of the pure water in the same colors that they present when directly seen.

"The valley teems with a rich and verdant herbage, which exhibits the amazing fecundity of the soil, and every thing here reminds us of all that is most picturesque and charming in a highly cultivated country.

"The stream is here twenty-five yards wide, inclosed upon each side by high, precipitous banks, which contain the water at the highest stages, and are lined with pecan, hackberry, black walnut, and other trees, which in many places along the lowlands spread out over spaces of considerable extent, constituting a goodly amount of timber suitable for building purposes or fuel.

"About six miles below the crossing the oak-timbered lands commence, and continue along the course of the stream upon both banks to its confluence with the main Brazos.

"The greater portion of the land in this direction is, however, taken up by individuals.

"The valley of the Clear Fork is, in this vicinity, from one quarter of a mile to two miles in width, and is every where bountifully supplied with cool fresh water spring-brooks. Limestone, which is here the predominating rock, is found in the greatest profusion, and is better adapted for building purposes than any I have ever seen before. It has been shaped out by natural causes into cubes and other symmetrical figures of convenient dimensions, with smooth surfaces and perfect angles in such a manner as to be already dressed for the hands of the mason.

"We were much rejoiced on arriving here to find evidences of civilization in this far Western Indian country.

"A former agent of the Comanches (Colonel J. Stem) some years since purchased a tract of land here, upon which he determined to open a farm.

"The experiment was made by turning over the sod with a prairie plow, and planting the seed (corn and oats) upon it. No other labor was expended in the way of hoeing or plowing, but it grew up most luxuriantly, and produced a very bountiful yield of grain.

"It has now been planted for three successive seasons, and in every instance with good results; while during the same period, in some of the populated sections farther east, the crops have failed. During the past summer, the universal drought throughout the Southwestern States caused an almost entire failure in the corn crop, but here they did not suffer in the least.

"Thus far the cultivation of this farm has realized handsome profits to its proprietor, and he finds a ready market for his produce at Fort Belknap, at good prices.

"These facts may seem foreign to the subject matter of a report of this character, but I have brought them to notice as an evidence of the fertility of the soil, and an argument in support of the adaptation of this locality to the wants of the Indians.

"There are numerous remains of old Comanche camps throughout the valley, showing that this has for many years been a favorite resort for them. All the best varieties of the gramma and mesquit grasses are found here, and animals require no other forage during the winter months; indeed, we are told that they thrive and keep in better condition during the winter than in the summer.

"There are not so many flies here as in the more heavily timbered districts to the east, from which cattle suffer severely, and I verily believe there is no place in the universe better suited to 'stock raising' than this.

"We made our encampment on the bank of the Clear Fork, at a large spring of cold, delicious water, which gushed forth from the bank about half a mile below Stem's ranch. As there is a vacant tract of land of sufficient extent for one reservation lying upon the river above here, we determined to make a halt for the purpose of examining it, and in the mean time send Ketumsee for the other chiefs of the Southern Comanches, who were about seventy miles off.

"On the following morning Major Neighbors and myself ascended the river about eight miles to the confluence of another tributary, called by the Comanches Qua-qua-hono, and by the whites Paint Creek. We ascended this branch to the crossing of the California road, where we bivouacked for the night, and I made my bed under the same tree where I pitched my tent in 1849. It was here that I met Senaco's band of Comanches upon that occasion.

"We turned our steps toward camp at an early hour on the next day, and passed down upon the north side of the river, thus making a careful examination of the tract of country noted as vacant upon the map furnished us from the General Land Office, which we find contains a good share of rich valley land along the borders of the stream, well suited to the culture of grain or plants. The uplands adjoining are undulating, with rich grassy slopes covered with mesquit-trees, well adapted for pasturage.

"As we were returning to camp we met two Indians from Senaco's camp, with a message from him desiring us to put no reliance in the statements of Ketumsee, as he did not authorize him to talk for the nation.

"Although Senaco is acknowledged by all to be the ruling spirit of the Southern Comanches, and claims and holds that position in their united deliberations, yet his band and that of Ketumsee are otherwise separate and independent. Ketumsee is an ambitious and astute leader, pursuing a discreet and complaisant policy in the government of his followers calculated to enhance his popularity, and he has already alienated several of Senaco's band, who have transferred their allegiance to him. This has engendered a feeling of ill will and jealousy between them that causes each to be suspicious of the motives of the other, and it was probably this that induced him to think he might be misrepresented to us.

"Senaco, with several sub-chiefs and a chief of the Middle Comanches, having arrived on the 20th, we assembled them in council in the evening, for the purpose of ascertaining their views upon the subject of the proposed settlement.

"As I had just come from Washington, the Indians were anxious I should tell them what their Great Father's wishes were. I accordingly stated to them that I had been sent into their country to select and survey a tract of land suitable for cultivating corn and raising cattle; that their agent had been appointed to assist me in this duty; that their Great Father at Washington was sorry to see his Red children upon the prairies suffering for food, and desired to place them in a situation where they would be more comfortable. To effect this, he proposed to locate them upon the lands we were about to select, and have them taught to cultivate it.

"In illustrating the benefits that would accrue to them, I remarked that the buffaloes had within a few years entirely left their hunting-grounds; the deer and other game were rapidly disappearing from the Plains, and in a few years they and their children would be compelled to resort to some other life than the chase for a subsistence.

"They would not be permitted to depredate upon their neighbors, and there would be no alternative left them but that of tilling the soil.

"That I had for twenty years lived near and become acquainted with several other tribes of Indians who once lived as they do, upon the uncertain results of the chase, but by the advice of the whites they were induced to give up their wandering habits, established permanent habitations, and learned to plant corn and raise cattle, and were now living like the whites, having an abundance to eat and wear during the entire year; and I believed it was only necessary for them to make the experiment to satisfy themselves that they and their children would be much benefited.

"I told them, farther, that I presumed the President would send them farmers to instruct them, and supply them with agricultural implements and provisions to subsist them until they could raise their first crop. That their agent and the military authorities stationed near them would see that they were not molested by the whites, and that their rights were respected by their neighboring brethren. But that, in return for these favors, they would be expected to obey all the orders of our government, and remain firm friends to the whites.

"In conclusion, I desired them to deliberate well upon what I had said, and when they had done so, we should be glad to hear what they had decided upon.

"After conferring together for some time in a low tone of voice, and passing around the pipe, Senaco rose, and, in a very dignified manner, said:

"'What I am about to say is the sentiment of all my people; what Senaco says the Comanche nation say. We have heard the talk which our Great Father has sent us by our friend Captain Marcy, and our reply to it will be straightforward and the truth.

"'We very well remember what our former chief "Mo-ko-cho-pe" told us before he died, and we endeavor to carry out his wishes after he is gone from us. He advised us to take the counsels of the whites and be governed by them, and they would benefit us. This has sunk deep into our hearts, and we shall not soon forget it.

"'We are very glad to hear the talk which has been sent us at this time; it makes our hearts warm, and we feel happy that our Great Father remembers his poor Red children in the prairies.

"'We accept the talk, and shall endeavor to accede to all that is required of us.

"'I am pleased to see Captain Marcy once more. I well remember meeting him five years since near this very place, and I was glad when I was told he was to meet us here.'

"After closing his remarks, we asked them many questions, the answers to which satisfied us that a majority of them were disposed to make a trial of the experiment in farming; yet, as it is altogether a new thing to them (neither they nor their forefathers from time immemorial having ever planted a seed), some of them are evidently fearful they will not be benefited by it, and they asked us why the government was so anxious to have them abandon their old mode of life at this particular time.

"They desired us to locate their land upon the Clear Fork of the Brazos, where they have been in the habit of spending the winter, and have very serious objections to settling farther north, as they say they entertain the same fears of the Northern Indians as their brethren upon the Brazos.

"After finishing the business of the council, Major Neighbors distributed among them the presents that had been purchased for them, which, with some rations I issued them, made them seemingly very happy, and their camp was a scene of feasting during the remainder of their stay with us. They, like other Indians, are extravagantly fond of corn, and the chief said he hoped we would give them a good allowance of this, as otherwise he would not be able to prevent the women from stealing it from the plantation in our vicinity.

"On the following morning, Major Neighbors and myself, leaving the command upon the Clear Fork, went in to Fort Belknap, for the purpose of making a more minute examination of the country below that post than we had been enabled to do previous to our departure upon our expedition up the Brazos.

"We found upon our map a vacant tract of country lying below the junction of the Clear Fork, and as this was the only available locality suited to the wishes of the Brazos Indians, we directed our attention exclusively to it. It is situated on both sides of the river, which divides it into two equal parts of four leagues each, and is in every particular well adapted to the uses of two separate tribes.

"There is a large body of valley land of the most pre-eminent fertility upon either side of the stream, extending throughout the entire length of the tract. This, upon both sides, is bordered by mesquit uplands, covered with luxuriant gramma grasses, affording the best pasturage, and adjoining this a range of mountains, covered with oak timber extends upon each side to the north and south lines, bounding the reservations.

"Each tract has a river front of upward of twenty-six

miles, affording an abundance of water at all seasons for their animals. Then there are several streams of fresh water, fed from springs, which will always supply them with water for their own use. The pure water of the Clear Fork (the largest confluent in this section) modifies the salts in the main stream to such a degree that animals drink it readily and thrive upon it.

"*Summary.*

"A brief and comprehensive glance at the general physical geography of this section of country, a portion of which has been noticed in detail in the foregoing narrative, will disclose the considerations which influenced us in making the selections for the Indian reservations.

"Before entering upon the discharge of the duties assigned us in our letters of instructions from the Departments of War and Interior, we procured from the General Land Office of Texas a map of that portion of the state to which our attention was directed, upon which all the vacant domain was indicated. A perusal of the foregoing journal will show that a great share of the most desirable lands, bordering the streams in the country over which we passed, has been disposed of by the state, and was not then available for Indian purposes. We, however, found many spots where all the natural requisites were at hand for making good farms, but, in almost every instance, these vacant tracts were not of sufficient magnitude to constitute reservations of the dimensions required.

"From the examination I had before made of that portion of Northern Texas lying upon the waters of Red, Witchita, and the Canadian Rivers, west of the 100th meridian of latitude, I was of the opinion that a much better locality could be found near the Big Witchita or the Brazos Rivers.

"The different confluents of Little Witchita are bordered by lands which are very highly productive to their very sources; and in that portion of the valley near Red River, woodland is sufficiently plenty for the purposes of the farmer, but this is appropriated, and in that section of the valley which is vacant there is a deficiency of timber. As I have observed before, however, the fine building-stone found throughout the valley may answer the purposes of a white population, and this may yet offer sufficient inducements to attract settlers.

"The country embraced within the valley of the Big Witchita presents in its physical aspect two remarkable divisions, distinct belts as it were, extending along the course of the stream, with entirely different topographical features. Commencing at Red River, and ascending the stream for seventy-five miles, the valley, which is from one to five miles wide, is smooth and regular, the soil highly fertile, and covered with a luxuriant vegetation. And upon the borders of this savanna a chain of bluffs terminates the elevated prairie lands adjoining, from whence issue many springs of pure, wholesome water; but, with the exception of a few cottonwood-trees upon the immediate borders of the river, there is no woodland throughout this section.

"The upper division of the river finds its way through a valley more contracted than that spoken of, and the soil is much more sterile, being a mixture of clay and sand unsuited to the rapid development of vegetation. The bluffs rise from the base to a much greater height, and approach nearer the river bank, and are covered with a variety of stunted red cedar bushes, indicating a great increase in the general elevation of the country. The surrounding plains assume a lonely, melancholy, and arid aspect, producing in the mind a sadness which contrasts strikingly with the feeling inspired upon the most unimpressible temperament by the beauty of a landscape embellished with verdant woodlands and smiling prairies, garnished with multitudes of gorgeous flowers.

"Above the sources of the Big Witchita a range of mountains stretch away to the south for about forty miles, embracing all the principal upper confluents of the Brazos. These mountains are composed principally of gypsum and sandstone, and stand out in bold relief upon the vast prairie lands surrounding. They are clothed with a scanty growth of dwarf cedar and cacti toward the bases, while the summits are denuded of all vegetation, which, with the rugged disposition of the strata, adds to the general imposing effect upon the beholder, and strangely contrasts with the smiling aspect of the prairies that sweep off to the east and south from below.

"The gypsum rock, which imparts to all the water in this section those peculiar and unpalatable properties that have been mentioned, will render this country uninhabitable by man for any great length of time.

"On leaving these dreary solitudes and turning to the east down the right bank of the Brazos, we soon enter a much more inviting section of country. We here encounter several tributaries of the Clear Fork, affording pure water, and the geological formation rapidly changes. The gypsum rock is only seen in detached masses, and its place is soon entirely occupied by lime and sandstone.

"Although in our expedition to the sources of the Big Witchita and the Brazos we were unsuccessful in discovering a suitable location for the Indians, yet it is thought that the results of our labors will not be entirely devoid of utility or interest. The geographical knowledge we have obtained of this hitherto unexplored region enables me to complete a sketch of the only tributaries of the Brazos that were before unknown. It will be observed that upon the map accompanying my report, a large stream (the Double

Mountain Fork of the Brazos), which has before been noted upon all the maps of this section, is wanting. This imaginary river has heretofore been supposed to enter the main Brazos about thirty miles above Fort Belknap, and is even found delineated upon the surveyor's maps that were sent us from the General Land Office of Texas, with surveys noted upon it. On our return from the head waters of the Brazos we traveled down the south bank of the stream until we arrived within forty miles of Fort Belknap, when we struck south for the Clear Fork, expecting to cross the Double Mountain Fork before we reached it, but, to our surprise, the Clear Fork was the first stream of magnitude we encountered, so that the Double Mountain Fork has no existence.

"On my return from New Mexico in 1849, I struck quite a large stream running to the east about thirty-five miles west of the crossing of Paint Creek. I was then given to understand by my Delaware guide that this was the 'Double Mountain Fork of the Brazos,' but our observations now prove it to have been Paint Creek.

"The geological information we have secured is also regarded as important.

"I had upon my former expeditions traced a great belt of gypsum from the Canadian River across the Plains in a southwesterly course for several hundred miles toward the Rio Grande.

"We have traced the continuation of this formation where it intersects the valley of the Big Witchita, and thence across the different branches of the Brazos. Near the head of the Brazos it presents a solid stratum of the enormous thickness of five hundred feet. It occurs in various shades of purity, from the common plaster of Paris to pure selenite, quite similar in appearance to that upon the Red and Canadian Rivers.

"In the journeys I had made before upon the Plains I had observed the mesquit-tree extending over vast tracts of country, and I had noticed some of its useful properties, such as its durability and its adaptation for fuel, but I was never so fully impressed with its many valuable qualities as during the past summer.

"It covered a great portion of the country over which we traveled, and our attention was especially attracted to an exudation of gum from its trunk and branches, which, upon tasting, we pronounced to be closely allied to the gum-arabic of commerce.

"This tree was first brought to the notice of the public by Dr. Edwin James, Assistant Surgeon United States Army, who met with it in his trip to the Rocky Mountains with Colonel Long, forty-seven years ago. It is a variety of the acacia, and possesses many properties in common with other species of that group of plants.

"What the exact geographical range of the tree is we are as yet (with a great portion of our territory unexplored) unable to define; my own observations, however, warrant me in asserting confidently that it is only indigenous to the great plains of the West and South, extending far beyond the limits of most other varieties of trees, and it would seem from its locality to have been planted by an all-wise Providence with special reference to the wants of the occupants of a section of country suitable to the growth of no other tree.

"Between the twenty-sixth and thirty-sixth parallels of north latitude, within the ninety-seventh and one hundred and third meridians of longitude, it is found abundantly, often constituting vast tracts of woodland, and is, indeed, almost the only silva of the section. It is also found in very many places between the Rocky Mountain range and the Pacific Ocean, but appears to flourish better and to attain greater dimensions in the vicinity of the Gila River than in any other locality I have heard of west of the Rio del Norte.

"In going north from the parallel of thirty-three degrees (in the direction I have traveled) the trees gradually become smaller and smaller, until at last they are mere bushes; and, finally, on arriving near the latitude of thirty-six degrees they entirely disappear.

"The vast geographical range of the mesquit-tree, and its many useful properties, some of which will be enumerated in the sequel, renders it available, and I have no doubt it is destined to become highly important to the future occupants of a large section of our new territory.

"It is a tree of short, scrubby growth, the stock averaging from four to fifteen inches in diameter, and seldom attaining a height, including its top, of more than twenty feet. The limbs are short, crooked, and thickly studded with long, sharp thorns; the leaves pinnated, and the leaflets are long and elliptical; the bark is a dark gray, resembling that of the peach-tree; the wood coarse-grained, very brittle; and the heart, which constitutes nearly the entire tree, somewhat like the darker varieties of mahogany.

"It burns readily, even when green, with a bright, cheerful flame, leaving a residue of coals almost as perfect in form as the original wood, making a very hot fire, and is, indeed, the best fuel I have ever seen, hickory not excepted.

"It possesses durability in an eminent degree, and is, in consequence, much used for building in Southern Texas and Mexico. As an evidence of its lasting qualities, I have seen pieces of the wood, in a perfect state of preservation, imbedded in the stones of an old ruin upon the Nueces River, in Texas, which must have been exposed to the weather for very many years, as the stones had become partially disintegrated, and were crumbling away with age, while the wood remained sound.

"The mesquit is often found upon the most elevated and arid prairies, far from water-courses, but will, I believe, only grow upon soil of the first quality; and so well is this fact established, that the mesquit groves, or 'flats,' as they are called, are sought after in Western Texas as the most desirable spots for cultivation, and they have thus far proved exceedingly productive. The trees stand at wide intervals, upon ground covered with a dense carpet of verdure, and a stranger, on approaching one of the groves, can not resist the impression that he has a peach orchard before him, so striking is the resemblance. The blossoms put forth in June, and a fruit appears in the form of a long, slender bean, from which the Mexicans make a cooling and pleasant beverage. These beans ripen in September, when they fall to the ground, and afford sustenance to wild horses, deer, antelope, and turkeys.

"The pod is highly saccharine and nutritious, and is used for food by the natives of the Plains, as well as those west of the Rocky Mountains. The Indians upon the Colorado and Gila Rivers pulverize and press them into cakes, which are said to be quite palatable.

"They make most excellent forage for horses and mules, and there are many instances where they have sustained those of the California emigrants upon some of those long 'journadas,' or sandy and barren deserts, toward the Pacific.

"A tree very similar to the mesquit, 'called the carob-tree,' is found in the south of Spain. It affords a bean like the mesquit, which is imported under the name of 'Algaroba bean.' It is used for food in Spain, and is there called 'St. John's Bread.' It was this bean that often constituted the only forage of the English cavalry horses during the war of 1811 and 1812.

"The species of acacia from which the gum-arabic of commerce is obtained (the acacia vera) is a hard, withered-looking tree, with a crooked stem and gray bark, very like, in external appearance, the mesquit.

"The gum of the mesquit exudes from the trunk and branches wherever there is an abrasion in the bark. It is also produced when a cut is made with a sharp instrument, in the same manner as the sap is drawn from the sugar maple. It commences exuding in July, and continues until the last of September. It is, at first, in a translucent and nearly fluid state, but soon hardens by exposure to the sun and air; and if there is no rain (and there seldom is any at this season), it forms in globules upon the bark, and can be collected in large quantities; and I have no doubt it will eventually become an important article of commerce, answering all the purposes of the gum-arabic of the shops.

"Specimens of the gum collected by us were submitted to Dr. John Torrey, who kindly returned to me the following remarks upon the subject, which, coming from so distinguished a source, will be read with interest:

"'The collection of plants made by Dr. James in his expedition to the Rocky Mountains was submitted to me for examination, an account of which, with descriptions of all the new species that it contained, I published in the "Annals of the New York Lyceum of Natural History" in 1827 (vol. ii., p. 161–254). The mesquit was found to be a new species of the genus Prosopis of Linnæus, to which I gave the name of P. glandulosa, and a figure of the plant accompanied the description. The eminent botanist, Mr. Bentham, who has made a special study of the Leguminosa, considers the section Algaroba of Prosopis as a distinct genus. His views were adopted in the "Flora of North America" by Dr. Gray and myself, so that the plant is there described as "Algaroba glandulosa" (Torr. and Gray, H. N. Amer., i., p. 399). Twelve or more other species are natives of Mexico and the western coast of South America. All of them bear a long, compressed pod, which is filled with a sweet, nutritious pulp. These pods were used for food by Major Long's party. They constitute, also, a most valuable fodder for animals.

" 'For several years I have known that a gum, allied to the gum-arabic, exuded from the trees, especially where they were wounded. Specimens of the gum were long ago brought to me by different travelers from New Mexico and Western Texas, but I never examined the substance particularly till I received a supply of it from you a few days ago. At your request I submitted it to examination, and compared it with the well-known gum-arabic.

" 'The mesquit or algaroba gum is intermediate in appearance between the darker kinds of gum-arabic and cherry-tree gum. Portions of it, however, are almost colorless, and have the roughish surface and cracked structure that belong to the better kinds of gum-arabic. The portion that you sent me was probably not gathered with particular care, for some of it has particles of bark attached to the lumps, or disseminated through them.

" 'On testing the solubility of the gum in cold water, it dissolved as readily as gum-arabic, and the mucilage, though of a brownish tint, was destitute of bitterness or other unpleasant flavor, and it is strongly adhesive. When the solution is poured into a shallow vessel, and left to spontaneous evaporation, it leaves the gum in transparent brilliant plates, having all the qualities of the original gum.' 'If the gum can not be gathered without a small portion of dirt being entangled in it, the best plan would be to dissolve it in water, and let the dirt subside, or separate it by straining. The mucilage might then be dried, the thin plates of gum bleached in the sun, and afterward pulverized.

" 'You are perhaps aware that the trees affording the mesquit gum and gum-arabic belong to the same natural group of plants, so it is not remarkable that they so strongly resemble each other.' "

As the history of the experiment of civilizing the Comanches may possess some interest to many of my readers, I remark, in concluding my account of these reservations, that Ketumsee and his followers settled upon the lands designed for them, and under the able superintendence of their agent, Major Neighbors, and the instruction of farmers provided by the United States government, they made commendable progress in the rudiments of agriculture. Their women and children worked in the fields and were cultivating good crops of grain, and their condition was undergoing such rapid improvement when contrasted with their former roving life and their precarious means of gaining a livelihood, that there is no question in my mind, if they had been unmolested, the next generation would have found them agriculturists and not hunters. But this desirable end was not destined to be consummated.

After they had made some considerable improvements upon their lands, their value was so much enhanced that they became an object worthy the attention of those lawless border robbers that inhabit Western Texas, and, as I was informed, they organized a large force, went to the reservation, and, without the slightest provocation from the Indians, attacked and indiscriminately murdered many of the men, women, and children. Those that escaped the foul massacre made their way into the Plains, and this pretty much broke up the settlement.

Major Neighbors, who subsequently commented severely upon the turpitude of the act, was shortly afterward shot in the back by one of the cowardly assassins, and died in a short time.

Senaco and his band never settled upon the reservation, but made war upon the whites for attempting to coerce them into the measure, and they continue to roam over the Plains to this day.

CHAPTER VIII.

WINTER EXPEDITION OVER THE ROCKY MOUNTAINS.

Winter Expedition over the Rocky Mountains.—Objects of the Expedition. —General Scott's Opinions.—Leaving Fort Bridger.—Desertion of Indian Guide.—Descending Mountain.—Singular Corral.—Reach Grand River. —Ute Indians.—Commence the Ascent of the Rocky Mountains.—Snow. —Cache Luggage.—Mules giving out and dying.—Provisions consumed. —Commence eating Mules.—Ptarmigan.—Getting lost.—New Guide.— Excellent Conduct of the Soldiers. — Destitute Condition. — Bivouac.— Reach the Summit of the Mountains.—Send Messengers to Fort Massachusetts. — Return of the Messengers.—Joy of the Party.—Mariano.— Overeating.—Arrival at Fort Massachusetts.—Arrival at Taos.—Comparative Qualities of different Animals in Snow.

During the month of November, 1857, while our troops were encamped at Fort Bridger, in Utah Territory, I was ordered, with a command of forty enlisted men, to cross the mountains by the most direct route into New Mexico, and procure supplies.

As but little, if any thing, is known to the public about this expedition, and as a great deal has been written and said concerning others of a similar character, which, perhaps, were of no more importance in their results than this, I trust that a brief account of some of the most prominent incidents connected with that journey will not prove uninteresting.

The objects of this march are set forth in the following extracts from the report of the Secretary of War for 1858. He says: "The destruction of our trains by the Mormons, and the disasters which necessarily flowed from it, drove

General Johnston to the necessity of sending a detachment of men to New Mexico for supplies essential to enable him to prosecute his march with all practicable dispatch.

"This expedition was intrusted to Captain R. B. Marcy, of the 5th Infantry; and, without intending to make an invidious comparison between the services of officers where all are meritorious, it is but just to bring the conduct of this officer and his command to your especial notice. It may be safely affirmed that, in the whole catalogue of hazardous expeditions scattered so thickly through the history of our border warfare, filled as many of them are with appalling tales of privation, hardship, and suffering, not one surpasses this, and in some particulars it has been hardly equaled by any.

"Captain Marcy left Fort Bridger on the 24th day of November, 1857, with a command of forty enlisted men, and twenty-five mountain men, besides packers and guides. Their course lay through an almost trackless wilderness, over lofty and rugged mountains, without a pathway or human habitation to guide or direct, in the very depth of winter, through snows, for many miles together, reaching to the depth of five feet. Their beasts of burden very rapidly perished until very few were left; their supplies gave out; their luggage was abandoned; they were driven to subsist upon the carcasses of their dead horses and mules; all the men became greatly emaciated; some were frost-bitten, yet not one murmur of discontent escaped the lips of a single man. Their mission was one of extreme importance to the movements of the army, and great disaster might befall the command if these devoted men failed to bring succor to the camp. They had one and all volunteered for this service, and, although they might freeze or die, yet they would not complain.

"After a march of fifty-one days, they emerged from the

forests, and found themselves at Fort Massachusetts, in New Mexico.

"During their whole march Captain Marcy shared all the privations of the common soldier, marching, sleeping, and eating as they did."

After my return to Fort Bridger, I had the honor of receiving the following letter:

"Head-quarters of the Army, New York, May 29, 1858.

"SIR,—I am instructed by the general-in-chief to say to you, in reply to your letter of the 29th of March (reporting my movements), that the unconquerable energy, patience, and devotedness to duty displayed by yourself and the command intrusted to your skillful guidance and direction, have been highly appreciated by himself, and that the unusual sufferings and hard labor to which the troops were exposed in accomplishing their arduous march in the depth of winter has been made known to the whole country by the public press. * * * * The general-in-chief will not fail to commend your admirable conduct to the special notice of the War Department.

"I am, very respectfully, your obedient servant,

(Signed) "GEO. W. LAY, *Lieut. Col. and A. D. C.*

"Captain R. B. Marcy, 5th Infantry."

When we left Fort Bridger there was only six inches of snow on the ground, and my guides, as well as other mountain men, were of opinion that we should not, at that early season, find over two feet of snow upon the summit of the mountains. They also believed that we could make the trip to Fort Massachusetts, New Mexico, in twenty-five days; but, to make sure of having enough provisions, I deemed it wise to take thirty days' supply, which, with our luggage, was packed upon sixty-six mules.

After bidding adieu to our friends at Fort Bridger, we proceeded down Henry's Fork to its confluence with Green River, where we forded the latter stream, and followed a trail that led us to the foot of the mountain dividing Green from Grand River. Here we found three lodges of Digger Utes, and engaged one of them to act as guide over the mountain. Our first day's march from here up a very circuitous cañon brought us to the top of this mountain, where we found the snow nearly two feet in depth. We encamped at the head of the cañon, and, after supper, our Indian guide came to me and expressed some doubt as to whether we were in possession of the articles he had been promised for his services, and Jim Baker, the interpreter, advised that they should be shown to him. Accordingly, the knife, powder, lead, and paint were spread out before him; and, although I rather disapproved the proceeding, Baker allowed him to take possession of them.

Before I lay down for the night I posted sentinels around the camp, and directed the guard to keep careful watch upon the Indian. About midnight I was awakened by the sergeant of the guard, who reported that he believed our Indian guide intended deserting, as he had placed his rifle and all his other effects in such a position that he could seize them instantly, and he appeared to be watching for an opportunity to break away. I repeated to the sergeant the order to guard him closely, and directed him, if he made any attempt at deserting us, to seize and tie him.

In the course of an hour the sergeant returned with the intelligence that, in spite of all his vigilance, the fellow had broken away from the guard and escaped. I regretted this, because we wanted his services to pilot us across the summit of the mountain on the following day. We were obliged, however, to set out without him, and, shortly after emerging from the cañon, found ourselves upon a level plateau about ten miles wide. Our track led us across this elevated table-land, which we found terminating in a towering and almost perpendicular cliff or bluff, bordering the valley of Grand River, and some two thousand feet above it. On reaching this lofty escarpment, it did not seem possible that our mules could descend it, and, indeed, I had been previously told that there was but one place for fifty miles along this cliff where the declivity was practicable for animals, and this was at a point where the Indians had cut out a narrow path along the face of the bluff, winding around over rocks and along the brinks of deep chasms.

We bivouacked in the snow directly upon the verge of this precipice, where we had a magnificent view of the valley of Grand River and the Rocky Mountains beyond. Immediately after we halted I sent out Baker to search for the trail leading into the valley, and it was not until late at night that he discovered it. In the morning we entered the tortuous defile and commenced the descent, which we found exceedingly precipitous and slippery. Our pack mules had great difficulty in keeping their footing. Occasionally one of them would fall, and, with his pack, roll over and over for thirty or forty feet down the rocks, until he was brought up by a tree or projecting crag. At length, however, after numerous tumbles and somersaults, we reached the valley at the base, and, to our surprise, found the grass green, and not a particle of snow upon the ground, while, as I said before, directly over our heads, upon the summit of the plateau, it lay two feet deep. We discovered at this place a naturally inclosed pasture, containing about two hundred acres, surrounded by an almost perpendicular trap wall some two hundred feet in height, and with but one opening of not more than a hundred yards wide. Our animals were all turned into this natural *corral*, and a herdsman stationed at the opening secured them as perfectly as if they had been shut up in a stable.

We picked up a horse here that had become very fat upon the rich *bunch* grass. He had probably been lost or abandoned by the Indians. We appropriated the animal, and subsequently used him for food in the mountains.

On the 8th of December we struck Grand River near the confluence of its two principal branches, the *Uncompadre* and the *Bunkara*. We forded them, but with much difficulty, as the water was deep and rapid, and filled with floating ice, and encamped at the base of the "Elk Mountain," near the remains of an old Indian trading establishment, which had formerly been occupied by a man named Robedeau, of St. Louis, who wandered out into this remote wilderness many years ago, but was subsequently driven away and his buildings burned by the Indians.

We were at this point within a few miles from the western base of the Rocky Mountains, which rose in formidable proportions in front of us, and appeared covered with a heavy coating of snow. Thus far our journey had been pleasant, and we had encountered no serious obstacles. Our animals had found abundance of grass, and were in fair condition.

But, as the guides informed me that we were to enter the mountains at this point, their appearance gave me serious apprehensions for the future. We here fell in with a large band of Digger Ute Indians, who were subsisting upon rabbits, bugs, crickets, etc. They came flocking around us as soon as we arrived, examining every thing, and begging for such articles as happened to take their fancy. They were a ragged, villainous-looking set, and we had our hands full in keeping the women from stealing every thing that came in their way.

They had a good many ponies; but, although we offered

large prices for some of them, we could not induce them to part with a single one. Their curiosity appeared a good deal exercised to ascertain our business in their country; and when we informed them that we were bound for New Mexico, they expressed great astonishment, and would point to the mountains and shiver as if with cold.

I endeavored to persuade the chief to accompany us as guide to the summit of the mountains, and offered him the value of three horses in goods, but he peremptorily refused, saying that he was not yet ready to die, and that, unless we turned back, or stopped and passed the winter with them, we would all inevitably perish. My interpreter asked him if he took us for a set of old women, who would be intimidated by a little snow; and added, that he had always before taken him for a warrior and a man, but now he had discovered his mistake, and he would advise him to go back to his lodge, cover up warm, and assist his squaw in tending the babies; that we were of the masculine gender; we had started to cross the mountains into New Mexico, and were going to accomplish it at all hazards, and if he did not feel disposed to go, we could dispense with his services. This taunt had no effect upon him, however. He persisted in refusing to go with us, saying that all we had would not be sufficient to induce him to attempt the journey. I then asked him how much snow he supposed we would find in the mountains? He replied that he was not positive as to the exact depth, but that he crossed over the same route we proposed to travel in the autumn, when the leaves were commencing to fall, and that he then found about one foot upon the summit; that there had been a great deal of rain in the valley since that time, which he presumed had its equivalent in snow upon the mountains, and he was of opinion that we might encounter from four to five feet, and perhaps even more than that. He concluded by saying,

"You may think I do not tell the truth, but if you will only cast your eyes toward the mountains you can see for yourselves that the snow is there."

On the following morning (the 11th day of December), in despite of the gloomy and discouraging prospects held out to us by the Digger chief, we packed up our mules and commenced the ascent of the western slope of the Rocky Mountains. We had proceeded but a few miles when the snow began very seriously to impede our progress. On the second day it became still deeper, with a crust upon the surface, which cut the legs of our animals seriously, and caused some of them to refuse their work. We, however, pushed on, until at length we found the snow so deep that they could no longer force their way through it, and I was now obliged to resort to a new order of march. Up to this time we had, for the security of our animals, adopted the plan of marching with an advanced guard, immediately followed by the pack mules, with the main party in rear.

I now placed the greater part of the command in front, in single rank, so as to break a track for the animals. This was, of course, very hard work upon a few of the leading men; and, in order to equalize the labor as much as possible, I directed that every man, as he came in front, should retain that position a certain length of time, after which he was permitted to turn out of the track and allow all the others to pass him, taking his place in rear. By these alternations the work was very much lightened, and, after all the party had passed, a good track was left for the animals. And they really required all our care, as, from the time we entered the mountains, they received no other sustenance than what they derived from the bitter pine-leaves. The effects of this novel and unwholesome forage soon began to manifest itself upon them. They became weak and exhausted, and at length began to give out and die. I was then obliged to *cache*, or hide, all our surplus luggage, which reduced the weight of the packs very considerably. Notwithstanding this, they continued to perish. One day we lost five, and another day as many as eight died out of our little stock. This gave me very serious uneasiness, as our supply of provisions was becoming very small, and I knew, after these were gone, our only dependence for subsistence must be upon our famished animals. Our beef cattle had nearly all been consumed, and our stock of bread was very limited. I felt the necessity of husbanding the strength of my men and animals as much as possible. I therefore ordered the command to throw away every article of baggage they had remaining excepting one blanket each and their arms and ammunition. They cheerfully complied with the order, and we thus made another very material reduction in the weight of our packs, which enabled our enfeebled animals to proceed with more ease.

The snow increased day after day as we ascended, until it was four feet deep, and was so dry and light that the men, walking in an upright position, would sink to their waists, and could not move. One of the guides made a pair of snow shoes, and attempted to walk upon them, but they sank so deep in the soft snow that it was impossible to use them.

Our only alternative now, in the deepest snow, was for the three or four leading men of the party to lie down and crawl upon their hands and feet, each man following in the tracks of the leader, and all placing their hands and feet in the same holes. This method packed the snow so that, after a few men had passed, it bore up the others, and was sufficiently firm to sustain the mules after all the men had traversed it.

The leading man was generally able to go about fifty

yards before he became exhausted; but I had one soldier, named McLeod, of the 10th Infantry, whose powers of endurance exceeded those of any other man I have ever known. He would generally, when his turn came to lead the party, make about four times the distance of any other man. He was always in good spirits, and never became weary or discouraged, and his example had a most cheering effect upon his comrades. One bitter cold day, after having labored very hard, we halted for a few moments, and made fires to warm our feet. While standing over the fire, I took out my pipe, and, cutting a little tobacco from a small piece I had remaining, indulged myself in a smoke, the men having used their last tobacco some ten days before. McLeod was standing near me at the time, and, being desirous of doing something to show my appreciation of his valuable sèrvice, I handed him the precious morsel of tobacco, and asked him if he would not like to smoke. He replied, "No, I thank you, captain, I never smoke." I suggested that he was very fortunate in not being addicted to the habit at a time when tobacco was so very scarce. After a moment's hesitation, he said, "*I sometimes take a chew*," when I told him to help himself, which he did, and immediately exclaimed, "I never tasted any thing so good in my life; I would have given ten dollars for that, captain."

Notwithstanding I reduced the rations one half, our provisions were all consumed long before we reached the top of the mountains, and we were then entirely dependent upon our famished animals for food.

Our first repast upon the novel regimen was from a colt belonging to Tim Goodale's Indian wife, who accompanied us, and underwent the hardships of the trip with astonishing patience and fortitude.

She cried very bitterly when the colt was killed, as it

had always been her pet; but she realized the necessity of the sacrifice, and was consoled upon my promising her another on our arrival in New Mexico.

We found the meat well-flavored, tender, and palatable.

Our next meal was from a very old, lean, and tough mare which had given out and could perform no farther service. This we found any thing but a "bonne bouche." We were, however, very hungry, and ate it.

After this our only diet for twelve days consisted of starved mules as they became exhausted and could go no farther. Twelve of my men had frozen their feet so badly as to be unable to walk, and we were obliged to appropriate all our serviceable animals to carry them. I had given up my own horse to one of these men, and took his place in the snow with the others. We had not a single morsel of any thing left to eat except these animals. If we had had some salt we would have done better, but that was all gone. I was in the habit of sprinkling a little gunpowder upon my mule-steaks, and it did not then require a very extensive stretch of the imagination to fancy the presence of both pepper and salt.

This lean meat did not, however, by any means satisfy the cravings of the appetite, and we were continually longing for fat meat. Although we consumed large quantities of the mule meat, yet within half an hour from the time we had finished our meals we would feel as hungry as before we had eaten.

One day, as we were making our weary way through the deepest snow near the summit of the mountains, and when we were suffering severely from the intense cold, and the piercing winds which sweep over those high altitudes, my guide, Tim Goodale, called out to me from the front, and pointing toward a snow-bank, said there were some birds he had never but once before seen.

I cast my eyes in the direction indicated, but could discern nothing until the birds rose up and flew away. We subsequently killed two of them, and, upon examination, found them about the size of the partridge of the North, or the pheasant of the South. They were as white as the snow itself, without a single colored feather, and their method of flying, and their appearance in other respects, was very similar to that of the grouse. I was quite confident we had discovered a new variety of that species of bird, until two specimens which were sent to Professor Baird, of the Smithsonian Institute, showed them to be the "*Sagopus leucurus*," or white-tailed ptarmigan, a species of which but two or three specimens are said to be found in any ornithological collections, and those are in Europe. This beautiful bird, which, in its winter plumage, is as white as the snow upon which we invariably found them, was before supposed to be confined to that part of the Rocky Mountain chain north of latitude 54° north. The specimens sent to Professor Baird are said by him to be the first indications of their occurrence within the limits of our possessions, and it extends their supposed range about a thousand miles to the south.

These birds were the only glimpses of animal life that we had met with, outside of our own party, during thirty days that we were struggling through the deep snow.

The following is an extract from my journal, written on the evening of the 1st of January.

"This morning dawned upon us with gloomy auspices, far from promising to us a happy New Year. We have been engaged since daylight this morning in wallowing along through snow at least five feet deep, and have only succeeded, by the severest toil, in making about two miles during the entire day. From our bivouac to-night we can see the fires of last night, and in the darkness they do not appear over a rifle-shot distant. The leading men have been obliged to crawl upon their hands and knees to prevent sinking to their necks, and could only go a few yards at a time before they were compelled, in a state of complete exhaustion, to throw themselves down and let others take their places.

"Gallant fellows! Many of them are almost barefooted, and several whose feet have been frozen have suffered intensely from pain and cold. Yet every soldier, without a single exception, has performed every thing I required of him cheerfully and manfully; they have never faltered, or uttered a murmur of complaint. I feel for them from the bottom of my heart, and I should be recreant to my duty as their commander if I neglected to give expression to my profound gratitude for the almost superhuman efforts put forth by them to extricate the party from our perilous position."

At one period of this toilsome journey, while we were ascending the Eagle-tail River, a branch of the Grand River, my guide made a mistake, and took the wrong direction for the "Cochetope Pass," the point at which we were aiming, and which was, as I was well aware, the only place where it was possible for us to cross the summit of the chain, as on the north and south of this passway the mountains were much more elevated, and the snow so deep at that season that it would have been utterly impossible for us, in our enfeebled and famished condition, to have forced our way through it. It was only fifty miles south of the Cochetope Pass that General Fremont attempted to penetrate these mountains from New Mexico, and encountered so much snow that all his animals perished, and he was forced to turn back, with the loss of several of his men, before the party was extricated from their perilous position. We traveled the greatest part of the day in the wrong direction; and after we had bivouacked for the night, one of my employés, a Mexican by the name of Miguel Alona, came to me and told me that we had left the right direction in the morning, and, pointing toward a depression in the mountains at right angles to the course we had taken, some thirty miles distant, said that was the Cochetope Pass. I asked him how it happened that he knew any thing about the country. He replied that he had been there before, and that he knew it well. Whereupon I called up the guide, and upon questioning him in regard to it, he admitted that the face of the country, buried as it was in deep snows, presented so different an appearance from what it did in the summer season, when he had traversed it before, that it was possible he might have been mistaken; but still he believed he was right. I did not blame him, as this might have occurred with any one; but this first exhibition of doubt on his part caused me great uneasiness, and I now regarded our situation as involving us in imminent peril. We had advanced too far to retrace our steps, and the only alternative left us was to go forward; and I asked the Mexican if he was willing to act as guide, telling him I would, in addition to his regular pay, make him a handsome present for his services, provided he conducted us in safety to New Mexico; but I also informed him that if at any time I discovered he was leading us in a wrong direction, I should hang him to the first tree.

He was quite displeased at this, saying that he was sorry I should think he would attempt to deceive me. I told him all I required was for him to be sure he was right, and to think over the matter deliberately, and come back and let me know if he was willing to enter into the agreement upon the terms proposed by me. He returned in a short time and said, "I'll risk my neck on it, captain." "Very well," I replied, "you are guide."

From this time the uncertainty of our position, and the knowledge of the fact that if we failed to strike the Cochetope Pass we must all inevitably perish, gave me great anxiety, and prevented me from sleeping for several nights. There was not the slightest sign of a road, trail, or footmark to guide us; all was one vast, illimitable expanse of snow as far as the eye could penetrate; and the mountains rose before us, peak upon peak, until they were lost in the clouds. Not a living animal outside of our own party was seen for many, many long days; all was dreary, desolate solitude; but my noble soldiers struggled manfully ahead, and not a single murmur or complaint ever was heard to come from them; on the contrary, they endeavored to give me encouragement, and requested the senior sergeant to inform me that they had observed for a few days past that I looked melancholy, and they desired him to say to me that they were willing to eat mule meat, or to undergo any other privations that I might think necessary, and that they would work for me as long as they could stand upon their legs. As before stated, I had already required them to throw away all their personal baggage except one blanket each, and the poor fellows were extremely destitute of every thing. They had worn out their shoes, and had patched them with mule hides as long as they would hang together, when some of them were obliged to wrap their feet in pieces of blankets or of their coat-tails to keep them from freezing. Many of them had worn out their pants, and their legs were greatly exposed.

The dazzling reflection of the sun's rays from the snow was very painful, and made several of the men snow blind; but we found a remedy for this by blacking our faces with powder or charcoal.

The greatest deprivation we experienced, however, and the one which caused more suffering among the men than any other, was the want of tobacco. All our tobacco was consumed long before we reached the summit of the mountains, and no one who has not been accustomed to the use of the weed can imagine the intense longing produced by being suddenly deprived of it.

An incident occurred while we were in the mountains which struck me at the time as being one of the most remarkable and touching evidences of devotion that I have ever known evinced among the brute creation.

On leaving Fort Leavenworth with the army for Utah in the previous summer, one of the officers rode a small mule, whose kind and gentle disposition soon caused him to become a favorite among the soldiers, and they named him "Billy." As this officer and myself were often thrown together upon the march, the mule, in the course of a few days, evinced a growing attachment for a mare that I rode. The sentiment was not, however, reciprocated on her part, and she intimated as much by the reversed position of her ears, and the free exercise of her feet and teeth whenever Billy came within her reach. But these signal marks of displeasure, instead of discouraging, rather seemed to increase his devotion, and whenever at liberty he invariably sought to get near her, and appeared much distressed when not permitted to follow her.

On leaving Camp Scott for New Mexico Billy was among the number of mules selected for the expedition. During the march I was in the habit, when starting out from camp in the morning, of leading off the party, and directing the packmen to hold the mule until I should get so far in advance with the mare that he could not see us; but the moment he was released he would, in spite of all the efforts of the packers, start off at a most furious pace, and never stop or cease braying until he reached the mare's side. We soon found it impossible to keep him with the other mules, and he was finally permitted to have his own way.

In the course of time we encountered the deep snows in the Rocky Mountains, where the animals could get no forage, and Billy, in common with the others, at length became so weak and jaded that he was unable any longer to leave his place in the caravan and break a track through the snow around to the front. He made frequent attempts to turn out and force his way ahead, but after numerous unsuccessful efforts he would fall down exhausted, and set up a most mournful braying.

The other mules soon began to fail, and to be left, worn out and famished, to die by the wayside. It was not, however, for some time that Billy showed symptoms of becoming one of the victims, until one evening after our arrival at camp I was informed that he had dropped down and been left upon the road during the day. The men all deplored his loss exceedingly, as his devotion to the mare had touched their kind hearts, and many expressions of sympathy were uttered around their bivouac fires on that evening.

Much to our surprise, however, about ten o'clock, just as we were about going to sleep, we heard a mule braying about half a mile to the rear upon our trail. Sure enough, it proved to be Billy, who, after having rested, had followed upon our track and overtaken us. As soon as he reached the side of the mare he lay down and seemed perfectly contented.

The next day I relieved him from his pack, and allowed him to run loose; but during the march he gave out, and was again abandoned to his fate, and this time we certainly never expected to see him more. To our great astonishment, however, about twelve o'clock that night the sonorous but not very musical notes of Billy in the distance aroused us from our slumbers, and again announced his approach. In an instant the men were upon their feet, gave three hearty cheers, and rushed out in a body to meet and escort him into camp.

But this well-meant ovation elicited no response from him. He came reeling and floundering along through the deep snow, perfectly regardless of these honors, pushing aside all those who occupied the trail or interrupted his progress in the least, wandering about until he found the mare, dropped down by her side, and remained until morning.

When we resumed our march on the following day he made another desperate effort to proceed, but soon fell down exhausted, when we reluctantly abandoned him, and saw him no more.

Alas! poor Billy! your constancy deserved a better fate; you may, indeed, be said to have been a victim to unrequited affection.

The method of constructing our bivouac was for each set of two or three men to dig a hole about seven or eight feet square down through the snow to the ground, where a bed was made of soft pine twigs, over which a blanket was spread. Two forked sticks were then set upright in the snow to the windward of the centre, and across them a horizontal pole was laid, and extending from this to the snow a thick covering of pine bushes was placed, forming a sort of roof that shielded us perfectly from the wind. This arrangement, with good fires at the bottom of the pits, enabled us to keep tolerably warm during the coldest nights. We suffered more from the cold during the daytime, and it was while marching that the men froze their feet.

From some cause or other which was incomprehensible to me, the men were often attacked with violent cramps in the stomach, even before they commenced eating mule meat, and the symptoms in all cases were nearly the same. I invariably administered for it a dose of about twenty grains of blue mass, which afforded temporary relief, but on the second or third day following the complaint generally returned in a more aggravated form than at first, and I then gave another dose of about thirty grains of the same medicine, which never failed to effect a permanent cure.

After I had placed Miguel in the position of guide, we struggled along up the western slope of the mountains as rapidly as the snow and our exhausted condition would permit, and, at the expiration of ten days, found ourselves upon the summit of a mountain, which the guide pronounced the long-looked-for Cochetope Pass — that Mecca of our most ardent aspirations.

Although I was by no means certain he was right, yet I was much rejoiced, and I now felt in a great measure relieved from the burden of responsibility which had given me such anxiety and distress of mind during the last twenty days and nights.

From the crest of the great continental vertebral column of the Rocky Mountain chain, with one foot standing upon the earth drained by the waters of the Pacific, and the other upon that from which flowed a tributary to the Atlantic, we could see in the east, stretching off from the foot of the mountains, a vast plain, extending to the south as far as the eye could reach. This, the guide informed me, was the valley of the Rio del Norte; and a mountain, which we could discern on the opposite side of this valley, apparently a hundred miles distant, he said was near Fort Massachusetts.

As we still had three good mules remaining, I determined to send forward Mariano and Miguel to Fort Massachusetts, to bring us back supplies, as we were now reduced to a state bordering on starvation. Accordingly, I wrote a letter to the commanding officer, telling him our situation, and requesting him to forward us succor as soon as possible.

These men took the good mules and started, and we followed on their tracks, expecting they would return to us with the supplies in about six or seven days; but we continued on the trail, until finally the snow had covered it up, so that we could no longer see it, and at length, after ten days, as the men did not return, we concluded they must have perished or been lost. On the eleventh day we reached the extended valley at the base of the mountains, and, for the first time in thirty days, found a little dry grass appearing above the snow. As our few remaining mules were greatly famished, I concluded to make a halt for a day at this place and let them graze. We had not yet seen a human being outside of our own party since we left Grand River, thirty-one days before, and we were all anxiously looking out for the return of our messengers from Fort Massachusetts. Nothing appeared, however, until near sunset, when one of the soldiers, upon an elevation near camp, cried out, "There comes two men on horseback;" and, sure enough, in a few moments, up galloped our long-absent companions upon fresh horses, firing their revolvers, and making other demonstrations of joy.

We knew from their fresh horses that they had reached the fort and that we were now saved, and the exhibition of joy manifest among the command exceeded any thing of the kind ever beheld. Some of the men laughed, danced, and screamed with delight, while others (and I must confess I was not one among the former) cried like children. I had not slept half an hour at a time for twenty days and nights, and was reduced from 170 to 131 pounds in weight, and, of course, my nervous system was not at that juncture under very good control. My joy was too great, under the circumstances, to find utterance in noise or levity; on the contrary, I mentally offered up sincere thanks to the Almighty for delivering us from the horrible death of starvation.

The mere accident of Miguel's happening to be with us, without any doubt, saved our lives, as without him we could never have found the pass, and must have perished in the mountain.

As soon as Mariano arrived he was surrounded by the men, eagerly entreating him for tobacco, when he produced a large plug of Cavendish, and threw it among them. It was in an instant torn to pieces and distributed, but one man had been omitted in the division, and I heard him offer ten dollars, or a month's pay, for a quid.

Mariano informed me that he had delivered my letter to Captain Bowman, the commanding officer at Fort Massachusetts, who at once dispatched three wagons with supplies for us; that these wagons left the fort with him, and were then probably about fifty miles back, as he had come very rapidly. I at once turned him back, with an order for the man in charge to drive night and day until he met us; and early on the following morning we resumed our march, and had not gone over ten miles, when, much to our delight, we met the wagons, and immediately went into camp. I was obliged to guard them very closely, to prevent the men from getting at the provisions, as I was fully aware of the danger of overeating after long abstinence.

Among other things which Captain Bowman had kindly sent me was a jug of brandy, and, as I thought this a proper occasion to indulge my men in the good cheer that they had been so long deprived of, I issued to each of them a moderate drink of the liquor, but, much to my astonishment, in a short time many of them were very much under the influence of it, and some even crazy drunk. It had acted upon their empty stomachs much more potently than I had anticipated, but I felt no inclination to censure them for this; on the contrary, I entertained a feeling somewhat similar to that of General Jackson when a charge of

ARRIVAL NEAR FORT MASSACHUSETTS.

drunkenness was made to him against an officer who had rendered conspicuous services in the war of 1812, and he replied that Colonel C.'s gallant conduct in battle authorized him to continue drunk during the remainder of his life, if he thought proper. I conceived that my men had a perfect right to get drunk after what they had endured.

We had a most luxurious supper, and all enjoyed it hugely; but during the night, several of the men, not feeling satisfied with the soup I had thought it wise to confine them to, had gone to the wagons and prevailed upon the sentinels to allow them to take enough to gorge themselves so much that the next morning found them suffering most excruciating torture, and one of the poor fellows died the next day.

On the fourth day after this we marched into Fort Massachusetts, and were most hospitably received by the officers and soldiers of the garrison, who supplied us with clothing, provisions, and every thing else we needed.

As we approached the fort, one of the officers complimented us by saying that he took us for a band of prairie Indians. Not more than one half of the men had any caps, and but few had any remains of trowsers below the knees. Their feet were tied up with mule hides, pieces of blankets, coat-tails, etc., and they certainly were rough and ragged-looking specimens of United States soldiers. As for myself, I am confident my own wife would not have recognized me. I had set out from Fort Bridger with a wardrobe of stout material suited to the rough work which I expected to encounter, but I had divided this among my destitute men until I was myself reduced to a scanty allowance. Among other garments I had remaining was a soldier's overcoat, from the skirts of which I was in the habit of cutting off pieces to patch my pants and stockings; and as rents in these were of every-day occurrence, by the time

I reached the fort there was but very little left of my original coat-tails.

Mariano and Miguel, whom I had sent forward with the message to the commanding officer, had experienced great suffering from hunger upon their trip, and had been obliged to kill one of their mules for food before they arrived at the fort.

Mariano took lodgings with a Mexican living in the fort, and immediately ordered a bountiful supper, which he said he devoured with exceeding gusto, and called for more. After this had been disposed of, he says he smoked his pipe and related incidents of his journey to the family until about nine o'clock, when he began to feel hungry again, and offered the hostess two dollars if she would cook him another supper, which she willingly did, and he again did ample justice to its merits. This he thought would suffice him until morning. Accordingly, he laid down and went to sleep; but during the night he awoke, and, to his surprise, found himself again very hungry. The family were all abed, and asleep at this time; the fire was out, and he was loth to disturb them, and he endured the cravings of his appetite for some time; but at length, not being able to stand it any longer, he called out to the woman of the house, telling her if she would be so kind as to get up and cook him one more supper he would give her five dollars. This tempting offer had the effect he desired, and he ate the fourth repast, which he smilingly informed me enabled him to worry through the remainder of the night.

Some of my readers may be incredulous regarding the powers of Mariano for accomplishing such gastronomic feats; but when it is considered that he was a half-breed Indian, and had been trained to their habits from infancy, it will not appear at all surprising to those who are familiar with Indian life.

From Fort Massachusetts we marched to Taos, New Mexico, where I paid off the citizens of my party, and of these Mariano received some five hundred dollars for his arduous and valuable services, which I thought would prove sufficient to supply all his wants for a long period; but my credulity was greatly taxed on the following morning when he told me his money was all gone, and asked me for a loan of five dollars. I said to him, "Is it possible you have been robbed?" He replied, "No, but me lose him all at monté, messieur." I gave him the modest loan he solicited, accompanied with an injunction against visiting the monté bank again.

He thanked me for the advice, but at the same time observed, raising his eyes and shrugging his shoulders, "Maybe some time me win, messieur."

A few days after this I dispatched him back to Fort Bridger, via the South Pass, with a letter to General Johnston reporting our arrival in New Mexico. The return journey he accomplished successfully, and was handsomely rewarded by the general for his services.

As it may be a subject of some interest to those who should ever have occasion to travel through deep snow to know the relative qualities of different animals, and their powers of endurance in this description of work, I will remark that I set out upon this journey with horses, mules, and oxen, the latter to be used as food.

I found, as soon as we struck snow three feet deep, that the mules directly became disheartened, laid down, and would not exert themselves. The horses seemed more ambitious, and would push their way through the snow as long as possible; but they soon became weary, and gave out from exhaustion; while the oxen slowly and deliberately plowed their way through the deep snow for a long time without becoming jaded. Moreover, they seemed to derive much better sustenance from the pine leaves, and from browsing upon other trees, than the horses and mules. I am so well satisfied upon this subject that, if I was ever obliged to make another journey over the mountains in winter (which God forbid), I would take no other animals but oxen. They could be packed with luggage, and used as beef when required. There is also less danger of their stampeding or being stolen by Indians than with horses or mules.

CHAPTER IX.

RETURN TRIP TO UTAH.

Return Trip to Utah.—Route of the March.—Organization of the Party.—Order to Halt.—*Fontaine-qui-bouille.*—Herd of Elk.—Arrival of Re-enforcements.—Terrible Snow-storm.—Stampede.—Storms.—Platte River.—Denver City.—Arrival at Fort Bridger.—Entrance into Salt Lake City.—Scarcity of Mormons.—Salt Lake.—Bathing.—Mormon Industry.—Proclamation by Brigham Young.—Mormon Depredations.—Order of Daniel H. Wells.—Interview with Captain Van Vliet.—Tone of the Pulpit and Press.—Benediction by Heber Kimball.

HAVING accomplished the objects of my mission to New Mexico by procuring animals and other supplies sufficient to enable the troops at Fort Bridger to make an early march into Salt Lake Valley, I, on the 15th day of March, left Fort Union on my return for Utah, intending to pass around the eastern base of the mountains near Pike's Peak, and the head waters of the Arkansas and Platte Rivers, following the Cherokee trail from the "*Cache la poudre.*" The command was well organized, and we made rapid progress for about two hundred and fifty miles, when, on the 27th day of March, I received an order from the general commanding in New Mexico to halt and await re-enforcements.

It appeared that General Johnston, commanding the troops in Utah, had received information that the Mormons intended sending out a force of their people to intercept our party, and stampede, scatter, or steal our animals. This information induced General Scott to believe that a force superior in numbers to that I had at my disposal was necessary to insure our safe return.

I regretted the delay caused by this order, as I felt confident we were sufficiently strong to cope with any force the Mormons would be likely to send against us. Moreover, I had anticipated that the "*Saints*" might take it into their heads to pay their respects to us before we reached Fort Bridger, and had made such dispositions in the organization of the party as in my judgment would have rendered us perfectly secure against any molestations from them. I had about a hundred of the best trailers, hunters, and Indian fighters in New Mexico, and I intended, as soon as we reached a point where there was any probability the Mormons would come, to keep these men continually scouting at least a day in advance of the main command with the animals and supplies. They would, I believed, have discovered the presence of the Mormons before the latter were aware of our proximity, and my plan was to have the Mexicans, who were perfectly *au fait* in all such matters, either take or stampede all the Mormons' animals, thereby turning the tables upon them, and placing them on foot. But I had no discretion. I was obliged to obey the order, and went into camp upon the head waters of a small tributary of the Arkansas called "*Fontaine-qui-bouille*," directly at the foot of Pike's Peak, and near a very peculiar spring, which gives the name to the stream.

This beautiful fountain issues from the centre of a basin, or rather bowl, about six feet in diameter, and throws out a column of water near the size of a man's arm. The receptacle, which is constantly filled, but never runs over, seems to have been formed by the deposit of salts from the water, and is as perfectly symmetrical and round as if it had been cut out with a chisel.

As the fountain is constantly playing and never overflows, it of course has a subterraneous outlet.

The most remarkable feature, however, in the *Fontaine-*

qui-bouille is the peculiar taste of the water. It is pungent and sparkling, and somewhat similar in taste to the water from the Congress Springs at Saratoga, but sweeter, and, to my palate, pleasanter. We drank it every day in large quantities without perceiving any ill effects from it, and the men made use of it instead of yeast in raising their bread, which induced the belief that it contained soda, or some other alkali. The Indians believe it to possess some mysterious powers, the purport of which I could not learn; but there were a great many arrows, pieces of cloth, and other articles that they had deposited in the spring, probably as offerings to the "big medicine" genius that presided over it.

We remained at this place a month, during which time we amused ourselves in hunting elk, mountain sheep, and black-tailed deer, all of which were very abundant in the surrounding country, and our larder was constantly supplied with the most delicious game.

I remember that one morning, just at daybreak, I was awakened by my servant, who told me there was a large herd of elk in close proximity to the camp. I ran out as soon as possible, and saw at least five hundred of these magnificent animals drawn up in line, like a troop of cavalry horses, with their heads all turned in the same direction, and from the crest of a high projecting cliff looking in apparent wonder and bewilderment directly down upon us. It was to me a most novel and interesting spectacle. The noise made in the camp soon frightened them, however, and they started for the mountains. They were pursued for some distance by our hunters, who succeeded in killing six before they escaped.

On the 30th day of April, our re-enforcements having joined us, we gladly resumed our march for Utah, and at about one o'clock encamped upon the ridge that divides the Arkansas from the Platte Rivers. The day was bright, cheerful, and pleasant, the atmosphere soft, balmy, and delightful, the fresh grass was about six inches high, the trees had put forth their new leaves, and all nature conspired in giving evidence that the sombre garb of winter had been cast aside for the more verdant and smiling attire of spring. Our large herds of animals were turned out to graze upon the tender and nutritious grass that every where abounded. Our men were enjoying their social jokes and pastimes after the fatigues of the day's march, and every thing indicated contentment and happiness.

This pleasant state of things lasted until near sunset, when the wind suddenly changed into the north: it turned cold, and soon commenced snowing violently, and continued to increase until it became a frightful winter tempest, filling the atmosphere with a dense cloud of driving snow, against which it was utterly impossible to ride or walk. Soon after the storm set in one of our herds of three hundred horses and mules broke furiously away from the herdsmen who were guarding them, and, in spite of their utmost efforts, ran at full speed, directly with the wind, for fifty miles before they stopped. Three of the herdsmen followed them as far as they were able, but soon became exhausted, bewildered, and lost on the prairie.

One of them succeeded in finding his way back to camp in a state of great prostration and suffering. One of the others was found frozen to death in the snow, and the third was discovered crawling about upon his hands and knees, in a state of temporary delirium, after the tempest subsided.

This terrific storm exceeded in violence and duration any thing of the kind our eldest mountaineers had ever beheld. It continued with uninterrupted fury for sixty consecutive hours, and during this time it was impossible to

STAMPEDE OF HORSES AND MULES.

move for any distance facing the wind and snow. One of our employés, who went out about two hundred yards from camp, set out to return, but was unable to do so, and perished in the attempt.

The instincts of all our animals, excepting the herds alluded to, led them to seek shelter in a grove of timber near camp, where they were somewhat protected from the fury of the gale. But several antelopes were found frozen upon the prairie after the storm.

We had with us a flock of sheep, which scattered throughout the timber in every direction during the storm, and afterward were nearly as wild as deer; they, like the insane herdsman, seemed to have lost their senses.

I have noticed that horses and mules, during a severe storm upon the prairies, will generally turn their heads from the wind, and stand quiet until it is over. For instance, while we were en route for Utah, on the 30th of July, 1857, near the Big Blue, a very severe storm suddenly arose, which soon brought with it hailstones as large as pigeon's eggs. These formidable missiles pelted the command so severely, that to me, who possess an exceedingly keen appreciation of the ridiculous, the cavalcade presented one of the most farcical and ludicrous pictures I ever beheld.

The instant the hailstones commenced striking the animals they probably supposed it a severe application of the whip, and started off furiously in every direction, without any regard to each other or to the road, and without submitting to the slightest control from their drivers or riders. The mules especially seemed perfectly frantic with terror. They plunged, kicked, and jumped, and in the mean time the hailstones rapidly increased in size, and added a corresponding re-enforcement to the momentum of their blows. The mules brayed with agony and fright; they threw off their riders, overturned many of the wagons, and produced a universal stampede among the entire command.

My own mule, which I was riding at the time, was no more quiet or reconciled to the existing condition of things than the others. She made several very desperate efforts at lofty vaulting when she felt the first hailstones, and came very near unseating me, but I managed to quiet her sufficiently to dismount, and attempted to hold her from running away. I soon found, however, that the hail was giving me some very severe raps upon my face and hands, and that it was necessary for me to seek some protection. I accordingly, with great difficulty, took off my saddle while the mule was plunging and kicking vigorously, and let her go, then squatted down upon the ground and covered my head with the saddle, which guarded it against the frozen missiles. My hands, however, projected over the edges of the saddle, and received several hard knocks that took off the skin.

After the animals broke loose, they soon discovered that they did not escape the hail by running, and they all of their own accord stopped, turned their tails to windward, and remained perfectly quiet in that position until the storm ceased.

In Western and Southern Texas, during the autumn and winter months, storms arise suddenly, and are generally accompanied by a north wind, which is very severe upon men and animals; and although the mercury seldom indicates the freezing point, yet these storms are sometimes so terrific as to compel travelers to hasten to the nearest sheltered spot to save their lives, and I have known of several instances where men and animals have perished in these "*Northers*," as they are called. During the winter season the climate here is generally as mild and genial as the May atmosphere in New York; but when a Norther appears, the temperature often undergoes a sudden depression of many degrees in a few minutes, the perspiration is checked, and the system receives a shock, against which it requires great vital energy to bear up. Men and animals are not in this latitude prepared for these capricious atmospheric changes, and, as I said before, they often perish under their effects.

While passing near the head waters of the Colorado of Texas in the autumn of 1849, I left one of my camps at daylight in the morning, with a mild and soft atmosphere, tempered with a gentle breeze from the south, but had traveled only a short distance when the wind suddenly whipped around into the north, bringing with it a furious chilling rain, and in a few minutes the ground became so soft and heavy, as to make the labor of pulling the wagons over it very exhausting upon our mules. When we went into camp the animals were in a profuse sweat, and the rain was pouring down in torrents upon them. It continued to rain incessantly, as hard as I ever saw it in a violent thunder-shower, for upward of thirty consecutive hours, and it seemed as if the heavens were pouring out upon us a second deluge.

A ravine near us, which was dry when we encamped, was, on the following morning, a rapid stream of sufficient magnitude to float an ocean steam-ship, and the ground was every where covered with water.

We had great difficulty, on our first arrival in camp, in making a fire; for, as soon as it was started a little, the rain would put it out, like dashing a bucket of water upon it, and we were obliged finally to hold blankets over it until the wood was thoroughly kindled.

Our mules were unharnessed as soon as we reached the camping-ground and turned out to graze, but, instead of feeding as usual, they turned their heads from the wind, and remained in that position, chilled and trembling, without making the least effort to move; and on the following morning, thirty-five out of our herd of one hundred and ten had perished, while those still alive could hardly be said to have any vitality left. They were drawn up with cold, and could with difficulty walk.

We cut up our tents and wagon-covers to protect them from the storm, which still continued with unabated fury, and drove them about until a little vital energy was restored, after which they commenced eating grass and recuperated, but it was three days before they were sufficiently recovered to resume the march.

I made a mistake in driving the mules after the "*Norther*" commenced. Had I halted at once, and encamped before they became heated and wearied, they would probably have eaten the grass, and this, I have no doubt, would have fortified them against the effects of the storm; but, as it was, their blood became heated from overwork, and the sudden chill brought on a reaction which proved fatal.

If an animal eats his forage plentifully, there is but little danger of his perishing with cold.

The loss of our animals obliged us to abandon several of our wagons, and every thing else we could possibly dispense with, before we were able to continue our journey.

I subsequently learned that the Comanches appropriated this property, and used the iron in making arrow-points and lance-heads.

With these observations in regard to the storms I have encountered in different latitudes, I will now invite the reader to return with me to Squirrel Creek, where we left the command in the snow-storm.

At the termination of this frightful tempest there was about three feet of snow upon the ground, but the warm rays of the sun soon melted it, and, after collecting together

THE PROPHET'S BLOCK.

our *stampeded* animals, we again set forward for Utah, and on the third day following struck the South Platte at its confluence with Cherry Creek.

We found the river at such a high stage, and so rapid, that we were compelled to encamp here for four days and construct a flat-boat, in which we crossed our entire party.

There was at that time but one white man living within one hundred and fifty miles of the place, and he was an Indian trader named Jack Audeby, upon the Arkansas.

While our ferry-boat was being constructed, one of our citizen employés washed from the sands of Cherry Creek a small amount of gold-dust, which he showed to me. Soon afterward he was discharged and went to St. Louis, and in a short time the miners commenced flocking to the locality, and laid out a town which has continued to flourish ever since, and at this time contains several thousand inhabitants. It is called "*Denver City*," and I feel quite confident that the representations made by our discharged teamster in St. Louis and other places were the origin of the location and establishment of a new city and Territory.

As we anticipated finding the North Platte River (some two hundred miles in advance) above a fording stage, we determined to haul our flat-boat to that point. Accordingly, we mounted it upon a stout wagon drawn by a team of twenty mules, and transported it the entire distance. We did not use it, however, as the river was fordable. We left the boat there, and it was often used by travelers afterward, and I believe it still remains at the same place.

Nothing worthy of special mention occurred to us after this, and we reached Fort Bridger with our supplies on the 9th day of June.

Soon after our arrival at Fort Bridger, General Johnston marched his command into Salt Lake Valley, and we encamped in a "church pasture" on the other side of Jordan, opposite to and about a mile distant from Salt Lake City.

We marched through the city with colors flying and bands playing, but, to our astonishment, we only saw here and there a very few persons. The city seemed to have been deserted, and those that we did see were apparently so busily occupied that they never even condescended to look toward our sacrilegious cavalcade of Gentiles. This was the first body of troops of any magnitude that had ever made its appearance in this remote part of the universe; yet one would have thought, from the perfect indifference with which our advent was looked upon by the *Saints*, that the event was of every-day occurrence.

While in the Territory, I visited that vast natural deposit of chloride of sodium, *Salt Lake*, and with several friends tried the experiment of bathing in it. We waded out from the shore until the water reached our arm-pits, when our feet were raised from the bottom and we remained suspended. The specific gravity of the water is so great that we were enabled to float upon the surface without moving hand or foot. We folded our arms and sat up in the lake, only sinking to near the arms, and we floated about like corks. The sensation was most novel and peculiar.

The fact is, that the entire volume of the lake is a saturated solution of salt, the water being charged to its maximum capacity, and we were told that four buckets of the water made, when evaporated, one fourth the volume of pure salt.

The wind was blowing quite fresh while we were in the lake, and the spray fell upon our heads and in our eyes, causing most acute pain. In a very few minutes after we came out of the water our bodies were incrusted with an armor of salt, and our hair was also frosted over with it, giving us the appearance of very great longevity. We felt exceedingly uncomfortable in this saline covering, and were puzzled as to how we should dispose of it, until some one suggested that we should go to a fresh-water spring near by, and dissolve the salt, which we did. We did not see a fish or any other living animal or reptile in the lake, and I doubt if animal life could be sustained there.

As is very generally known, this vast body of water (something like eighty by thirty miles in extent) receives several quite large fresh-water streams, but has no visible outlet.

Ever since it was first discovered it has been constantly contracting, and the water receding from the shores. The water of the Salt Lake has a greater specific gravity, and a greater amount of solid matter than any other known, with the exception of that of the Dead Sea.

One hundred parts of the water by weight were found to contain, after evaporation, 22.422 of solid matter, in which were the following constituents:

Chloride of Sodium	20.196
Sulphate of Soda	1.834
Chloride of Magnesium	0.252
	22.282,

with a trace of Chloride of Calcium.

The analysis of the Salt Lake waters, as given by Colonel Fremont, for 100 parts of solid matter, is as follows:

Chloride of Sodium	97.80
" " Calcium	0.61
" " Magnesium	0.24
Sulphate of Soda	0.23
" " Lime	1.12
	100.00

One hundred parts in weight of the Dead Sea water gave 24.580 of solid contents, or 2.298 more than the water of Salt Lake.

The following analysis of the Dead Sea water at different dates and by different chemists, shows some very different constituents from those in Salt Lake.

	Dr. Marcet. 1807.	Gay-Lussac. 1818.	Dr. Apjohn. 1839.
Chloride of Calcium	3.920	3.980	2.438
" Magnesium	10.246	15.310	7.370
" Sodium	10.360	6.950	7.839
" Manganese..........			0.005
" Potassium...........			0.852
Bromide of Magnesium			0.201
Sulphate of Zinc..................	0.054		0.075
Water............................	75.420	73.760	81.220

The specific gravity of the Dead Sea water, as given by the above-named authorities, is as follows. The water was taken at the boiling point, and contrasted with the pure water at 1000.

Dr. Marcet, 1211. Gay-Lussac, 1228. Dr. Apjohn, 1153.

Specific gravity of Salt Lake Water.............................. 1.170

Stanley, in his work on Sinai and Palestine, gives the level of the Dead Sea as 1300 feet below that of the Mediterranean, while the level of Salt Lake is 4200 feet above the ocean. Both of these peculiar lakes receive fresh-water Jordans, and have no outlets.

The Mormons are a very industrious people, and no one is allowed to remain idle in their community. Their principal occupation is farming, which they pursue with unremitting patience and perseverance.

The cultivation of the soil in this valley is attended with a vast amount of labor, as the soil produces nothing without artificial irrigation, and this involves the necessity of excavating canals for long distances to bring the water from the mountain streams, after which it is distributed over the fields in small ditches.

The construction, repairs, and tending of these numerous water-communications requires so much extra labor that one man can cultivate only about four acres of ground, or not much more than one tenth the amount that he could in the Eastern States, where no irrigation is required.

In view of these facts, it struck me that no other people

but the Mormons or Mexicans would ever think of becoming farmers in Utah, when there is so much vacant, uncultivated domain east of the mountains, where the rains from heaven irrigate and fertilize the soil.

Before we reached Utah we heard many rumors concerning the unfriendly disposition of the Mormons toward the United States government, and their determination to resist by force, if necessary, our entrance into Salt Lake Valley, but we did not give much credence to these reports until we received the following proclamation of Brigham Young:

"*Proclamation by the Governor.*

"*Citizens of Utah*,—We are invaded by a hostile force, who are evidently assailing us to accomplish our overthrow and destruction.

"For the last twenty-five years we have trusted officials of the government, from constables and justices to judges, governors, and presidents, only to be scorned, held in derision, insulted, and betrayed. Our houses have been plundered and then burned, our fields laid waste, our principal men butchered while under the pledged faith of the government for their safety, and our families driven from their homes to find that shelter in the barren wilderness, and that protection among hostile savages which were denied them in the boasted abodes of Christianity and civilization.

"The Constitution of our common country guarantees to us all that we do now, or have ever claimed.

"If the constitutional rights which pertain unto us as American citizens were extended to Utah according to the spirit and meaning thereof, and fairly and impartially administered, it is all that we could ask, all that we ever asked.

"Our opponents have availed themselves of prejudice existing against us because of our religious faith, to send out a formidable host to accomplish our destruction. We have had no privilege, no opportunity of defending ourselves from the false, foul, and unjust aspersions against us before the nation.

"The government has not condescended to cause an investigating committee, or other person, to be sent to inquire into and ascertain the truth, as is customary in such cases.

"We know those aspersions to be false, but that avails us nothing. We are condemned unheard, and forced to an issue with an armed mercenary mob, which has been sent against us at the instigation of anonymous letter-writers, ashamed to father the base, slanderous falsehoods which they have given to the public; of corrupt officials, who have brought false accusations against us to screen themselves in their own infamy; of hireling *priests* and *howling editors*, who prostitute the truth for filthy lucre's sake.

"The issue which has been thus forced upon us compels us to resort to the great first law of self-preservation, and stand in our own defense, a right guaranteed to us by the genius of the institutions of our country, and upon which the government is based.

"Our duty to ourselves, to our families, requires us not tamely to be driven and slain, without an attempt to preserve ourselves. Our duty to our country, our holy religion, our God, to freedom and liberty, requires that we should not quietly stand still and see those fetters forging around which are calculated to enslave and bring us in subjection to an unlawful military despotism, such as can only emanate (in a country of constitutional law) from usurpation, tyranny, and oppression.

"*Therefore*, I, Brigham Young, Governor and Superintendent of Indian Affairs for the Territory of Utah, in the name of the people of the United States in the Territory of Utah,

"1st. Forbid all armed forces of every description from coming into this Territory, under any pretense whatever.

"2d. That all the forces in said Territory hold themselves in readiness to march at a moment's notice to repel any and all such invasion.

"3d. Martial law is hereby declared to exist in this Territory from and after the publication of this proclamation, and no person shall be allowed to pass or repass into or through, or from the Territory, without a permit from the proper officers.

"Given under my hand and seal at Great Salt Lake City, Territory of Utah, this 15th day of September, A.D. 1857, and of the Independence of the United States of America the 82d.

(Signed) "BRIGHAM YOUNG."

With this proclamation came, by express from Salt Lake City, the following:

"Governor's Office, Utah Territory,
Great Salt Lake City, Sept. 29, 1857.

"To the officer commanding the forces now invading Utah Territory:

"SIR,—By reference to the Act of Congress passed September 9, 1850, organizing the Territory of Utah, published in a copy of the Laws of Utah, herewith forwarded, p. 146–7, you will find the following: 'Section 2. *And be it further enacted*, That the executive power and authority in and over said Territory of Utah shall be vested in a governor, who shall hold his office for four years, *and until his successor shall be appointed and qualified*, unless sooner removed by the President of the United States. The governor shall reside within said Territory, shall be commander-in-chief of the militia thereof,' etc.

"I am still the Governor and Superintendent of Indian Affairs for this Territory, no successor having been appointed and qualified, as provided by law, nor have I been removed by the President of the United States. By virtue of the authority thus vested in me, I have issued and forwarded you a copy of my proclamation forbidding the entrance of armed forces into this Territory. This you have disregarded" (great presumption, this!). "I now farther direct that you retire forthwith from the Territory, by the same route you entered. Should you deem this impracticable, and prefer to remain until spring in the vicinity of your present position at Black's Fork or Green River, you can do so in peace and unmolested, on condition"—(now comes the cream of the joke)—"that you deposit your arms and ammunition with Lewis Robinson, Quarter-master-general of the Territory, and leave in the spring as soon as the condition of the roads will permit you to march. And should you fall short of provisions, they can be furnished you upon making the proper applications therefor.

"General D. H. Wells will forward this, and receive any communication you may have to make.

"Very respectfully, etc.,

(Signed) "BRIGHAM YOUNG, Governor, etc."

Shortly after this the Mormons burned two of our supply trains, containing a large amount of stores for the use of the troops during the winter. They drove off our cattle, and committed other acts of hostility toward us.

On the 16th of October I caught some Mormons carrying supplies to the parties that were committing depredations upon us, and upon the person of one of them (a major) I found several papers, one of which was as follows:

"Head-quarters Eastern Expedition,
Camp near Cashecove, Oct. 4, 1857.

"MAJOR JOSEPH TAYLOR,—You will proceed with all possible dispatch, without injuring your animals, to the Oregon Road, near the head of Bear River, north by east of this place. Take close and correct observations of the country on your route. When you approach the road, send scouts ahead to ascertain if the invading troops have passed that way. Should they have passed, take a concealed route and get ahead of them. Express to Colonel Burton, who is now on that road and in the vicinity of the troops, and effect a junction with him, so as to operate in concert.

"On ascertaining the locality or route of the troops, proceed at once to annoy them in every possible way. Use every exertion to stampede their animals, and set fire to their trains. Burn the whole country before them and on their flanks. Keep them from sleeping by night surprises. Blockade the road by felling trees, or destroying the fords when you can. Watch for opportunities to set fire to the grass on their windward, so as, if possible, to envelop their trains. Leave no grass before them that can be burned. Keep your men concealed as much as possible, and guard against surprise. Keep scouts out at all times, and communication open with Colonel Burton, Major McAllister, and O. P. Rockwell, who are operating in the same way. Keep me advised daily of your movements, and every step the troops take, and in which direction.

"God bless you and give you success.

"Your brother in Christ,

(Signed) "DANIEL H. WELLS.

"P.S.—If the troops have not passed, or have turned in this direction, follow in their rear, and continue to annoy them, and stampede or drive off their animals at every opportunity. D. H. WELLS."

Brigham Young, in an interview with Captain Van Vliet, of the Army, who was sent to Salt Lake City to confer with the Mormon authorities, complained that our government officials had taken for truth *ex parte* statements, made against them by men of notoriously immoral characters, who had become prejudiced against them without cause, and, without giving them any opportunity to defend themselves, had made premature decisions adverse to his people.

He thought it due to him and his followers, especially while he regarded himself as *ex officio* the chief magistrate of the Territory, to have given him a hearing. Instead of this, he said, the government had instituted proceedings of a most unusual and rigorous character, sending out a very large armed force, with a menacing aspect, to coerce them into subjection to laws which they had always respected and obeyed. He added, "I can, with my people, keep out the forces now approaching us, and I shall most positively do so. No United States soldier shall enter this valley. And if they attempt to pass Fort Bridger, I shall first have all the grass between that point and this city burned up. If that does not stop them, I shall then make use of all the means within my control to resist by force, if necessary, their approach."

Captain Van Vliet said to him that he might possibly succeed in keeping out during the winter the troops now en route, but that he must be aware that this step would be looked upon by our government as an insult of no ordinary character, and that a sufficient number of troops to chastise them would certainly be sent out in the spring.

He replied, "I am conscious of that; but I have four years' supply of provisions on hand; and before we will submit to a military rule, we will burn and destroy every house, fence, tree, and other vestige of improvement in this valley, and retreat to the mountains, where we can live unmolested in the enjoyment of our religion."

He was then asked how he would receive Governor

Cummings on his arrival. He replied, "I would very quietly place him in a carriage, and politely escort him out of the Valley."

The foregoing proclamation, and orders subsequently issued, show conclusively that Brigham was sincere in what he said to Captain Van Vliet.

The Mormon leaders were all intensely exercised upon the subject of our approach, and gave vent to their feelings in the pulpit and in their papers.

In an article which I saw in the Deseret News, the writer very ably and ingeniously set forth the grievances of the Saints from the time of Joe Smith up to that moment. His arguments were, however, somewhat specious and sophistical, and not in all respects sustained by fact; as, for example, he said that the United States had not sent armed forces into other Territories to assist the Federal authorities in the execution of law, when he must have known that troops had repeatedly been employed in similar service, and that a portion of the very force designed for Utah was at that moment detained in Kansas for precisely the same object. He also said that the people of other Territories had always been allowed to elect their own rulers, when it was known to every body that the people of the Territories generally have nothing to do with the appointment of Territorial officers; that, on the contrary, these officers are in almost all cases selected from other places, and sent to the Territories. Utah, in that regard, had been more favored than any other Territory, as their prophet and ruler had been permitted to occupy the governor's seat a longer period than usual.

In one of the numbers of the Deseret News were several speeches made by the leaders, all of which breathed forth sentiments teeming with war to the knife. Brigham said "he had always prophesied that there was a time coming when the cord that bound the Saints to the world must be severed, and when a military force was sent to Utah to kill him and his people, then would be the time to cut it."

The following racy specimen of pulpit oratory, although not very chaste or classic in its character, emanated from the fulminating and explosive brain of that "*father in Israel*," Brother Heber Kimball, about that time. It was in the form of a benediction to his flock.

"May the Almighty bless you; may the peace of God be with you, and with your children, and with your children's children forever and ever; and may God Almighty curse our enemies (voices, 'Amen!'). I feel to curse my enemies; and when God won't bless them, I do not think he will ask me to bless them. If I did, it would be to put the poor curses to death who have brought death and destruction on me and my brethren, upon my wives and children that I buried on the road between the States and this place.

"Did I ever wrong them out of a dime? No; but I have fed thousands when I never received a dime. Poor rotten curses! and the President of the United States, inasmuch as he has turned against us, and will take a course to persist in pleasing the ungodly curses that are howling around him for the destruction of this people, he shall be cursed in the name of Israel's God; and I curse him, and all his coadjutors in their cursed deeds, in the name of Jesus Christ, and by the authority of the holy priesthood, and all Israel shall say 'Amen!'

"Send two thousand five hundred troops here, my brethren, to make a desolation of this people! God Almighty helping me, I will fight until there is not a drop of blood in my veins. Good God! I have wives enough to whip out the United States! Amen."

In speaking of the approach of the army upon another

occasion, we have the following Biblical illustration from the same orator. "Will we have manna? Yes, the United States have seven hundred wagons loaded with about two tons to each wagon, with all kinds of things, and then seven thousand head of cattle; and there is said to be two thousand five hundred troops with this, and that, and the other.

"That is all right. Suppose the troops don't get here, but all these goods and cattle come? well, that would be a mighty help to us; that would clothe up the boys and girls, and make them comfortable; and then remember there is fifteen months' provisions besides. I am only talking about this. Suppose it extends four or five years, and they send one hundred thousand troops and provisions, and goods in proportion, and every thing else got here and they did not, etc., etc."

The sequel of the Mormon expedition is well known to the public.

CHAPTER X.

UNEXPLORED TERRITORY.

Unexplored Territory.—Lack of geographical Information in 1849.—Wagon Road from Fort Smith.—New Road from Dona Ana.—Great Cañon of the Colorado.—Visit of the Spaniards.—Mr. Kern's Opinions.—Tall Race of Men.—Height of the Cañon.—Attempts to explore it.—Splendid Scenery.—Mineral Considerations.—Method for exploring the Cañon suggested.

PREVIOUS to our occupation of the Territory of New Mexico in 1846, but little was known concerning the physical features of the greater part of that country, and almost the entire section of Northwestern New Mexico embraced between the Rio del Norte and the Rio Colorado of California had been, up to that period, a "*terra incognita.*" Indeed, as late as 1849, our authorities at Washington possessed so little information in regard to the country west of the Rio del Norte, that I was ordered to escort emigrants from Fort Smith, Arkansas, to Santa Fé, New Mexico, under the supposition that there were direct practicable wagon-roads from the latter point to San Francisco; but, on our arrival at Santa Fé, we learned, from the most experienced guides of the country, that the most direct known wagon-route to the Pacific coast left the Rio del Norte some three hundred miles below Santa Fé, thus making a deflection of a right angle from the course which we had traveled. We had discovered and rendered passable an excellent wagon-road from the point of our departure in Arkansas to Santa Fé, according to our instructions, but the information regarding the country west of Santa Fé showed conclusively that our road, in connection with that down the Gila, deviated so much from a direct track across the continent, that it would not subserve the purposes of subsequent emigration. I therefore made inquiries from all persons I could meet with who knew any thing about the country east of the Del Norte in regard to the practicability of making a wagon-road directly back from the point on that river where the emigrants turned west toward the Gila to Fort Smith. The greater part of the guides of the country informed me that there were several ranges of mountains intervening, and were of the opinion that I would have difficulty in finding a passage through them. I, however, heard of a Comanche Indian, living among the Mexicans, who was reported to be familiar with the section over which I desired to pass, and I consulted him. He said he knew the country as far east as the head waters of the Brazos, and that he could guide me over a route that was entirely safe for wagons from Dona Ana to that stream, and he would insure us water every night. Our own guide, Black Beaver, was confident he could pilot us from the Brazos to Fort Smith; accordingly, we returned over that route directly across the country indicated, making a most excellent road, which was traveled for several years afterward by California emigrants.

Since that time several exploring parties have traversed portions of northwestern New Mexico, and the information gained by our officers who have campaigned against the Indians in that section has added greatly to our stock of geographical knowledge; but it presents such an exceedingly barren, rough, and forbidding aspect, and has been so difficult of access on account of the hostility of the Indians, that but few white men have ventured into it, so that some portions still remain unexplored. There is, for example, a section of some two hundred miles or more of the Colorado

River that has never, so far as we have any record, been traversed by a white man, and that I believe to be at the present moment about the only part of our vast possessions of which we have not some knowledge.

I refer to that portion of the Colorado extending from near the confluence of Grand and Green Rivers, which is known as the "Big Cañon of the Colorado." This cañon is without doubt one of the most stupendous freaks of Nature that can be found upon the face of the earth. It appears that by some great paroxysmal convulsive throe in the mysterious economy of the wise laws of Nature, an elevated chain of mountains has been reft asunder, as if to admit a passage for the river along the level of the grade at the base. The walls of this majestic defile, so far as they have been seen, are nearly perpendicular; and although we have no exact data upon which to base a positive calculation of their altitude, yet our information is amply sufficient to warrant the assertion that it far exceeds any thing of the kind elsewhere known.

The first published account of this remarkable defile was contained in the work of Castenada, giving a description of the expedition of Don Francisco Vasquez de Coronado in search of the "seven cities of Cibola" in 1540–1.

He went from the city of Mexico to Sonora, and from thence penetrated to Cibola; and while there, dispatched an auxiliary expedition, under the command of Don Garcia Lopez de Cardenas, to explore a river which emptied into the Gulf of California, called "*Rio del Tison*," and which, of course, was the *Rio Colorado.*

On reaching the vicinity of the river, he found a race of natives of very great stature, who lived in subterranean tenements covered with straw or grass. He says, when these Indians traveled in cold weather, they carried in their hands a firebrand, with which they kept themselves warm.

Captain Sitgreaves, who in 1852 met the Mohave Indians on the Colorado River, says "they are over six feet tall;" and Mr. R. H. Kern, a very intelligent and reliable gentleman, who was attached to the same expedition, and visited the lower part of the great cañon of the Colorado, says, "The same manners and customs (as those described by Castenada) are peculiar to all the different tribes inhabiting the valley of the Colorado, even to the use of the brand for warming the body. These Indians, as a mass, are the largest and best-formed men I ever saw, their average height being an inch over six feet."

The Spanish explorer says he traveled for several days along on the crest of the lofty bluff bordering the cañon, which he estimated to be three leagues high, and he found no place where he could pass down to the water from the summit. He once made the attempt at a place where but few obstacles seemed to interfere with the descent, and started three of his most active men. They were gone the greater part of the day, and on their return informed him that they had only succeeded in reaching a rock about one third the distance down. This rock, he says, appeared from the top of the cañon about six feet high, but they informed him that it was as high as the spire of the cathedral at Seville in Spain.

The river itself looked, from the summit of the cañon, to be something like a fathom in width, but the Indians assured him it was half a league wide.

Antoine Lereux, one of the most reliable and best-informed guides in New Mexico, told me in 1858 that he had once been at a point of this cañon where he estimated the walls to be *three miles high.*

Mr. Kern says, in speaking of the Colorado: "No other river in North America passes through a cañon equal in depth to the one alluded to. The description (Castenada's) is made out with rare truth and force. We had a view of it from the San Francisco Mountain, N. M., and, judging from our own elevation, and the character of the intervening country, I have no doubt the walls are at least five thousand feet in height."

The mountaineers in Utah told me that a party of trappers many years since built a large row-boat and made the attempt to descend the river through the defile of the cañon, but were never heard from afterward. They probably dashed their boat in pieces, and were lost by being precipitated over sunken rocks or elevated falls.

In 185– Lieutenant Ives, of the United States' Engineers, was ordered to penetrate the cañon with a steamer of light draught. He ascended the river from the Gulf as high as a little above the mouth of the gorge, but there encountered rapids and other obstacles of so serious a character that he was forced to turn back and abandon the enterprise, and no other efforts have since been made under government auspices to explore it.

A thorough examination of this cañon might, in my opinion, be made by taking small row-boats and ascending the river from the debouche of the gorge at a low stage of water. In this way there would be no danger of being carried over dangerous rapids or falls, and the boats could be carried around difficult passages. Such an exploration could not, in my judgment, prove otherwise than intensely interesting, as the scenery here must surpass in grandeur any other in the universe.

Wherever we find rivers flowing through similar formations elsewhere, as at the "*dalles*" of the Columbia and Wisconsin Rivers, and in the great cañons of Red and Canadian Rivers, although the escarpments at those places have nothing like the altitude of those upon the Colorado, yet the long-continued erosive action of the water upon the rock has produced the most novel and interesting combinations of beautiful pictures. Imagine, then, what must be the effect of a large stream like the Colorado traversing for two hundred miles a defile with the perpendicular walls towering five thousand feet above the bed of the river. It is impossible that it should not contribute largely toward the formation of scenery surpassing in sublimity and picturesque character any other in the world. Our landscape painters would here find rare subjects for their study, and I venture to hope that the day is not far distant when some of the most enterprising of them may be induced to penetrate this new field of art in our only remaining unexplored territory. I am confident they would be abundantly rewarded for their trouble and exposure, and would find subjects for the exercise of genius, the sublimity of which the most vivid imaginations of the old masters never dreamed of.

A consideration, however, of vastly greater financial and national importance than those alluded to above, which might, and probably would result from a thorough exploration of this part of the river, is the development of its mineral wealth.

In 1849 I met in Santa Fé that enterprising pioneer, Mr. F. X. Aubrey, who had just returned from California, and *en route* had crossed the Colorado near the outlet of the *Big Cañon*, where he met some Indians, with whom, as he informed me, he exchanged leaden for golden rifle-balls, and these Indians did not appear to have the slightest appreciation of the relative value of the two metals.

That gold and silver abound in that region is fully established, as those metals have been found in many localities both east and west of the Colorado. Is it not, therefore, probable that the walls of this gigantic crevice will exhibit many rich deposits? Companies are formed almost daily, and large amounts of money and labor expended in sinking shafts of one, two, and three hundred feet, with the confident expectation of finding mineral deposits; but here Nature has opened and exposed to view a continuous shaft two hundred miles in length and five thousand feet in depth. In the one case we have a small shaft blasted out at great expense by manual labor, showing a surface of about thirty-six hundred feet, while here Nature gratuitously exhibits ten thousand millions of feet extending into the very bowels of the earth.

Is it, then, at all without the scope of rational conjecture to predict that such an immense development of the interior strata of the earth—such a huge gulch, if I may be allowed the expression, extending so great a distance through the heart of a country as rich as this in the precious metals, may yet prove to be the *El Dorado* which the early Spanish explorers so long and so fruitlessly sought for; and who knows but that the government might here find a source of revenue sufficient to liquidate our national debt?

Regarding the exploration of this river as highly important in a national aspect, I in 1853 submitted a paper upon the subject to the War Department, setting forth my views somewhat in detail, and offering my services to perform the work; but there was then no appropriation which could be applied to that object, and the Secretary of War for this reason declined ordering it.

CHAPTER XI.

HUNTING.

Hunting.—Its Benefits to the Soldier.—Disposition of Fire-arms.—Namaquas. — Tracking. — Horse Tracks. — Elk Hunt. — Faculties of Indians. —Deer Hunting.--Rifles.—Antelope.—Bear.—Lassoing Grizzlies.—Amateur Sportsman.—Big-Horn.—Buffalo.—Rapidly diminishing.--H. H. Sibley's Remarks. — Range of the Buffalo. — Chasing on Horseback. — Stalking.—Winter Hunting.—The Beaver.—The Prairie Dog.--Hints to Sportsmen.

I KNOW of no better school of practice for perfecting men in target-firing, and the use of fire-arms generally, than that in which the frontier hunter receives his education. One of the first and most important lessons that he is taught impresses him with the conviction that, unless his gun is in good order and steadily directed upon the game, he must go without his supper; and if ambition does not stimulate his efforts, his appetite will, and ultimately lead to success and confidence in his own powers.

The man who is afraid to place the butt of his piece firmly against his shoulder, or who turns away his head at the instant of pulling trigger (as soldiers often do before they have been drilled at target-practice), will not be likely to bag much game or to contribute materially toward the result of a battle. The successful hunter, as a general rule, is a good shot, will always charge his gun properly, and may be relied upon in action. I would, therefore, when in garrison or at permanent camps, encourage officers and soldiers in field-sports. If permitted, men very readily cultivate a fondness for these innocent and healthy exercises, and occupy their leisure time in their pursuit; whereas, if confined to the narrow limits of a frontier camp or garrison, having no amusements within their reach, they are prone to indulge in practices which are highly detrimental to their physical and moral condition.

By making short excursions about the country they acquire a knowledge of it, become inured to fatigue, learn the art of bivouacking, trailing, etc., etc., all of which will be found serviceable in border warfare; and, even if they should perchance now and then miss some of the minor routine duties of the garrison, the benefits they would derive from hunting would, in my opinion, more than counterbalance its effects. Under the old regime it was thought that drills, dress-parades, and guard-mountings comprehended the sum total of the soldier's education, but the experience of the last ten years has taught us that these are only the rudiments, and that to combat successfully with Indians we must receive instruction from them, study their tactics, and, where they suit our purposes, copy from them.

The union of discipline with the individuality, self-reliance, and rapidity of locomotion of the savage is what we should aim at. This will be the tendency of the course indicated, and it is believed by the writer that an army composed of well-disciplined hunters will be the most efficient of all others against the only enemy we now have to encounter within the limits of our vast possessions.

I find some pertinent remarks upon this subject in a very sensible essay by "a late captain of infantry" (U. S.). He says:

"It is conceived that scattered bands of mounted hunters, with the speed of a horse and the watchfulness of a wolf or antelope, whose faculties are sharpened by their necessities; who, when they get short of provisions, separate and look for something to eat, and find it in the water, in the ground, or on the surface; whose bill of fare ranges from grass-seed, nuts, roots, grasshoppers, lizards, and rattlesnakes up to the antelope, deer, elk, bear, and buffalo, and who have a continent to roam over, will be neither surprised, caught, conquered, overawed, or reduced to famine by a rumbling, bugle-blowing, drum-beating town passing through their country on wheels at the speed of a loaded wagon.

"If the Indians are in the path and do not wish to be seen, they cross a ridge, and the town moves on, ignorant whether there are fifty Indians within a mile or no Indian within fifty miles. If the Indians wish to see, they return to the crest of the ridge, crawl up to the edge, pull up a bunch of grass by the roots, and look through or under it at the procession."

Although I would always encourage men in hunting when permanently located, yet, unless they are good woodsmen, it is not safe to permit them to go out alone in marching through the Indian country, as, aside from the danger of encountering Indians, they would be liable to become bewildered and perhaps lost, and this might detain the entire party in searching for them. The better plan upon a march is for three or four to go out together, accompanied by a good woodsman, who will be able with certainty to lead them back to camp.

The little group could ascertain if Indians are about, and would be strong enough to act on the defensive against small parties of them; and, while they are amusing themselves, they may perform an important part as scouts and flankers.

An expedition may have been perfectly organized, and every thing provided that the wisest forethought could suggest, yet circumstances beyond the control of the most experienced traveler may sometimes arise to defeat the best concerted plans. It is not, for example, an impossible contingency that the traveler may, by unforeseen delays, consume his provisions, lose them in crossing streams, or have them stolen by hostile Indians, and be reduced to the necessity of depending upon game for subsistence. Under these circumstances, a few observations upon the habits of the different animals that frequent the Plains, and on the best methods of hunting them, may not be altogether devoid of interest or utility in this connection.

Previous to describing the methods of hunting the different animals, I propose to give a few useful hints regarding fire-arms, and other items of information which will be found important to those who should have occasion to go out into the Plains. First I notice the disposition of fire-arms.

The mountaineers and trappers exercise a very wise precaution, on lying down for the night, by placing their arms and ammunition by their sides, where they can be seized at a moment's notice. This rule is never departed from, and they are therefore seldom liable to be surprised. In Parkyns's "Abyssinia" I find the following remarks upon this subject:

"When getting sleepy, you return your rifle between your legs, roll over, and go to sleep. Some people may think this is a queer place for a rifle; but, on the contrary, it is the position of all others where utility and comfort are most combined. The butt rests on the arm, and serves as a pillow for the head; the muzzle points between the knees, and the arms encircle the lock and breech, so that you have a smooth pillow, and are always prepared to start up armed at a moment's notice."

I have never made the experiment of sleeping in this way, but I should imagine that a gun-stock would make rather a hard pillow.

Many of our experienced frontier officers prefer carrying their pistols in a belt at their sides to placing them in holsters attached to the saddle, as in the former case they are always at hand when they are dismounted; whereas, by the other plan, they become useless when a man is unhorsed, unless he has time to remove them from the saddle, which, during the excitement of an action, would seldom be the case.

Notwithstanding Colt's army and navy sized revolvers have been in use for a long time in our army, officers are by no means of one mind as to their relative merits for frontier service. The navy pistol, being more light and portable, is more convenient for the belt, but it is very questionable in my mind whether these qualities counterbalance the advantages derived from the greater weight of powder and lead that can be fired from the larger pistol, and the consequent increased projectile force.

This point is illustrated by an incident which fell under my own observation. In passing near the "Medicine-Bow Butte" during the spring of 1858, I most unexpectedly encountered and fired at a full-grown grizzly bear; but, as my horse had become somewhat blown by a previous gallop, his breathing so much disturbed my aim that I missed the animal at the short distance of about fifty yards, and he ran off. Fearful, if I stopped to reload my rifle, the bear would make his escape, I resolved to drive him back to the advanced guard of our escort, which I could see approaching in the distance; this I succeeded in doing, when several mounted men, armed with the navy revolvers, set off in pursuit. They approached within a few paces, and discharged ten or twelve shots, the most of which entered the animal, but he still kept on, and his progress did not seem materially impeded by the wounds. After these men had exhausted their charges, another man rode up armed with the army revolver, and fired two shots, which brought the stalwart beast to the ground. Upon skinning him and making an examination of the wounds, it was discovered that none of the balls from the small pistols had, after passing through his thick and tough hide, penetrated deeper than about an inch into the flesh, but that the two balls from the large pistol had gone into the vitals and killed him. This test was to my mind a decisive one as to the relative efficiency of the two arms for frontier service, and I resolved thenceforth to carry the larger size.

Several different methods are practiced in slinging and carrying fire-arms upon horseback. The shoulder-strap, with a swivel to hook into a ring behind the guard, with the muzzle resting downward in a leather cup attached by a strap to the same staple as the stirrup-leather, is a very handy method for cavalry soldiers to sling their carbines; but, the gun being reversed, the jolting caused by the motion of the horse tends to move the charge and shake the powder out of the cone, which renders it liable to burst the gun and to miss fire.

An invention of the Namaquas, in Africa, described by Galton in his Art of Travel, is as follows:

"Sew a bag of canvas, leather, or hide, of such bigness as to admit the butt of the gun pretty freely. The straps that support it buckle through a ring in the pommel, and the thongs by which its slope is adjusted fasten round the girth below. The exact adjustments may not be hit upon by an unpracticed person for some little time, but, when they are once ascertained, the straps need never be shifted. The gun is perfectly safe, and never comes below the arm-pit, even in taking a drop leap; it is pulled out in an instant by bringing the elbow in front of the gun and close to the side, so as to throw the gun to the outside of the arm; then, lowering the hand, the gun is caught up. It is a bungling way to take out the gun while its barrel lies between the arm and the body. Any sized gun can be carried in this fashion. It offers no obstacle to mounting or dismounting."

This may be a convenient way of carrying the gun; I have never tried it. Of all methods I have used, I prefer, for hunting, a piece of leather about twelve inches by four, with a hole cut in each end; one of the ends is placed over the pommel of the saddle, and with a buckskin string made fast to it, where it remains a permanent fixture. When the rider is mounted, he places his gun across the strap upon the saddle, and carries the loose end forward over the pommel, the gun resting horizontally across his legs. It will now only be necessary occasionally to steady the gun with the hand. After a little practice the rider will be able to control it with his knees, and it will be found a very easy and convenient method of carrying it. When required for use, it is taken out in an instant by simply raising it with the hand, when the loose end of the strap comes off the pommel.

The chief causes of accidents from the use of fire-arms arise from carelessness, and I have always observed that those persons who are most familiar with their use are invariably the most careful. Many accidents have happened from carrying guns with the cock down upon the cap. When in this position, a blow upon the cock, and sometimes the concussion produced by the falling of the gun, will explode the cap; and, occasionally, when the cock catches a twig, or in the clothes, and lifts it from the cap, it will explode. With a gun at half-cock there is but little danger of such accidents; for, when the cock is drawn back, it either comes to the full-cock, and remains, or it returns to the half-cock, but does not go down upon the cone. Another source of very many sad and fatal accidents resulting from the most stupid and culpable carelessness is in persons standing before the muzzles of guns and attempting to pull them out of wagons, or to draw them through a fence or brush in the same position. If the cock encounters an obstacle in its passage, it will, of course, be drawn back and fall upon the cap. These accidents are of frequent occurrence, and the cause is well understood by all, yet men continue to disregard it, and their lives pay the penalty of their indiscretion. It is a wise maxim, which applies with especial force in campaigning on the prairies, "*Always look to your gun, but never let your gun look at you.*"

An equally important maxim might be added to this: *Never to point your gun at another, whether charged or uncharged, and never allow another to point his gun at you.* Young men, before they become accustomed to the use of arms, are very apt to be careless, and a large percentage of gun accidents may be traced to this cause. That finished sportsman and wonderful shot, my friend Captain Martin Scott, than whom a more gallant soldier never fought a battle, was the most careful man with fire-arms I ever knew, and up to the time he received his death-wound upon the bloody field of Molino del Rey he never ceased his cautionary advice to young officers upon this subject. His extended experience and intimate acquaintance with the use of arms had fully impressed him with its importance, and no man ever lived whose opinions upon this subject should carry greater weight. As incomprehensible as it may appear to persons accustomed to the use of fire-arms, recruits are very prone, before they have been drilled at target practice with ball cartridges, to place the ball below the powder in the piece. Officers conducting detachments through the Indian country should therefore give their special attention to this, and require the recruits to tear the cartridge and pour all the powder into the piece before the ball is inserted.

As accidents often occur in camp from the accidental discharge of fire-arms that have been capped, I would recommend that the arms be continually kept loaded in campaigning, but the caps not placed upon the cones until they are required for firing. This will cause but little delay in an action, and will conduce much to security from accidents.

When loaded fire-arms have been exposed for any considerable time to a moist atmosphere, they should be discharged, or the cartridges drawn, and the arms thoroughly cleaned, dried, and oiled. Too much attention can not be given in keeping arms in perfect firing order.

TRACKING.

I know of nothing in the woodman's education of so much importance, or so difficult to acquire, as the art of trailing or tracking men and animals. To become an adept in this art requires the constant practice of years, and with some men a life-time does not suffice to learn it.

Almost all the Indians whom I have met with are proficient in this species of knowledge, the faculty for acquiring which appears to be innate with them. Exigencies of woodland and prairie life stimulate the savage from childhood to develop faculties so important in the arts of war and of the chase.

I have seen very few white men who were good trailers, and practice did not seem very materially to improve their faculties in this regard; they have not the same acute perceptions for these things as the Indian or the Mexican. It is not apprehended that this difficult branch of woodcraft can be taught from books, as it pertains almost exclusively to the school of practice, yet I will give some facts relating to the habits of the Indians that will facilitate its acquirements.

A party of Indians, for example, starting out upon a war

excursion, leave their families behind, and never transport their lodges; whereas, when they move with their families, they carry their lodges and other effects. If, therefore, an Indian trail is discovered with the marks of the lodge-poles upon it, it has certainly not been made by a war-party; but if the track do not show the trace of lodge-poles, it will be equally certain that a war or hunting party has passed that way, and if it is not desired to come in conflict with them, their direction may be avoided. Mustangs or wild horses, when moving from place to place, leave a trail which is sometimes difficult to distinguish from that made by a mounted party of Indians, especially if the mustangs do not stop to graze. This may be determined by following upon the trail until some dung is found, and if this should lie in a single pile, it is a sure indication that a herd of mustangs has passed, as they always stop to relieve themselves, while a party of Indians would keep their horses in motion, and the ordure would be scattered along the road. If the trail pass through woodland, the mustang will occasionally go under the limbs of trees too low to admit the passage of a man on horseback.

An Indian, on coming to a trail, will generally tell at a glance its age, by what particular tribe it was made, the number of the party, and many other things connected with it astounding to the uninitiated.

I remember, upon one occasion, as I was riding with a Delaware upon the prairies, we crossed the trail of a large party of Indians traveling with lodges. The tracks appeared to me quite fresh, and I remarked to the Indian that we must be near the party. "Oh no," said he, "the trail was made two days before, in the morning," at the same time pointing with his finger to where the sun would be at about eight o'clock. Then, seeing that my curiosity was excited to know by what means he arrived at this conclusion, he called my attention to the fact that there had been no dew for the last two nights, but that on the previous morning it had been heavy. He then pointed out to me some spears of grass that had been pressed down into the earth by the horses' hoofs, upon which the sand still adhered, having dried on, thus clearly showing that the grass was wet when the tracks were made.

At another time, as I was traveling with the same Indian, I discovered upon the ground what I took to be a bear-track, with a distinctly-marked impression of the heel and all the toes. I immediately called the Indian's attention to it, at the same time flattering myself that I had made quite an important discovery, which had escaped his observation. The fellow remarked with a smile, "Oh no, captain, maybe so he not bear-track." He then pointed with his gun-rod to some spears of grass that grew near the impression, but I did not comprehend the mystery until he dismounted and explained to me that, when the wind was blowing, the spears of grass would be bent over toward the ground, and the oscillating motion thereby produced would scoop out the loose sand into the shape I have described. The truth of this explanation was apparent, yet it occurred to me that its solution would have baffled the wits of most white men.

Fresh tracks generally show moisture where the earth has been turned up, but after a short exposure to the sun they become dry. If the tracks be very recent, the sand may sometimes, where it is very loose and dry, be seen running back into the tracks, and by following them to a place where they cross water, the earth will be wet for some distance after they leave it. The droppings of the dung from animals are also good indications of the age of a trail. It is well to remember whether there have been any rains within a few days, as the age of a trail may sometimes be conjectured in this way. It is very easy to tell whether tracks have been made before or after a rain, as the water washes off all the sharp edges.

It is not a difficult matter to distinguish the tracks of American horses from those of Indian horses, as the latter are never shod; moreover, they are much smaller.

In trailing horses, there will be no trouble while the ground is soft, as the impressions they leave will then be deep and distinct; but when they pass over hard or rocky ground, it is sometimes a very slow and troublesome process to follow them. Where there is grass, the trace can be seen for a considerable time, as the grass will be trodden down and bent in the direction the party has moved; should the grass have returned to its upright position, the trail can often be distinguished by standing upon it and looking ahead for some distance in the direction it has been pursuing; the grass that has been turned over will show a different shade of green from that around it, and this often marks a trail for a long time.

Should all traces of the track be obliterated in certain localities, it is customary with the Indians to follow on in the direction it has been pursuing for a time, and it is quite probable that in some place where the ground is more favorable it will show itself again. Should the trail not be recovered in this way, they search for a place where the earth is soft, and make a careful examination, embracing the entire area where it is likely to run.

Indians who find themselves pursued and wish to escape, scatter as much as possible, with an understanding that they are to meet again at some point in advance, so that, if the pursuing party follows any one of the tracks, it will invariably lead to the place of rendezvous. If, for example, the trail points in the direction of a mountain pass, or toward any other place which affords the only passage through a particular section of country, it would not be worth while to spend much time in hunting it, as it would probably be regained at the pass.

As it is important in trailing Indians to know at what gaits they are traveling, and as the appearance of the tracks of horses are not familiar to all, I have in the following cut

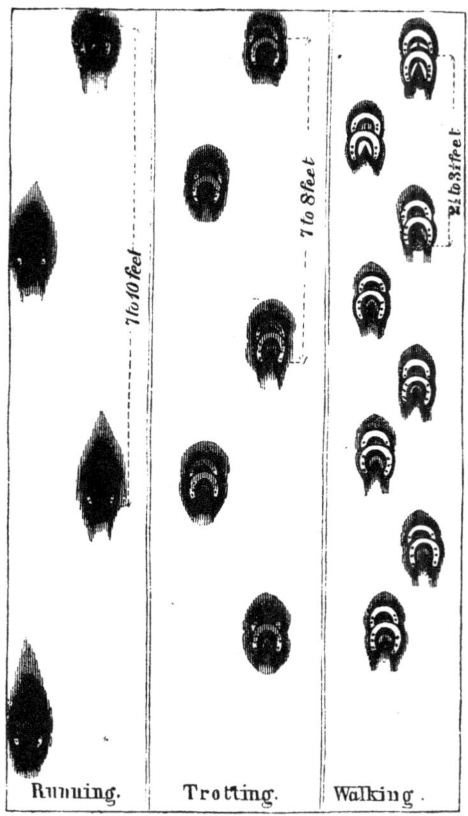

HORSE-TRACKS AT ORDINARY SPEED.

represented the prints made by the hoofs at the ordinary speed of the walk, trot, and gallop, so that persons, in following the trail of Indians, may form an idea as to the probability of overtaking them, and regulate their movements accordingly.

In traversing a district of unknown country where there are no prominent landmarks, and with the view of returning to the point of departure, a pocket compass should always be carried, and attached by a string to a button-hole of the coat, to prevent its being lost or mislaid; and on starting out, as well as frequently during the trip, take the bearing, and examine the appearance of the country when facing toward the starting-point, as a landscape presents a very different aspect when viewed from opposite directions. There are few white men who can retrace their steps for any great distance unless they take the above precautions in passing over an unknown country for the first time; but with the Indians it is different; the sense of locality seems to be innate with them, and they do not require the aid of the magnetic needle to guide them.

Upon a certain occasion, when I had made a long march over an unexplored section, and was returning upon an entirely different route without either road or trail, a Delaware, by the name of "Black Beaver," who was in my party, on arriving at a particular point, suddenly halted, and, turning to me, asked if I recognized the country before us. Seeing no familiar objects, I replied in the negative. He put the same question to the other white men of the party, all of whom gave the same answers, whereupon he smiled, and in his quaint vernacular said, "Injun he don't know nothing. Injun big fool. White man mighty smart; he know heap." At the same time he pointed to a tree about two hundred yards from where we were then standing, and informed us that our outward trail ran directly by the side of it, which proved to be true.

Another time, as I was returning from the Comanche

country over a route many miles distant from the one I had traveled in going out, one of my Delaware hunters, who had never visited the section before, on arriving upon the crest of an eminence in the prairie, pointed out to me a clump of trees in the distance, remarking that our outward track would be found there. I was not, however, disposed to credit his statement until we reached the locality, and found the road passing the identical spot he had indicated.

This same Indian would start from any place to which he had gone by a sinuous route, through an unknown country, and keep a direct bearing back to the place of departure; and he assured me that he has never, even during the most cloudy or foggy weather, or in the darkest nights, lost the points of compass. There are very few white men who are endowed with these wonderful faculties, and those few are only rendered proficient by matured experience.

I have known several men, after they had become lost in the prairies, to wander about for days without exercising the least judgment, and finally exhibit a state of mental aberration almost upon the verge of lunacy. Instead of reasoning upon their situation, they exhaust themselves running ahead at their utmost speed without any regard to direction. When a person is satisfied that he has lost his way, he should stop and reflect upon the course he has been traveling, the time that has elapsed since he left his camp, and the probable distance that he is from it; and if he is unable to retrace his steps, he should keep as nearly in the direction of them as possible; and if he has a compass, this will be an easy matter; but, above all, he should guard against following his own track around in a circle with the idea that he is in a beaten trace.

When he is traveling with a train of wagons which leaves a plain trail, he can make the distance he has traveled from camp the radius of a circle in which to ride around, and before the circle is described he will strike the trail. If the person has no compass, it is always well to make an observation, and to remember the direction of the wind at the time of departure from camp; and as this would not generally change during the day, it would afford a means of keeping the points of the compass.

In the night Ursa Major (the Great Bear) is not only useful to find the north star, but its position, when the pointers will be vertical in the heavens, may be estimated with sufficient accuracy to determine the north even when the north star can not be seen. In tropical latitudes, the zodiacal constellations, such as Orion and Antares, give the east and west bearing, and the Southern Cross the north and south, when Polaris and the Great Bear can not be seen.

It is said that the moss upon the firs and other trees in Europe gives a certain indication of the points of compass in a forest country, the greatest amount accumulating upon the north side of the trees. But I have often observed the trees in our own forests, and have not been able to form any positive conclusions in this way.

In the autumn of 1844 I made a hunting excursion upon the peninsula of Michigan, in the vicinity of Saginaw Bay. That part of the country was then perfectly in a state of nature, and probably continues so to this day, as it is a cold, barren region, covered with heavy pine and tamarack trees, growing upon a miserable soil, illy adapted to the purposes of the agriculturist. In this wild and lonely section there were at that time a good many elk, and I started out for the purpose of trying my skill in hunting the noble beast, which I had then never had the pleasure of seeing. I engaged for a guide an old Chippeway Indian named "*Petowanquad*," who had passed the greater portion of his life in hunting moose, elk, bears, and deer in that very locality, and was perfectly well acquainted with the haunts and habits of those animals.

He told me that, many years before this, he was hunting here in the winter season at a time when the snow was so deep that he was obliged to use snow-shoes; that during the course of his hunt he struck the tracks of seven moose, which he followed until he came within rifle range, and succeeded in killing two of them. The other five made their escape for the time, but he proceeded on the trail until he killed another, and thus he went on for three days, bivouacking at night upon the tracks, and at the expiration of this time he had killed the entire gang, with a large black bear which he encountered during the time. He then returned home and called out a sufficient number of Indians to go with hand-sleds and bring in the meat.

After we had reached the hunting-ground we made our bivouac in the woods, and prepared to try our luck the following morning.

Petowanquad, who was master of ceremonies upon the occasion, cautioned us against firing our guns or making other noises, as he said the sense of hearing in the elk was so very acute that at the slightest unusual noise they would take alarm and run away.

At daylight the next morning Petowanquad and myself shouldered our rifles and started out with two dogs in leash, and we had not gone far before I saw some tracks which to me appeared fresh, but the Indian said they were made the day previous, and that the animals then were probably far off. We soon saw others, which he said had been made during the past night, but these were not sufficiently fresh to answer his purposes. Afterward we came to others, which he decided to have been made some three hours before; but still he did not seem inclined to follow them, and so we traveled on until it got to be about ten o'clock, when we struck the tracks of five elk, which the Indian, in a low tone of voice, informed me had just passed, and were in all probability close by us at that time, whereupon we unleashed the dogs, who instantly bounded away upon the tracks into a dense thicket of brush, and in a very few minutes we heard them giving tongue most vociferously on the other side, and rapidly making their way up the bank of a small creek. The Indian was nearly as much excited as I was myself, and we started in pursuit at the top of our speed. After we had run about half a mile my ardor began to abate somewhat; I became thoroughly blown, and seated myself upon a log to rest, telling the Indian to follow the sound of the dogs, and keep them within hearing until they brought the animals to bay, but under no circumstances to fire at them, as I was ambitious to have the honor of killing them myself. He proceeded on, and in a few minutes I heard him call to me. On joining him he informed me that the dogs had brought a large buck elk "to bay" in the creek just above where we then were, whereupon I approached the sound of the dogs' voices, and saw an immense elk, with antlers at least five feet long, standing in the bed of the creek, with his head erect, and the two dogs jumping up and biting his nose and ears, at the same time keeping up a furious barking. I leveled my rifle and placed an ounce of lead directly back of his shoulder, at which he trotted off, but the excellent dogs brought him to bay again directly, when with the Indian's rifle I gave him another shot near the same place, but it was not until I had fired another ball into his head that I brought him down. He was a magnificent fellow, weighing at least five hundred pounds, and his horns were so large that they were a full load for the Indian in returning to our camp. This was my first elk, and, as may be imagined, I felt very proud of the exploit.

The main object I had in view in describing this hunt here was to show the great accuracy with which the experienced Indian hunter will at a glance, from the appearance of a track, approximate to the time when the game passed. I endeavored to learn from the Indian the secret of this wonderful faculty; he could not, however, enlighten me, saying that it was in his head, but he could not explain it; I am therefore convinced that a knowledge of this art can only be attained by long-continued practical application and experience.

From our camp to the point where we struck the fresh elk tracks was some eight or ten miles in a direct line, over a densely-timbered, flat country, without a single hill, stream, or other landmark to break the monotony of the surface. I noticed, in passing over it in the morning, that the Indian would occasionally kick up some dry leaves with his feet, and, in returning, I observed that we passed near some of these places; but my astonishment was very great when he stopped suddenly and requested me to fire off my rifle, which I did, and immediately our companions in the camp called out to us but a short distance off. Although I considered myself a tolerably good woodsman, yet I had not the slightest conception we were then any where near our camp that we had left in the morning.

There was so much sameness in the appearance of this section that one of our young Indians got lost on the same day, and did not find his way back until he went to the lake and followed out our trail.

THE DEER.

Of all game quadrupeds indigenous to this continent, the common red deer is probably more widely dispersed from north to south and from east to west over our vast possessions than any other. They are found in all latitudes from

Hudson's Bay to Mexico, and they clamber over the most elevated peaks of the western sierras with the same ease that they range the eastern forests or the everglades of Florida. In summer they crop the grass upon the summits of the Rocky Mountains, and in winter, when the snow falls deep, they descend into sheltered valleys, where they fall an easy prey to the Indians.

Besides the common red deer of the Eastern States, two other varieties are found in the Rocky Mountains, viz., the "black-tailed deer," which takes its name from the fact of its having a small tuft of black hair upon the end of its tail, and the *long-tailed* species. The former of these is considerably larger than the Eastern deer, and is much darker, being of a very deep-yellowish iron-gray, with a yellowish red upon the belly. It frequents the mountains, and is never seen far away from them. Its habits are similar to those of the red deer, and it is hunted in the same way. The only difference I have been able to discern between the long-tailed variety and the common deer is in the length of the tail and body. I have seen this animal only in the neighborhood of the Rocky Mountains, but it may resort to other localities.

Although the deer are still abundant in many of our forest districts in the East, and do not appear to decrease very rapidly, yet there has within a few years been a very evident diminution in the numbers of those frequenting our Western prairies. In passing through Southern Texas in 1846, thousands of deer were met with daily, and, astonishing as it may appear, it was no uncommon spectacle to see from one to two hundred in a single herd; the prairies seemed literally alive with them; but in 1855 it was seldom that a herd of ten was seen in the same localities. It seemed to me that the vast herds first met with could not have been killed off by the hunters in that sparsely-populated section, and I was puzzled to know what had become of them. It is possible they may have moved off into Mexico; they certainly are not in our territory at the present time.

Sportsmen have never been, and probably never will be, unanimous in their opinions regarding the best arm for deer-hunting. The relative efficiency of the rifle and the smooth-bored fowling-piece has been a fruitful theme for discussion among the respective advocates of each for many years, and some very cogent arguments have been adduced in support of both sides of the question.

In driving deer with dogs, where the hunter is stationed upon a "runway," and seldom has an opportunity of getting any other than a running shot, and this oftentimes in dense cover, I should unquestionably give the preference to a large gauged shot-gun. I should also choose the same description of gun to hunt deer on horseback in thick cover, where the game is lying down, and generally springs up suddenly and is out of sight before a rifle could be brought to bear with much certainty upon it; but when it comes to still-hunting deer, there is no comparison, in my judgment, between the relative merits of the two arms.

Any one who has been in the habit of deer-stalking knows that it is generally difficult to approach nearer to them than about one hundred yards; he also will be aware of the fact that a smooth-bored gun, even when charged with Ely's wire buck-shot cartridges, is a very uncertain weapon at greater distances than about sixty or seventy yards; while, on the other hand, it will be equally apparent to him that a good rifle, in the hands of an experienced shot, is perfectly reliable at all distances under one hundred and fifty yards.

That man who can not kill a deer at one hundred yards with a good rifle had better throw it aside, take the shot-gun, and turn his attention to smaller game, for he certainly never will become proficient as a deer-hunter.

One of the most conclusive arguments I know of upon this subject is found in the fact that all our frontier hunters, who rely exclusively upon their guns to furnish them subsistence, use only the rifle; and, indeed, I have never known a very expert deer-stalker that would make use of any other arm.

The rifles that are manufactured in the Eastern States are designed for small game or target practice, and are, for the most part, of small calibre, carrying from about eighty to one hundred round balls to the pound. While it is admitted that these missiles, when fired with great accuracy through the vitals of a deer, will bring him to the ground, yet it is contended that if they only penetrate the fleshy parts of the animal, or even pass through the entrails, they are often insufficient to stop him; whereas, if a deer be wounded with a large ball, he will bleed much more freely, and will sooner become exhausted.

I have always been much more successful with a large-calibred rifle than with a small one; and I am of the opinion that a gauge admitting about thirty-two round balls to the pound is the most efficient, not only for deer-shooting, but for all the other large-game quadrupeds found upon our continent.

A hunting rifle should not be shorter in the barrel than thirty inches (I prefer thirty-four inches), as this length insures a good line of sight, and gives a desirable balance to the gun when brought to the shoulder. A shorter barrel may throw the ball with as much accuracy, but it is more easily thrown out of the proper line of direction, and does not allow sufficient interval between the front and back sights.

The weight of metal in the barrel is a consideration of

importance, but will depend somewhat upon the physical powers of the individual. A heavy barrel recoils less than a light one, and, consequently, throws the projectile with more precision; but a delicate man can not carry a very heavy rifle upon his shoulder all day without too great a tax upon his powers of endurance. Some of our stout and hardy frontiermen, like the Swiss mountaineers, may carry a rifle of twenty pounds' weight, but this I deem unnecessarily large. A rifle weighing entire from ten and a half to twelve pounds is, in my judgment, heavy enough for hunting purposes. It does not recoil perceptibly when properly charged, and is not cumbersome for men of ordinary physique.

A great variety of complicated elevating back-sights have been brought to the notice of the public within the past few years, and some of them received with favor among military men. They are graduated, and designed to be elevated or depressed as the firing distance increases or diminishes. Theoretically they are correct in principle, and perhaps, for military arms, they may be found advantageous when the distances can be determined with accuracy; but when the enemy is manœuvring, and continually occupying different positions, the distances must, for the most part, be estimated. Under such circumstances, it strikes my mind that but little, if any, practical utility will be attained from the use of this awkward and cumbersome appendage.

The open back-sight is, in my opinion, the only one that should ever be used upon a hunting-rifle. After it is firmly attached to the gun, the point-blank distance can be ascertained by experiment, and the sights adjusted to the proper distance. If the object is at a greater or less distance, the hunter draws a coarser or finer sight, and by practice he will become enabled to make this estimate with a good deal of accuracy; whereas, if he have the elevating sight upon his rifle, he must stop to regulate it to the distance the game happens to show itself before he can fire, and by the time this is done, unless the game is more accommodating than I have usually found it, he will be disappointed.

The only objection I have discovered in the use of the open sight is, that when the sun's rays strike it at particular angles it produces a glimmering in the notch, which prevents drawing a fine sight; but this difficulty is, in a great degree, overcome by a very ingenious and simple device, which originated with one of my Rocky Mountain guides. It consists in having a semi-spherical concavity drilled into the top of the sight, with the circumference tangent to the outer front and rear edges of it. The notches are then cut so as to be in a vertical plane with the axis of the piece when the sight is fixed in position. This orifice effectually screens the notches and prevents any glimmering.

The front sights upon the rifles found in the shops in Northeastern States are generally too short, and our Western hunters always knock them off and put on others. This sight should be about an inch long, and shaped according to the opposite diagram. The hunters generally make them of a piece of silver cut from the edge of a half dollar.

Twenty years' experience in deer-hunting has taught me several facts relative to the habits of the animal, which, when well understood, will be found of much service to the inexperienced hunter, and greatly contribute to his success. The best target-shots are not necessarily the most skillful deer-stalkers. One of the great secrets of this art is in knowing how to approach the game without giving alarm, and this can not easily be done unless the hunter sees it be-

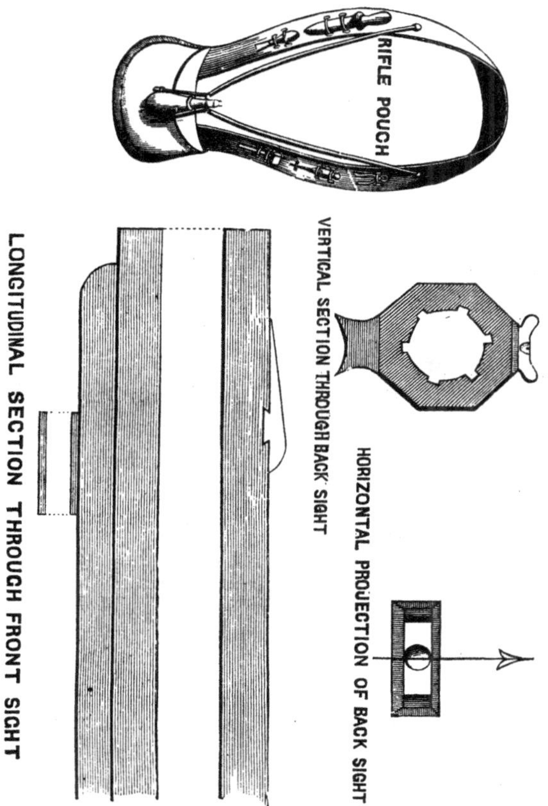

fore he is himself discovered. There are so many objects in the woods resembling the deer in color that none but a practiced eye can often detect the difference.

When the deer is reposing he generally turns his head from the wind, in which position he can see an enemy approaching from that direction, and his nose will apprise him of the presence of danger from the opposite side. The best method of hunting deer, therefore, is *across the wind.*

While the deer are feeding, early in the morning and a short time before dark in the evening are the best times to stalk them, as they are then busily occupied and less on the alert. When a deer is espied with his head down, cropping the grass, the hunter advances cautiously, keeping his eyes constantly directed upon him, and screening himself behind intervening objects, or, in the absence of other cover, crawls along upon his hands and knees in the grass, until the deer hears his step and raises his head, when he must instantly stop and remain in an attitude fixed and motionless as a statue, for the animal's vision is his keenest sense. When alarmed he will detect the slightest movement of a small object, and, unless the hunter stands or lies perfectly still, his presence will be detected. If the hunter does not move, the deer will, after a short time, recover from his alarm and resume his grazing, when he may be again approached. The deer always exhibits his alarm by a sudden jerking of the tail just before he raises his head.

I once saw a Delaware Indian walk directly up within rifle range of a deer that was feeding upon the open prairie and shoot him down; he was, however, a long time in approaching, and made frequent halts whenever the animal flirted his tail and raised his head. Although he often turned toward the hunter, yet he did not appear to notice him, probably taking him for a stump or tree.

When the deer are lying down in the smooth prairie, unless the grass is tall, it is difficult to get near them, as they are generally looking around, and become alarmed at the least noise.

The most auspicious season of the year for still-hunting deer in a northern latitude is immediately after the first light falls of snow during the early part of winter. The game is then "*in season*," fat, well-flavored, and the fawns sufficiently grown to take care of themselves.

When the ground is covered with a soft carpet of three or four inches of snow, the hunter passes over it without making much noise by the crackling of twigs or the rustling of leaves under his feet.

Moccasins are preferable for this kind of hunting to boots or shoes, especially in the cold and dry weather, for the reason that they are more soft and yielding, and do not occasion so much noise by crushing twigs or striking against hard substances, and are therefore less liable to startle the game.

In starting out at early dawn, after there has been a light snow during the preceding night, the hunter may be certain, should he encounter a track, that it is fresh, and that the animal is not very far distant. He then, in a region where the deer are not very abundant, takes the trail and follows it; but, in doing this, he should not keep his eyes constantly fixed upon the ground, but walk cautiously along near the track, carefully avoiding stepping upon dry brush, or breaking off overhanging limbs of trees, and attentively scrutinizing all the ground in front within rifle range.

Where the deer has been moving directly along, without stopping to lie down or wandering about to eat, it will not be necessary to exercise so much caution, as the animal will probably be found some distance in advance; but whenever the track takes a direction toward a thicket of brush, a morass covered with tall grass or rushes, or, indeed, toward any other place affording dense cover, where the animal might be likely to lie down, the hunter should at once leave the trail and make a wide detour around upon the lee side of such covert, keeping his eyes intently occupied in scrutinizing every object within the area. After passing entirely around the copse in this manner, and arriving at the point of departure, if he has not crossed the track on the opposite side, he knows that the deer is within the circle he has described, and he then makes sure that his rifle is in good firing order; and, carrying it in such a position that it can be brought to bear upon the object in the shortest possible time, he begins to contract the circle by gradually approaching nearer the covert, and keenly searching every place where it is possible for the deer to make his bed. To insure success in the execution of this very adroit and strategic approach, it is absolutely necessary that the hunter should move with a slow and regular gait, but on no account stop, or make any unusual demonstration, until he discovers the game and is in readiness to deliver his shot, as, in the event of his being very near, the deer will oftentimes jump up and run at the instant he makes a halt, whereas if he moves steadily along with a measured step, as if he intended to pass by, they will generally lie close, and sometimes I have even seen them lower their heads upon the ground to hide from the hunter.

The antlers of the bucks, before they shed them, can often be seen over the tops of the tall grass or low brush when they are lying down, and the long erect ears of the does are the first objects that make their appearance under the same circumstances.

The hunter must be careful not to allow his eyes to catch those of the deer when he discovers him, as I am informed by a finished sportsman and an experienced deer-stalker (although I have never observed the fact myself) that in such event the animal will instantly jump up and run.

During the "*running season*" the bucks follow on the trail of the does in a fast walk or slow trot, and, as they are then eagerly occupied in the pursuit of their object, they are not easily diverted from it. The hunter may then fall in behind them after they pass him, and, following up rapidly, approach within rifle range without difficulty.

The "running season" in the Northern States generally

commences in October, and lasts about a month; but in the Southern States it is about a month later. During this season the bucks run themselves down, become poor, their necks swell to an enormous size, and the venison is then rank and unfit for the table.

A wounded deer can be followed without difficulty upon the snow; and if the blood that flows from the wound is of a light red or pink color, it is a certain indication that the animal has been struck in the vitals, and will not run far. In the summer season a wounded deer will generally seek the water, and, hiding under the shelving banks of rivers, or in the grass upon the borders of ponds, sink his body, only keeping his head exposed; it then becomes necessary to search very closely to discover his hiding-place.

When a deer has been alarmed by a hunter upon his track, he often runs a long distance before he recovers from his fright, and it requires a long and exhausting chase to come up with him again; even then he will be likely to keep an eye to the rear for a considerable time, and it will require great caution to approach within shooting distance. I have always, under such circumstances, thought it better to abandon the track and look for another.

When a deer has but one leg broken he makes good running, and a man on foot will find it very difficult to overtake him without a dog to bring him "to bay." I remember one instance where I broke both fore legs of a doe just above the knees, yet, notwithstanding these severe wounds, she ran off upon the stumps nearly half a mile before I succeeded in securing her.

Another very successful method of deer-stalking, which is practiced a good deal in the sparsely-populated districts of Texas and Mexico, where the game is abundant, and accustomed to grazing in the vicinity of cattle and horses, is by making use of a gentle and tractable horse or mule, and approaching as near the deer as can conveniently be done without giving alarm (about 300 yards); the hunter then dismounts, attaches one end of his wiping-stick, or other small rod, to the bridle-bit by means of a string; he then takes the opposite end of the rod in one hand, his rifle in the other, and, placing himself near the horse's shoulder on the opposite side from the deer, so as to be screened from their observation by the horse, he moves off very slowly in a direction not directly toward the game, but so as to pass within the desirable rifle range, and upon the lee side. With the stick he is enabled to guide his horse, stop him, or turn him in any direction he may desire. In this manner he proceeds in a slow walk, carefully covering himself behind the horse, and gradually bearing toward the deer.

During the approach the deer will sometimes take alarm, raise their heads, and cast a startled and inquiring look at the horse. Should this occur, the hunter will at once stop and allow his horse to crop the grass, while he himself lowers his head so as to be entirely screened from the deer. As soon as they regain their composure and resume their grazing, he proceeds again, and will generally be able to get within short rifle range, when he can stoop down and fire under his horse's belly or neck. If, however, the stalking-horse has not been trained to this particular method of hunting, or is alarmed at the report of fire-arms, the hunter should carry the lariat rope in his hand, and, when he is sufficiently near the deer, drop the guiding-stick, and allow his horse to pass on, while he remains upon the ground behind, and places himself in position to fire at the instant he is uncovered by the horse. I have often hunted in this way, and with good success. I observed, however, after a particular herd had been stalked several times, that they became wary, after which it was necessary to unsaddle before commencing the approach.

Another successful, but not very sportsmanlike method of deer-stalking is resorted to by the unscrupulous pot-hunters in Western Texas and Mexico, and which is so entirely different from any other I have ever heard of that it is worthy of a notice for its originality. It consists in making use of a dry and stiff ox-hide, to one end of which a rope is attached. A yoke of well-trained and gentle oxen are then hitched to the rope, and the hunter drives out into the prairies where the deer resort. When he discovers a herd, and has approached as near as can be done without disturbing them, he seats himself upon the hide, and, without speaking or making any other noise, directs the team with his whip toward the game. During the approach, he allows his cattle to move slowly, and occasionally to stop and crop the grass. He is well screened by the oxen and the prairie grass, and will find it a very easy matter to drive within short rifle range without being discovered. After killing a deer, he places it upon his drag, and drives on in search of others.

The Indians are in the habit of using a small instrument which imitates the bleat of the young fawn, with which they lure the doe within range of their rifles. The young fawn gives out no scent upon its track until it is sufficiently grown to make good running, and instinct teaches the mother that this wise provision of nature to preserve the helpless little quadruped from the ravages of wolves, panthers, and other carnivorous beasts, will be defeated if she remains with it, as her tracks can not be concealed. She therefore hides her fawn in the grass, where it is almost impossible to see it, even when very near it, goes off to some neighboring thicket within call, and makes her bed alone. The Indian pot-hunter, who is but little scrupulous as to the means he employs in accomplishing his ends, sounds the bleat along near the places where he thinks the game is lying, and the unsuspicious doe, who imagines that her offspring is in distress, rushes with headlong impetuosity toward the sound, and often goes within a few yards of the hunter to receive her death-wound.

This is cruel sport, and can only be justified when meat is scarce, which is very frequently the case in the Indian's larder.

It does not always comport with a man's feelings of security, especially if he happens to be a little nervous, to sound the deer-bleat in a wild region of country. I once undertook to experiment with the instrument myself, and made my first essay in attempting to call up an antelope which I discovered in the distance. I succeeded admirably in luring the wary victim within shooting range, had raised upon my knees, and was just in the act of pulling trigger, when a rustling in the grass on my left drew my attention in that direction, where, much to my surprise, I beheld a huge panther within about twenty yards, bounding with gigantic strides directly toward me. I turned my rifle, and in an instant, much to my relief and gratification, its contents were lodged in the heart of the beast.

Many men, when they suddenly encounter a deer, are seized with nervous excitement, called in sporting parlance the "*buck fever*," which causes them to fire at random. Notwithstanding I have had much experience in hunting, I must confess that I am never entirely free from some of the symptoms of this malady when firing at large game, and I believe that in four out of five cases where I have missed the game my balls have passed too high. I have endeavored to obviate this by sighting my rifle low, and it has been attended with more successful results. The same remarks apply to most other men I have met with. They fire too high when excited.

CALLING UP ANTELOPES.

THE ANTELOPE.

This animal frequents the most elevated bleak and naked prairies in all latitudes from Mexico to Oregon, and constitutes an important item of subsistence with many of the prairie Indians. It is the most wary, timid, and fleet animal that inhabits the Plains. It is about the size of a small deer, with a heavy coating of coarse, wiry hair, and its flesh is more tender and juicy than that of the deer. It seldom enters a timbered country, but seems to delight in cropping the grass from the elevated swells of the prairies. When disturbed by the traveler, it will circle around him with the speed of the wind, but does not stop until it reaches some prominent position whence it can survey the country on all sides, and nothing seems to escape its keen vision. They will sometimes stand for a long time and look at a man, provided he does not move or go out of sight; but if he goes behind a hill with the intention of passing around and getting nearer to them, he will never find them again in the same place. I have often tried the experiment, and invariably found that, as soon as I went where the antelope could not see me, he moved off. Their sense of hearing, as well as vision, is very acute, which renders it difficult to stalk them. By taking advantage of the cover afforded in broken ground, the hunter may, by moving slowly and cautiously over the crests of the irregularities in the surface, sometimes approach within rifle range.

The antelope possesses a greater degree of curiosity than any other animal I know of, and will often approach very near a strange object. The experienced hunter, taking advantage of this peculiarity, lies down and secretes himself in the grass, after which he raises his handkerchief, hand, or foot, so as to attract the attention of the animal, and thus often succeeds in beguiling him within shooting distance.

In some valleys near the Rocky Mountains, where the pasturage is good during the winter season, they collect in immense herds. The Indians are in the habit of surrounding them in such localities and running them with their horses until they tire them out, when they slay large numbers.

The antelope makes a track much shorter than the deer, very broad and round at the heel, and quite sharp at the toe; a little experience renders it easy to distinguish them.

THE BEAR.

Besides the common black bear of the Eastern States, several others are found in the mountains of California, Oregon, Utah, and New Mexico, viz., the grizzly, brown, and cinnamon varieties; all have nearly the same habits, and are hunted in the same manner.

From all I had heard of the grizzly bear, I was induced to believe him one of the most formidable and savage animals in the universe, and that the man who would deliberately encounter and kill one of these beasts had performed a signal feat of courage which entitled him to a lofty position among the votaries of Nimrod. So firmly had I become impressed with this conviction, that I should have been very reluctant to fire upon one had I met him when alone and on foot. The grizzly bear is assuredly the monarch of the American forests, and, so far as physical strength is concerned, he is perhaps without a rival in the world; but, after some experience in hunting, my opinions regarding his courage and his willingness to attack men have very materially changed.

In passing over the elevated table-lands lying between the two forks of the Platte River in 1858, I encountered a full-grown female grizzly bear, with two cubs, very quietly reposing upon the open prairie, several miles distant from any timber. This being the first opportunity that had ever occurred to me for an encounter with the ursine monster, and being imbued with the most exalted notions of the beast's proclivities for offensive warfare, especially when in the presence of her offspring, it may very justly be imagined that I was rather more excited than usual. I, however, determined to make the assault. I felt the utmost confidence in my horse, as she was afraid of nothing; and, after arranging every thing about my saddle and arms in good order, I advanced to within about eighty yards before I was discovered by the bear, when she raised upon her haunches and gave me a scrutinizing examination. I seized this opportune moment to fire, but missed my aim, and she started off, followed by her cubs at their utmost speed. After reloading my rifle, I pursued, and, on coming again within range, delivered another shot, which struck the large bear in the fleshy part of the thigh, whereupon she set up a most distressing howl and accelerated her pace, leaving her cubs behind. After loading again I gave the spurs to my horse and resumed the chase, soon passing the cubs, who were making the most plaintive cries of distress. They were heard by the dam, but she gave no other heed to them than occasionally to halt for an instant, turn around, sit up on her posteriors, and give a hasty look back; but, as soon as she saw me following her, she invariably turned again and redoubled her speed. I pursued about four miles and fired four balls into her before I succeeded in bringing her to the ground, and from the time I first saw her until her death-wound, notwithstanding I was often very close upon her heels, she never came to bay or made the slightest demonstration of resistance. Her sole purpose seemed to be to make her escape, leaving her cubs in the most cowardly manner.

Upon three other different occasions I met the mountain

bears, and once the cinnamon species, which is called the most formidable of all, and in none of these instances did they exhibit indications of anger, but invariably ran from me. While I was returning from New Mexico to Utah in 1858, I encountered a large gray bear, which I drove for two miles in the same manner that a wild cow is driven. I was well mounted, and could ride around the bear whenever I desired, and this enabled me to turn the animal in any direction, and thus I drove him directly back to the command, where he was killed.

Such is my experience with this formidable monarch of the mountains. I believe that if a man came suddenly upon the beast in a thicket, where it could have no previous warning, he might be attacked; and it is possible that a large grizzly bear might attack a man on foot in the open prairie, and in some instances they have been known to make war upon men on horseback; but I have always observed that an acquaintance with the larger wild animals of our country makes them much less formidable than they are represented to us when in the distance.

It has generally been considered a very daring feat for General Putnam when he entered a cave and killed a wolf, and the spot is to this day pointed out as the scene of a most wonderful performance; whereas those persons who understand the cowardly nature of the wolf, and are familiar with their habits, are perfectly aware that such an undertaking is not attended with the slightest danger. I knew a woman who, in the night-time, hearing a disturbance in her poultry-yard, went out and met a large wolf carrying off one of her turkeys. She had a very great appreciation for her turkeys, as they were the only ones within a hundred miles, and she pursued the wolf, made him drop the turkey, and run away.

If any one should have any doubt regarding this statement, I beg to refer him to my wife, who was the owner of the turkeys. She, however, did not know what animal she had pursued until a sentinel saw the wolf.

It is my opinion, from all I have seen of the grizzly bear, that if he gets *the wind* or sight of a man on horseback at any considerable distance, he will endeavor to get away as soon as possible. I am so fully impressed with this conviction, that I should hunt the animal (provided I was well mounted on a reliable horse) with a feeling of as much security as I would have in hunting the buffalo. My experience in hunting the grizzly bear differs materially from that of some of my acquaintances.

General Van Vliet, who at one time was stationed at Fort Laramie, was hunting in the Black Hills, when he suddenly came into close proximity with a large grizzly bear, and gave him a shot, wounding him in one of the fore legs. This only served to exasperate the animal, and, instead of running away, he took the offensive, and charged upon the general, who was mounted upon a good horse, but he had never before seen one of the hideous-looking monsters, and was so much terrified at his appearance that he became almost paralyzed, and could hardly move; and the most vigorous application of the spurs had no effect in accelerating his speed, until the bear came up and struck him in the buttock with one of his huge paws, which restored his powers of locomotion, and he bounded off with lightning speed, and carried his rider out of danger. The general subsequently killed the bear.

My first bear was killed in rather a novel manner, in the hills bordering Pecan Bayou, Texas, in 1850, while I was examining the country with the view of establishing a new military post. Attached to my command were several Delaware hunters, to whom I had expressed an earnest desire of adding the ursine monarch to the list of my hunting trophies, and they very obligingly promised to afford me every facility in their power to gratify my ambition.

One day, while hunting alone, in an exceedingly wild and solitary locality, I heard in the distance the sound of loud whooping and screaming of Indians, who apparently were approaching toward me. I was in the woods at the time, and could not discern objects very far off, but as this was in a section frequented by wild Indians, I thought it by no means improbable that the sounds proceeded from some of them, and I hastened to a position behind a large rock where I could screen myself and horse, and at the same time observe every thing in front. The sound continued to advance, until at length, to my great relief (for I must confess I was considerably excited just then), I discovered a black bear emerge from the woods, with three of the Delawares whooping most vociferously in hot pursuit, and all coming directly to where I stood. I mounted my horse, and, joining in the chase, had the good fortune to kill the bear at the first shot.

The Indians informed me that they had driven the animal for nearly a mile, and were on the way back to the command for the express purpose of giving me an opportunity to kill it. He had, several times during the *drive*, taken to trees, but in every instance they had climbed up and shaken him down. They laughed most heartily in describing to me the efforts of the animal to make his escape from them, and congratulated me on the occasion of killing my "*first bear.*"

Black Beaver says he was once in a canoe pursuing a black bear that had taken the water to cross the Missouri River. On coming near the animal he gave him a shot, but the ball only grazed the top of his head, and he turned, swam up to the canoe, and, placing his paws upon the gunwale, seemed determined to get in. Not feeling inclined to

THE GRIZZLY.

take such a passenger into his frail craft, he endeavored to keep him off by striking him over the head with his discharged rifle, but this only had the effect to infuriate him, and make him the more persistent in his apparent determination to embark in the *dug-out.* He then resorted to an expedient he had heard of, but never before practiced. It was, to lay his paddle across upon the top of the bear's neck, which caused him to let go his hold upon the canoe, seize the paddle on each side of his neck, and immediately sink to the bottom, and he was drowned.

The grizzly, like the black bear, hibernates in winter, and makes his appearance in the spring, with his claws grown out long, and very soft and tender; he is then poor, and unfit for food.

I have heard a very curious fact stated by several old mountaineers regarding the mountain bears, which, of course, I can not vouch for, but it is given by them with great apparent sincerity and candor. They assert that no instance has ever been known of a female bear having been killed in a state of pregnancy. This singular fact in the history of the animal seems most inexplicable to me, unless she remains concealed in her brumal slumber until after she has been delivered of her cubs.

I was told by an old Delaware Indian that when the bear has been traveling against the wind and wishes to lie down, he always turns in an opposite direction, and goes some distance away from his first track before making his bed. If an enemy then comes upon his trail, his keen sense of smell will apprise him of the danger. The same Indian mentioned that when a bear had been pursued and sought shelter in a cave, he had often endeavored to eject him with smoke, but that the bear would advance to the mouth of the cave, where the fire was burning, and put it out with his paws, then retreat into the cave again. This would indicate that

Bruin is endowed with some glimpses of reason beyond the ordinary instincts of the brute creation in general, and, indeed, is capable of discerning the connection between cause and effect. Notwithstanding the extraordinary intelligence which this quadruped exhibits upon some occasions, upon others he shows himself to be one of the most stupid brutes imaginable. For example, when he has taken possession of a cavern, and the courageous hunter enters with a torch and rifle, it is said he will, instead of forcibly ejecting the intruder, raise himself upon his haunches and cover his eyes with his paws, so as to exclude the light, apparently thinking that in this situation he can not be seen. The hunter can then approach as close as he pleases and shoot him down.

LASSOING GRIZZLY BEARS.

The Spanish *vaqueros* of California, who, by the constant exercise of their vocation, become astonishingly expert in throwing the lasso, occasionally capture the grizzly bear with it. As this curious and somewhat hazardous method of hunting is well described by Mr. J. Ross Browne, in his interesting book on California, I do not know how to give a better idea of it than to quote his own words. It appeared that while he was in the valley of the Santa Marguerita, he saw a large animal coming toward him pursued by four horsemen, upon which he concealed himself in a ravine. He says: "Scarcely had I partially concealed myself when I heard a loud shouting from the men on horseback, and, peeping over the bank, saw within fifty or sixty paces a huge grizzly bear, but no longer retreating. He had faced round toward his pursuers, and now seemed determined to fight. The horsemen were evidently native Californians, and managed their animals with wonderful skill and grace. The nearest swept down like an avalanche toward the bear, while the others coursed off a short distance in a circling direction to prevent his escape. Suddenly swerving a little to one side, the leader whirled his lasso once or twice around his head, and let fly at his game with unerring aim. The loop caught one of the fore paws, and the bear was instantly jerked down upon his haunches, struggling and roaring with all his might. It was a striking instance of the power of the rider over the horse, that, wild with terror as the latter was, he dared not disobey the slightest pressure of the rein, but went through all the evolutions, blowing trumpet-blasts from his nostrils, and with eyes starting from their sockets. Despite the strain kept upon the lasso, the bear soon regained his feet, and commenced hauling in the spare line with his fore paws so as to get within reach of the horse. He had advanced within ten feet before the nearest of the other horsemen could bring his lasso to bear upon him. The first throw was at his hind legs—the main object being to stretch him out—but it missed. Another more fortunate cast took him round the neck. Both riders pulled in opposite directions, and the bear soon rolled on the ground again, biting furiously at the lassos, and uttering the most terrific roars. The strain upon his neck soon choked off his breath, and he was forced to let loose his grasp upon the other lasso. While struggling to free his neck, the two other horsemen dashed up, swinging their lassos and shouting with all their might so as to attract his attention. The nearest, watching narrowly every motion of the frantic animal, soon let fly his lasso, and made a lucky hitch around one of his hind legs. The other, following quickly with a large loop, swung it entirely over the bear's body, and all four riders now set up a yell of triumph, and began pulling in opposite directions. The writhing, pitching, and straining of the powerful monster were now absolutely fearful. A dust arose over him, and the earth flew up in every direction. Sometimes by a desperate effort he regained his feet, and actually dragged one or more of the horses toward him by main strength; but whenever he attempted this, the others stretched their lassos, and either choked him or jerked him down upon his haunches. It was apparent that his wind was giving out, partly by reason of the long chase, and partly owing to the noose around his throat. A general pull threw him once more upon his back. Before he could regain his feet, the horsemen, by a series of dexterous manœuvres, wound him completely up, so that he lay perfectly quiet upon the ground, breathing heavily, and utterly unable to extricate his paws from the labyrinth of lassos in which he was entangled. One of the riders now gave the reins of his horse to another and dismounted. Cautiously approaching, with a spare *riata* he cast a noose over the bear's fore paws, and wound the remaining part tightly round the neck, so that what strength might still have been left was speedily exhausted by suffocation. This done, another rider dismounted, and the two succeeded in binding their victim so firmly by the paws that it was impossible for him to break loose. They next bound his jaws together by means of another *riata*, winding it all the way up around his head, upon which they loosened the fastening around his neck so as to give him air. When all was secure, they freed the lassos and again mounted their horses."

The bear was secured, and subsequently hauled away for a grand bull-fight.

AN AMATEUR SPORTSMAN.

Although four expert *vaqueros* might with safety attempt and succeed in capturing a full-grown grizzly bear, yet I should imagine that it would hardly be advisable for one or two men to undertake the same feat.

LASSOING THE GRIZZLY.

I have heard it stated that a naval officer many years ago made the experiment of hunting the animal with the lasso, but his success was by no means as decisive as in the instance related by Mr. Browne. This officer had, it appeared, by constant practice upon the ship while making the long and tiresome voyage round the Horn, acquired very considerable proficiency in the use of the lasso, and was able, at twenty or thirty paces, to throw the noose over the head of the negro cook at almost every cast. So confident had he become in his skill, that on his arrival upon the coast of Southern California he employed a guide, and, mounted upon a well-trained horse, with his lasso properly coiled and ready for use, he one morning set out for the mountains with the firm resolve of bagging a few grizzlies before night. He had not been out a great while before he encountered one of the largest specimens of the mighty beast, whose terrific aspect amazed him not a little; but, as he had come out with a firm determination to capture a grizzly, in direct opposition to the advice of his guide he resolved to show him that he was equal to the occasion. Accordingly he seized his lasso, and, riding up near the animal, gave it several rapid whirls above his head in the most artistic manner, and sent the noose directly around the bear's neck at the very first cast; but the animal, instead of taking to his heels and endeavoring to run away as he had anticipated, very deliberately sat up on his haunches, facing his adversary, and commenced making a very careful examination of the rope. He turned his head from one side to the other in looking at it; he felt it with his paws, and scrutinized it very closely, as if it was something he could not comprehend. In the mean time the officer had turned his horse in the opposite direction, and commenced applying the rowels to his sides most vigorously, with the confident expectation that he was to choke the bear to death and drag him off in triumph; but, to his astonishment, the horse, with his utmost efforts, did not seem to advance. The great strain upon the lasso, however, began to choke the bear so much that he soon became enraged, and gave the rope several violent slaps, first with one paw and then with the other; but, finding that this did not relieve him, he seized the lasso with both paws, and commenced pulling it in hand over hand, or rather paw over paw, and bringing with it the horse and rider that were attached to the opposite extremity. The officer redoubled the application of both whip and spurs, but it was all of no avail; he had evidently "caught a Tartar," and, in spite of all the efforts of his horse, he recoiled rather than advanced. At this intensely exciting and critical juncture he cast a hasty glance to the rear, and, to his horror, found himself steadily backing toward the frightful monster, who sat up with his eyes glaring like balls of fire, his huge mouth wide open and frothing with rage, and sending forth the most terrific and deep-toned roars. He now, for the first time, felt seriously alarmed, and cried out vociferously for his guide to come to his rescue. The latter responded promptly, rode up, cut the lasso, and extricated the amateur gentleman from his perilous position. He was much rejoiced at his escape, and, in reply to the inquiry of the guide as to whether he desired to continue the hunt, he said it was getting so late that he believed he would capture no more grizzlies that day.

I do not, of course, pretend to vouch for the authenticity of the foregoing narrative; I have merely given it in the way it was related to me, as a good story, the truth of which the reader can judge of as well as myself. I have no doubt, however, that an animal of such extraordinary proportions, possessing such enormous development of bone and muscle, and whose strength is asserted as sufficient to enable him to drag off a full-grown buffalo, could compete successfully with a California horse in a contest of physical powers. I therefore see nothing improbable in the account given above.

THE BIG-HORN.

The big-horn or mountain sheep, which has a body like the deer, with the head of a sheep, surmounted by an enormous pair of short, heavy horns, is found throughout the Rocky Mountains, and resorts to the most inaccessible peaks and to the widest and least-frequented glens. It clambers over almost perpendicular cliffs with the greatest ease and celerity, and skips from rock to rock, cropping the tender herbage that grows upon them.

It has been supposed by some that this animal leaps down from crag to crag, lighting upon his horns, as an evidence of which it has been advanced that the front part of the horns is often much battered. This I believe to be erroneous, as it is very common to see horns that have no bruises upon them.

The old mountaineers say they have often seen the bucks engaged in desperate encounters with their huge horns, which, in striking together, made loud reports. This will account for the marks sometimes seen upon them.

The flesh of the big-horn, when fat, is more tender, juicy, and delicious than that of any other animal I know of, but it is a *bon bouche* which will not grace the tables of our city epicures until a railroad to the Rocky Mountains affords the means of transporting it to a market a thousand miles distant from its haunts.

In its habits the mountain sheep greatly resembles the chamois of Switzerland, and it is hunted in the same manner. The hunter traverses the most inaccessible and broken localities, moving along with great caution, as the least unusual noise causes them to flit away like a phantom, and they will be seen no more. The animal is gregarious, but it is seldom that more than eight or ten are found in a flock. When not grazing they seek the sheltered sides of the mountains, and repose among the rocks.

BISON OR BUFFALO.

This largest and most useful animal, that is indigenous to this continent, was first seen by Europeans in an individual specimen exhibited to Cortez and his followers in a kind of menagerie, or zoological collection of Montezuma at Mexico in 1521. The animal had been procured in the north, and brought here by the natives, to whom the Aztec monarch intrusted the collection of rare birds and quadrupeds.

It was not, however, until the expedition of Coronado into New Mexico in 1541 that the vast ranges of the quadruped were discovered. The Spanish explorers found none throughout the mountainous districts of New Mexico, but met with the herds in countless numbers in the prairies east of the Del Norte, in the region about the South Fork of the Arkansas.

Castenada's narrative has the following: "On Coronado went, traversing immense plains, seeing nothing for miles together but skies and herds of bison; hundreds of these were killed."

De Soto, in the same year, met with the buffalo after he crossed the Mississippi River, and penetrated into the country now embraced within the limits of Arkansas and Missouri. De Soto applied the term *vaca* to the animal, and the word *bœuf* was afterward given by the French, which merely indicated its identity with the species of our domestic cattle. Linnæus gave it the name of bison, in contradistinction to the Asiatic buffalo; but the name by which the peculiar species in our country is generally known is "buffalo."

In a work published at Amsterdam in 1637, called "New English Canaan," by Thomas Morton, one of the first settlers of New England, he says: "The Indians have also made description of the great heards of well-growne beasts that live about the parts of this lake (Erocoise), now Lake Champlain, such as the Christian world (until this discovery) hath not bin made acquainted with. The beasts are of the bigness of a coue, their flesh being very good foode, their hides good leather, their fleeces very useful, being a kind of woole, as fine almost as the woole of the beaver, and the salvages do make garments thereof. It is tenne yeares since first the relation of these things came to the eares of the English."

It is stated by another author (Purchas) that as early as in 1613 the adventurers in Virginia discovered a "slow kinde of cattell as bigge as kine, which were good meate."

In a work published in London in 1589, by Hakluyt, it is said that in the island of Newfoundland were found "mightie beastes, like to camels in greatness, and their feete were cloven." He adds: "I did see them farre off, not able to descerne them perfectly; but their steps (tracks) showed their feete were cloven, and bigger than the feete of camels. I suppose them to be a kind of buffes, which I read to bee in the countreys adjacent, and very many in the firme land."

It is supposed by some that these animals may have been the musk-ox. They were found by Captain Franklin as high as 60° north latitude. I am inclined to doubt this, however, as the musk-ox has not, I believe, been found in large herds.

What were formerly the precise limits of the buffalo range the history of the early settlement of the country does not inform us. That it embraced nearly all that vast area lying between the Mississippi and the Rocky Mountains there is abundant evidence to show. They were also found in Illinois and Indiana, and extended south as far as Ohio and Kentucky; but there is no record of their having ever been seen within the present limits of Florida, although it is only a few years since they were abundant in the same latitude on the opposite side of the Gulf, in Texas. It is but a few years since some of the animals were seen in the timbered country near the head of the St. Francis River, in Arkansas. They formerly thronged the present area of Kentucky, and they were said to have extended their eastern range to the shores of Lake Erie. They were also at one time abundant in Southern Wisconsin, and crossed the Mississippi above the Falls of St. Anthony, in Minnesota, for the last time, it is believed, in 1820.

Two buffaloes were killed by the Sioux Indians upon the "Trempe à l'Eau," in Upper Wisconsin, in 1832, "and they are supposed to have been the last specimens of the noble bison which trod, or will ever again tread the soil of the region lying east of the Mississippi River" (H. H. Sibley).

If the statements of Morton, Purchas, and Hakluyt are to be relied upon, the buffalo formerly extended his wanderings as far east of the Alleghany range as the Atlantic Ocean.

The western limits of the buffalo range at an early period are not certainly defined, but they have seldom been seen on the western slope of the Rocky Mountains.

They go into high northern latitudes even to the present day, and often pass the winter in the mountainous districts, where the snow remains upon the ground during the entire winter. Early in the spring of 1858 I found them in the mountains at the head of the Arkansas and South Platte Rivers, and there was every indication that this was their permanent abiding-place. It is not more than half a century since the buffalo thronged in countless multitudes over nearly all that vast area included between Mexico and the British Possessions. Lewis and Clarke, in descending the Missouri in July, 1806, estimated that at one place they beheld twenty thousand buffaloes at a single view. At another place they saw such a multitude of the animals crossing the river that the stream for a mile was so filled up they could not proceed until the herd had passed.

The buffaloes formerly ranged free and uninterrupted over the Great Plains of the West, only guided in their course by that faithful instinct which invariably led them to the freshest and sweetest pastures. Their only enemy then was the Indian, who supplied himself with food and clothing from the herds around the door of his lodge, but would have looked upon it as sacrilege to destroy more than barely sufficient to supply the wants of his family. Thus this monarch of the Plains was allowed free range from one extremity of the continent to the other. But this happy state of things was not destined to continue. With the advent of the European an enemy appeared, who made war upon them, and the insatiate slaughter inflicted upon them by this avaricious stranger in a few years produced a very sensible diminution in their numbers, and greatly contracted the limits of their wanderings. This enemy, in his steady advance, also caused the original proprietor of the soil to recede before him, and to diminish in numbers almost as rapidly as the buffalo. Thousands of these animals were annually slaughtered for their skins, and often for their tongues alone; animals whose flesh is sufficient to afford sustenance to a large number of men are sacrificed to furnish a *bon bouche* for the rich epicure. This wholesale slaughter on the part of the white man, with the number consumed by the Indians, who are constantly on their trail, migrating with them as regularly as the season comes round, with the ravenous wolves that are always at hand to destroy one of them if wounded, gives the poor beast but little rest or prospect of permanent existence. It is only fourteen years since the western borders of Texas abounded with buffaloes; but now they seldom go south of Red River, and their range upon the east and west has also very much contracted within the same time, so that they are at present confined to a narrow belt of country between the outer settlements and the Rocky Mountains. With this rapid diminution in their numbers, they must, in the course of a very few years, become exterminated.

In a very interesting paper upon this matter, written by the Hon. H. H. Sibley, of Minnesota, who is himself an excellent sportsman, and perfectly well acquainted with the subject upon which he treats, I find the following:

"The multitudes of these animals (buffaloes) which have hitherto darkened the surface of the great prairies on the west of the 'Father of Waters' are fast wasting away under the fierce assaults made upon them by the white man as well as the savage. From data which, although not mathematically correct, are sufficiently so to enable us to arrive at conclusions approximating the truth, it has been estimated that for each buffalo robe transported from the Indian country at least five animals are destroyed. If it be borne in mind that very few robes are manufactured of the hides of buffalo, except of such as, in hunter's parlance, are killed when they are in season—that is, during the months of November, December, and January, and that even of these a large proportion are not used for that purpose, and also that the skins of cows are principally converted into robes, those of the males being too thick and heavy to be easily reduced by the ordinary process of scraping, together with the fact that many thousands are annually destroyed through sheer wantonness by civilized as well as savage men, it will be found that the foregoing estimate is a moderate one. From the Missouri region, the number of robes received varies from 40,000 to 100,000 per annum, so that from a quarter to half a million of buffalo are destroyed in the period of each twelve months. So enormous a drain must soon result in the extermination of the whole race; and it may be asserted with certainty that in twenty years from this time, the buffalo, if existing at all, will be only found in the wildest recesses of the Rocky Mountains. The savage bands of the West, whose progenitors have from time immemorial depended mainly upon the buffalo, must, with them, disappear from the earth, unless they resort to other means of subsistence, under the fostering care of the general government."

The traveler, in crossing the Plains from Texas or Arkansas, through Southern New Mexico to California, does not, at the present day, encounter the buffalo. Upon the direct route from Fort Leavenworth to Santa Fé they are almost invariably met with between the 99th and 102d meridians of longitude, and they are often seen upon the South Platte, along the road from St. Joseph to Denver and Fort Laramie, in the vicinity of Fort Kearney.

In 1859 I passed across from the Missouri River at Fort Randall to Fort Laramie, a distance of three hundred and sixty miles, over a country that has very seldom been traveled by a white man, and, to my surprise, I did not see a buffalo, and there was no indication of their having been upon the immediate track I followed for three years. They are rapidly disappearing, and a very few years will, at the present rate of destruction, be sufficient to exterminate the species.

There are two methods generally practiced in hunting the buffalo, viz., running them on horseback, and stalking, or still hunting. The first method requires a sure-footed and tolerably fleet horse that is not easily frightened. The buffalo cow, which makes much better beef than the bull, when pursued by the hunter runs rapidly, and, unless the horse be fleet, it requires a long and exhausting chase to overtake her.

When the buffaloes are discovered, and the hunter intends to give chase, he should first dismount, arrange his saddle-blanket and saddle, buckle the girth tight, and make every thing about his horse furniture snug and secure. He should then put his arms in good firing order, and, taking the lee side of the herd, so that they may not get "*the wind*" of him, he should approach in a walk as close as possible, taking advantage of any cover that may offer. His horse then, being cool and fresh, will be able to dash into the herd, and probably carry his rider very near the animal he has selected before he becomes alarmed.

If the hunter be right-handed, and uses a pistol, he should approach upon the left side, and when nearly opposite and close upon the buffalo, deliver his shot, taking aim a little below the centre of the body, and about eight inches back of the shoulder. This will strike the vitals, and generally render another shot unnecessary.

When a rifle or shot-gun is used the hunter rides up on the right side, keeping his horse well in hand, so as to be able to turn off if the beast charges upon him; this, however, never happens except with a buffalo that is wounded, when it is advisable to keep out of his reach.

The buffalo has immense powers of endurance, and will run for many miles without any apparent effort or diminution in speed. The first buffalo I ever saw I followed about ten miles, and when I left him he seemed to run faster than when the chase commenced.

As a long buffalo-chase is very severe labor upon a horse, I would recommend to all travelers, unless they have a good deal of surplus horse-flesh, never to expend it in this sport.

Still hunting, which requires no consumption of horse-flesh, and is equally successful with the other method, is recommended. In stalking on horseback, the most broken and hilly localities should be selected, as these will furnish cover to the hunter, who passes from the crest of one hill to another, examining the country carefully in all directions. When the game is discovered, if it happen to be on the lee side, the hunter should endeavor, by making a wide detour, to get upon the opposite side, as he will find it impossible to approach within rifle range with the wind.

When the animal is upon a hill, or in any other position where he can not be approached without danger of disturbing him, the hunter should wait until he moves off to more favorable ground, and this will not generally require much time, as they wander about a great deal when not grazing; he then pickets his horse, and approaches cautiously, seeking to screen himself as much as possible by the undulations in the surface, or behind such other objects as may present themselves; but if the surface should offer no cover, he must crawl upon his hands and knees when near the game, and in this way he can generally get within rifle range.

Should there be several animals together, and his first shot take effect, the hunter can often get several other shots before they become frightened. A Delaware Indian and myself once killed five buffaloes out of a small herd before the remainder were so much disturbed as to move away. Although we were within the short distance of twenty yards, yet the reports of our rifles did not frighten them in the least, and they continued grazing during all the time we were loading and firing.

The sense of smelling is exceedingly acute with the buffalo, and they will take the wind from the hunter at as great a distance as a mile.

When the animal is wounded, and stops, it is better not to go near him until he lies down, as he will often run a great distance if disturbed; but if left to himself, will in many cases die in a short time.

When buffaloes are grazing upon an open flat prairie where the grass is short, affording no cover, the Indians stalk them by covering themselves with a light-colored blanket, and crawling along the ground on their hands and knees to the leeward of the herd, and at the same time dragging their guns or bows and arrows along with them. If proper caution is used, they are thus enabled to reach the desired proximity, and may even approach directly into the midst of the herds without giving alarm.

It very rarely happens that there is any danger resulting from this method of approach unless the hunter by a careless shot gives an animal a slight flesh-wound, which only tends to irritate him. Instances have occurred under such circumstances when the hunter's life has been exposed to imminent jeopardy. I once knew a case of this kind in which an experienced buffalo-hunter was pursued by a young bull for several hundred yards, and he only effected his escape by passing over an elevated swell in the prairie and hiding in some tall grass which he was so fortunate as to find at this critical juncture. The buffalo, on reaching the top of the eminence, cast a glance around, but, not discovering his adversary, abandoned the pursuit and walked away in another direction.

When a man on foot is pursued by a buffalo, if he will drop some object, such as his coat, hat, or other article of dress, this will often divert the animal's attention, and he will stop and vent his rage upon it, thus giving the hunter time to get out of danger.

When a herd of buffalo is pursued they generally run in a solid mass, keeping close together, but with the cows near the front and inside, so that it is necessary, in order to reach them, to penetrate the dense phalanx of bulls occupying the outside. This may be done by riding along with the herd and gradually inclining toward the centre as openings present themselves; this, however, is a feat attended with some hazard, and should not be attempted by any one without a well-trained and sure-footed horse, as, in the event of being unhorsed, the hunter would inevitably be trampled to pieces under the feet of the buffalo.

It is dangerous to chase a herd of buffalo when they raise such a dust as to make it difficult to see them or to judge accurately of their position.

The hunter should never leave his horse near a herd of buffalo without tying him, as horses will often start off with the buffalo, and are sometimes irretrievably lost in this way. One of our officers, en route to Utah, jumped from his horse, and, leaving him without tying, ran forward to shoot a buffalo, when, much to his astonishment, his horse suddenly took to his heels, joined the fleeing herd with saddle, bridle, and other accoutrements, continued with it far over the prairies out of sight, and has not, I believe, been heard from since.

The tongues, humps, and marrow-bones are regarded as the choice parts of the animal. The tongue is taken out by ripping open the skin between the prongs of the lower jawbone, and pulling it out through the orifice. The hump may be taken off by skinning down on each side of the shoulders and cutting away the meat, after which the hump ribs can be unjointed where they unite with the spine. The marrow, when roasted in the bones, is delicious.

My friend, General Sibley, in the interesting paper before

alluded to, makes some pertinent remarks upon the buffalo chase, from which I take the liberty of quoting the following:

"The chase of the buffalo on horseback is highly exciting, and by no means unattended with danger. The instinct of that animal leads him, when pursued, to select the most broken and difficult ground over which to direct his flight, so that many accidents occur to horse and rider from falls, which result in death, or dislocation of the limbs of one or both. When wounded, or too closely pressed, the buffalo will turn upon his antagonist, and not unfrequently the latter becomes the victim in the conflict, meeting his death upon the sharp horns of an infuriated bull.

"In common with the moose, the elk, and others of the same family, Nature has furnished the buffalo with exquisite powers of scent, upon which he principally relies for warning against danger. The inexperienced voyager will often be surprised to perceive the dense masses of these cattle urging their rapid flight across the prairie, at a distance of two or three miles, without any apparent cause of alarm, unaware, as he is, of the fact that the tainted breeze has betrayed to them his presence while still far away.

"The bow and arrow, in experienced hands, constitute quite as efficient a weapon in the chase of the buffalo as the fire-arm, from the greater rapidity with which the discharges are made, and the almost equal certainty of execution. The force with which an arrow is propelled from a bow, wielded by an Indian of far less than the ordinary physical strength of white men, is amazing. It is generally imbedded to the feather in the buffalo, and sometimes even protrudes on the opposite side. It is reported among the Dacotahs or Sioux Indians, and generally credited by them, that one of their chiefs, Wah-na-tah by name, who was remarkable, up to the close of his life, for strength and activity of frame, and who was equally renowned as a hunter and warrior, on one occasion discharged an arrow with sufficient force entirely to traverse the body of a female buffalo, and to kill the calf by her side. For the accuracy of this statement I do not, of course, pretend to vouch. The arrow is launched from the bow while the body of the victim is elongated in making his forward spring, and the ribs, being then separated from each other as far as possible, allow an easy entrance to the missile between them.

"The same instant is taken advantage of by such of the Western Indians as make use of long lances wherewith to destroy the buffalo. Approaching sufficiently near to the particular cow he has selected for his prey, the hunter allows the weapon to descend and rest upon her back, which causes her at first to make violent efforts to dislodge it. After a few trials the poor beast becomes accustomed to the touch, and ceases farther to notice it in her great anxiety to escape from her pursuer, who then, by a dexterous and powerful thrust, sheathes the long and sharp blade into her vitals, and withdraws it before the animal falls to the ground. This mode of slaughter is successful only with those who have fleet and well-trained horses, and who have perfect reliance upon their own coolness and skill.

"When the alternate thawing and freezing during the winter months have formed a thick crust upon the deep snows of the far Northwest, the buffalo falls an easy victim to the Indian, who glides rapidly over the surface upon his snow-shoes, while the former finds his powers of locomotion almost paralyzed by the breaking of the icy crust beneath his ponderous weight. He can then be approached with absolute impunity, and dispatched with the gun, the arrow, or the lance.

"It sometimes happens that a whole herd is surrounded and driven upon the clear ice of a lake, in which case they spread out and fall powerless, to be mercilessly massacred by their savage pursuers. It is a well-known fact that, several years since, nearly a hundred buffaloes attempted to cross *Lac qui Parle*, in Minnesota, upon the ice, which, not being sufficiently strong to bear so enormous a pressure, gave way, and the whole number miserably perished. The meat furnished a supply of food for many weeks to the people at the neighboring trading-post, as well as to the Indians, and to the wolves and foxes.

"In the northern part of Minnesota, on both sides of the line dividing the United States from the British Possessions, there is to be found a large population, consisting mostly of mixed bloods. These men possess, in an eminent degree, the physical energy and powers of endurance of the white man, combined with the activity, subtlety, and skill in hunting of the Indian. They are fine horsemen, and remarkably dexterous in the chase of the buffalo. Half farmer and half hunter, they till the ground, and raise fine crops of wheat and other cereals, while semi-annually they repair to the buffalo region to procure meat, which they cure in divers ways, and dispose of to our own citizens, and to the Hudson Bay Company for the supply of their inland trading-posts. Being numerous, and well supplied with horses, oxen, and carts, the number of buffaloes annually slaughtered by them is astonishing."

It has been thought by many persons that the buffalo would cross with the domestic cattle, and I have several times seen domestic animals upon the frontier which were said to have been hybrids of the two species of the Bos family, but I am very firm in the belief that there are no properly authenticated instances where these animals have bred together. A trader among the Chickasaws collected about forty buffalo some years since, and, although they were herded with his domestic cattle for two years, he informed me that they never crossed.

THE BEAVER.

I know of no animal concerning which the accounts of travelers have been more extraordinary, more marvelous or contradictory, than those given of the beaver.

By some he has been elevated in point of intellect almost to a level with man. He has been said, for instance, to construct houses with several floors and rooms; to plaster the rooms with mud in such a manner as to make smooth walls, and to drive stakes of six or eight inches in diameter into the ground, and to perform many other astounding feats, which I am induced to believe are not supported by credible testimony.

Laying aside these questionable statements, there is quite sufficient in the true natural history of the animal to excite our wonder and admiration.

On the 12th of June, 1852, I encamped upon a small tributary of the North Fork of Red River, near where a community of beavers had just completed the construction of a new dam.

Upon an examination of their works, we were both astonished and delighted at the wonderful sagacity, skill, and perseverance which they displayed.

In the selection of a suitable site, and in the erection of the structure, they appeared to have been guided by something more than mere animal instinct, and exhibited as correct a knowledge of hydrostatics, and the action of forces resulting from currents of water, as the most scientific millwright would have done.

Having chosen a spot where the creek was narrow, and the banks on each side sufficiently high to raise a head of about five feet, they selected two cottonwood-trees some fifteen inches in diameter, situated above this point, and having an inclination toward the stream; these they cut down with their teeth (as the marks upon the stumps plainly showed), and, floating them down to the position for the dam, they were placed across the stream with an inclination downward, the butt ends uniting in the centre. These constituted the foundation upon which the superstructure of brush and earth was placed, in precisely the same manner as a brush dam is built by our millwrights, with the bushes and earth alternating and packed closely, the butts in all cases turned down the stream.

After this was raised to a sufficient height, the top was covered with earth except in the centre, where there was a sluice or waste-wier to let off the superfluous water when the creek rose so high as to endanger the structure. In examining the results of the operations of these ingenious quadrupeds, it occurred to me that the plan of constructing our brush dams may have been originally suggested by witnessing those made by the beavers, as they are so very much alike.

I observed at one place above the pond where they had commenced another dam, and had progressed so far as to cut down two trees on opposite sides of the creek; but as they did not fall in the right direction to suit their purposes, the work was abandoned.

During the month of April, 1858, I found upon one of the head branches of the South Platte River, in the mountains near Pike's Peak, a place where the beavers had dammed the creek for three miles in such a manner as to form a continuous succession of ponds or slack-water for the entire distance. There were a large number of dams, and all in good repair, which, with the stumps of the freshly-cut willows, showed conclusively that there were an immense number of the animals there; yet, although we were upon the creek for several hours, we did not see one of them. They are exceedingly timid and shy, and at the slightest noise take alarm and hide themselves in their houses, the entrance to which are hidden beneath the surface of the water.

The only way they can be seen is to lay concealed and quiet near their dams about sunset, when they will come out to work or play, and in this manner they are often killed by the hunters.

A friend of mine related to me an amusing incident connected with a pet beaver which he had caught when he was quite young, and raised.

He was in the habit of leaving him in his cabin, with the door fastened, while he visited his traps.

Upon one of these occasions, he found on his return that the beaver had accidentally upset the water-bucket, and, seeing the stream running down the floor, he had attempted to make a dam to stop it. All the tables, benches, blankets, skins, and every thing else movable in the cabin had been piled across the floor in the vain effort of the animal to prevent the escape of his favorite element.

PRAIRIE DOG.

This interesting and gregarious little specimen of the mammalia of our country is indigenous to the most of our far Western prairies, from Mexico to the northern limits of our possessions, and has often been described by those who have traveled on the Plains; but as there are some facts in relation to their habits that I have never seen mentioned in any published account of them, I trust I shall be pardoned if I add a few remarks to what has already been said.

In the selection of a site or position for their towns, they appear to have special reference to their food, which is a species of short, wiry grass, and a variety of cactus growing upon the Plains, where there is often no water near; indeed, I have sometimes seen their towns upon the elevated table-lands of New Mexico, where there was no water upon the surface of the ground within twenty miles, and where it could not probably have been found by excavating a hundred feet. This fact has induced me to believe that they do not require that element, without which most other animals perish in a short time.

As there are generally no rains or dews during the summer months where these dog communities are found, and as the animals never wander far from home, I think I am warranted in coming to the conclusion that they require no water beyond what the grass affords. That they hibernate, passing the winter in a lethargic or torpid state, is evident from the fact that they lay up no sustenance for the winter, and that the grass in the vicinity of their burrows dries up in the autumn; the earth freezes hard, and renders it utterly impossible for them to procure food in the usual manner.

When the prairie dog first feels the approach of the sleeping season (generally about the last days of October), he closes all the passages to his dormitory, to exclude the cold air, and betakes himself to his brumal slumber with the greatest possible regularity and care. He remains housed until the warm days of spring, when he removes the obstructions from his door, and again appears above ground as lively and frolicsome as ever. I have been informed by the Indians that a short time before a cold storm in the autumn all the prairie dogs may be seen industriously occupied with weeds and earth closing the entrances to their burrows. They are sometimes, however, observed reopening them while the weather is still cold and stormy, but mild and pleasant weather is always certain to follow. It appears, therefore, that instinct teaches the little quadruped when to expect good or bad weather, and to make his arrangements accordingly.

In passing through their villages the traveler is often obliged to turn out of his course to avoid the mounds of earth thrown up around their holes. The animals are seen in countless numbers sitting upright at the mouths of their domicils, and presenting in the distance very much the appearance of the stumps of small trees; and so incessant is the clatter of their barking, that it requires but little effort of the imagination to fancy one's self surrounded by the busy hum of a city.

The immense numbers of these animals in some of these towns or warrens may be conjectured from the large area which they cover.

One near the head of Red River which we passed was about thirty miles long. Supposing its dimensions in other directions to have been the same, it would have embraced a space of six hundred and twenty-five square miles, or eight hundred and ninety-six thousand acres. Estimating the burrows to have been twenty yards apart, and each family containing four or five dogs, the aggregate population would have excelled in numbers any city of the universe.

A species of small owl, about the size of a quail, is frequently found in the mouths of the burrows occupied by the dogs, whether for the purpose of procuring food, or for some other object, I do not know. They do not, however, as some have asserted, burrow with the dogs; and when approached, instead of entering the holes, they invariably fly away.

It has also been said that the rattlesnake is a constant companion of the prairie dog; but this is a mistake, for I have sometimes passed for days through their towns without seeing one. They are, however, often met with in the burrows with the dogs, and for this reason it has been supposed by some that they were welcome guests with the proprietors of the establishments; but we have satisfied ourselves that this is a domestic arrangement entirely at variance with the wishes of the dogs, as the snakes prey upon them, and consequently must be considered as intruders. One snake which we killed was found to have swallowed a full-grown dog.

When the prairie dog is full grown he is of a light brown color, about the size of a gray rabbit, with a bushy tail some four inches long, and shaped very much like a young bull pup.

HINTS TO SPORTSMEN.

To those persons who are desirous of participating in the exciting amusement of a buffalo chase, and doubtless there are many such, a few words in regard to the most comfortable and expeditious routes for reaching the localities where the animals can with certainty be met with will not be amiss in this connection. I have known several English sportsmen who crossed the Atlantic for no other purpose but that of enjoying the pleasures of a buffalo hunt, who, on their arrival, seemed to be impressed with the idea that the best, if not, indeed, the only route to the hunting-grounds was by St. Paul, and thence to the Red River of the North. This is a very erroneous notion, as it is seldom that buffalo are found within four or five hundred miles of St. Paul; besides, in the section of country west of Red River, the ranges of the buffalo are so variable and uncertain that it is seldom they can be found two consecutive seasons in the same eastern localities, the courses taken by the herds from year to year depending in a great measure on the way they are driven by the Indians, and upon other circumstances contingent upon grass, water, etc., which are without the scope of anticipation or previous calculation. This, however, is not the case in the direction of New Mexico and Colorado, where the ranges are more uniform and reliable.

A party leaving New York City can by rail reach the Missouri River at St. Joseph or Atcheson in less than three days, and from thence the overland stages will, in three or four days more, carry them with absolute certainty near the buffalo on either the Fort Kearney or Fort Riley routes. At these forts the most accessible hunting localities can be ascertained, and some of the officers, or other persons who are acquainted with the country, will generally be found ready to join the hunt.

Should the aspirations of any of our Eastern sportsmen induce them to venture an encounter with the grizzly bear, they will, unless they go to the Pacific or ascend the Missouri River very high, be obliged to travel a long distance over the Plains in order to accomplish the object. In 1858 these animals were abundant about the head waters of the Arkansas and Platte Rivers, and they were often seen in the vicinity of Pike's Peak and the present site of Denver City; but as that country has been so much frequented and settled since I visited it, I doubt if many are left there at the present time. The Black Hills, in the neighborhood of Fort Laramie, I should regard as the most likely place for finding the animal now.

From the Missouri River at Atcheson or Leavenworth to Fort Laramie is about seven hundred miles, but the road is excellent, and the grass, wood, and water are abundant upon the entire route. While the Indians remain hostile it would not, of course, be safe for a small party to venture into that section for pleasure; but, after the Indian difficulties are terminated, I know of no summer excursion that would be more delightful or conducive to health than for a party of gentlemen, who are fond of shooting and excitement, to start out from the Missouri River with their own transportation and camping arrangements, passing through the buffalo range south of Fort Kearney, and along the North Platte River to the Black Hills, thence turning south, skirting the eastern base of the mountains, crossing the head waters of the Laramie and other branches of the Platte River, and through the Parks to Denver City; returning home by the Arkansas or the Republican Fork of the Kansas, upon either of which routes buffalo are always found. Nothing can be imagined more pure, elastic, and invigorating than the summer atmosphere in the country that would be traversed in this way. The climate of the plains and the mountains is of so salubrious a character, that invalids, whose healths have been seriously impaired by sedentary occupations in the damp, changeable, and foul atmosphere of our crowded cities, often derive great benefit from it, and are rapidly restored to perfect health. Several cases of this character have come under my own observation, one of which was a gentleman of New York City, who had for several years been suffering from a complication of complaints that kept him almost continually in the hands of the physicians, without any apparent prospect of restoration to health. He accompanied me for four months upon the Plains, and returned home entirely free from disease, and has been hale, hearty, and robust ever since. He has "thrown physic to the dogs," and the doctors have lost one of their very best patrons.

Besides the grizzly bears that would be found upon the route I have indicated, elk, black-tailed deer, antelope, and occasionally mountain sheep will be met with in the vicinity of the mountains.

The most favorable season of the year for leaving the Missouri River is about the middle of May. The grass then affords good pasturage for animals, the roads are dry and firm, and the temperature is mild and agreeable.

An outfit of wagons, teams, and other requisites for the expedition can be procured at reasonable rates at St. Joseph, Atcheson, Leavenworth City, and at other points of departure on the Missouri River. A guide who knows the country is indispensable, especially after reaching the mountains, and one such can generally be found at the places mentioned.

CHAPTER XII.

PIONEERS OF THE WEST.

Pioneers of the West.—Frontier Settlers.—Night at a Log Cabin.—Effects of drinking Mint Juleps.—A young Cadet's Arrival at West Point.—Prairie Belle.—Texas Surveyor.—Dinner in Arkansas.—Night in Arkansas.—New Use of Tea.—Yankee Curiosity illustrated.—Propensity for roaming.—Meeting a Fellow-statesman in Mexico.—An old Acquaintance.—Southern Curiosity.—Virginia Hospitality.—Perversion of the English Language.—Arrival in the Settlements in 1849.—A Texas Clergyman's Experience.—Frontier Settlers of Texas.—Major Neighbors's Experience.—The Six-man Team.—Texas Volunteers.—Recuperative Character of the Frontiersman illustrated.

THE object I have in view in the following pages is to contribute something, in as attractive and reliable a form as I am able, to perpetuate the true characteristics of the frontiersman, the greater part of which I have obtained from long personal intercourse and observation. My sketches may perhaps be regarded as crude and unfinished, but, so far as they extend, they may be relied on as faithful representations of real existing specimens, and without any coloring of romance.

It may be thought by some that I am endowed with a more vivid conception of the ludicrous and mirthful than is desirable in the character of a historian or a biographer; indeed, I am rather inclined to this opinion myself. The farcical always possessed far greater attractions for me than the tragic; in fact, I may say that tragedy is my abhorrence. I seldom read the newspaper accounts of horrible murders; and when I visit a theatre, it is not for the purpose of getting my feelings wrought up to the crying pitch, but I go there for the express object of indulging in a good hearty laugh. The ordinary every-day affairs of life have enough commingling of tragedy to answer my aspirations, without the necessity of paying for a box in which to undergo three hours' agony and torture from listening to a mock representation of it. Let it not, therefore, surprise the reader if he should find that in the following illustrations I have drawn largely from the comic elements in the characters of the classes represented.

FRONTIER SETTLERS.

The ideas, habits, and language of the population upon the borders of Arkansas and Texas are eminently peculiar, and very different from those of any other people I have ever before met with in my travels; they seem to constitute an anomalous and detached element in our social structure. Their sparsely scattered forest habitations, being far removed from towns or villages, and seldom visited by travelers, almost entirely exclude them from intercourse with the civilized world, and they are nearly as ignorant of what is transpiring outside their own immediate sphere as the savages themselves. They seldom or never see a newspaper, and could not read it if they did; and I honestly believe that many of them could not tell whether General Jackson, Mr. Lincoln, or Mr. Johnson is President of the United States at the present time.

Some of the most salient traits in the character of this singular type of the Anglo-Saxon race have been exhibited in a conspicuous light among the specimens I have encountered upon the frontier, and I now propose to introduce some of them to the notice of the reader.

I remember, upon one occasion, after riding all day through a dense forest region in Northwestern Texas, in the winter of 1850–1; without the slightest indication of a road or even trail to guide me, and during a severe storm of snow and rain, and without having met with a single human being during the entire day, that I suddenly came out into a small clearing, in the centre of which was a very diminutive log cabin, from whence arose a cheerful smoke, indicating the presence of occupants. This was a very pleasant surprise to me, as I had confidently calculated on being obliged to bivouac for the night alone in the woods, and this, during such a cold storm, would have been any thing but agreeable. I therefore gladly turned my jaded horse toward the hut, and, on my approach, a woman, some half a dozen children, and about as many dogs emerged therefrom.

After passing the customary salutations of the country, and exchanging particular inquiries as to the past and present condition of each other's health, I begged to inquire if I could be accommodated with lodgings for the night, to which the woman very obligingly replied, "Wall, now, stranger, my ole man he ar out on a bar track, but I sort-o-reckon maybe you mought git to stay;" she, however, for my consideration, added "that thar war narry show of vittles in the house barrin some sweet taters and a small chance of corn." As I was very hungry, and did not feel disposed to put up with such meagre fare, I dismounted, tied my horse, took my rifle, and went out into the woods in quest of something more substantial for supper, and fortunately had not gone far before I succeeded in killing a deer, which I *packed* to the house, and, by the aid of my "*couteau de chasse*," soon had nicely dressed. My hostess and the children seemed highly delighted at my success, as they had seen no meat for several days, and the old lady complimented me by asking "what my name mought be;" and upon my informing her that it was Marcy, she said "she knowd a heap o' Massys down in ole *Massasip*," and that "me an him (Davy, her husband) allers 'lowed that them thar Massys was considdible on bar and other varmints." She then told me, if I would grind some corn in a coffee-mill which was fastened against the corner of the house, that she would bake a poen for me. Accordingly, I set to work, and, after about half an hour's steady application, succeeded in producing from the rickety old machine about a quart of meal, which was speedily converted into a cake. This, with some of the ribs of the fat venison well roasted, and a cup of good coffee produced from my saddle-bags, made a most substantial and excellent supper. After this was over I lighted my pipe, and, seating myself before the cheerful log fire, for the first time since my arrival took a survey of the establishment.

It consisted of one room about fourteen feet square, with the intervals between the logs not *chinked*, and wide enough in places to allow the dogs to pass in and out at their pleasure. There was an opening for the door, which was closed with a greasy old beef's hide, but there were no windows, and no floor excepting the native earth. The household furniture consisted of two small benches of the most primitive construction imaginable, and two bedsteads, each made by driving four forked stakes into the ground, across which poles were placed, and then covered transversely by flour-barrel staves, the whole structure surmounted by a sack of prairie hay, upon which I observed the remains of an antiquated coverlid that had evidently seen much service. The table furniture consisted of one tin milk-pan, three tin cups, two knives and three forks, two of the latter having but one prong each. The *tout ensemble* gave every indication of the most abject destitution and poverty; indeed, the hostess informed me that she had not, previous to my arrival, tasted sugar, tea, or coffee for three months; yet, as strange as it may appear, she seemed entirely contented with her situation, and considered herself about as well to do in the world as the most of her neighbors. She had emigrated to this remote and solitary spot from Mississippi about two years previously, and not the slightest trace of a road or trail had since been made leading to the locality from any direction, and she informed me that her nearest neighbor was some fifteen miles distant.

Upon her remarking that her husband was occasionally absent for several days at a time, I inquired if she was not afraid to stay alone in this wild, out-of-the-way place. She said "No; that when Davy was away the dogs kept the varmints off, and that mighty few humans ever com'd that-a-way."

After finishing my pipe, and getting my clothes well dried, and feeling quite fatigued and sleepy, I asked the woman where I should sleep. She replied, "Stranger, you take that thar bed with the boys, and I'll take this yere with the gals."

Now the width of the bed indicated for my use was measured with a flour-barrel stave, and was already occupied by three boys, two on the back side and one at the foot. It therefore became a question of some considerable interest to me as to how I should manage to stow myself away in such contracted quarters, especially in view of the fact that my longitudinal meridian was some twelve inches greater than the space allotted me. Nevertheless, as I was not very exclusive or particular in my notions, I turned in, and for some time tried to sleep, but my position between the three bedfellows was so much cramped and distorted that I found it impossible to get any repose. I did not, however, like the idea of disturbing the boys, but the case seemed to me a desperate one: I must have some sleep, and the only alternative, under the circumstances, was to make the effort to secure a greater area; I therefore very quietly administered a pinch upon my nearest juvenile neighbor, who was sound asleep, which caused him to scream most lustily. His mother, probably thinking that he was dreaming, or suddenly taken with the nightmare, called out from the other bed, "Now, Dave, ef yer don't get shut o' that thar yellin, yer'l wake up the stranger." This admonition quieted him for a while, but as soon as he was asleep again I gave him another sharp pinch, which made him cry out more vociferously than before, while at the same time I was exerting my utmost efforts in giving a good imitation of the loftiest pitch of snoring. The mother then got up, came to our bed, and shaking the boy, told him "ef he didn't dry up that hollerin she woodn't 'low him to sleep 'long with the stranger no more, no how." Another well-timed and vigorous pinch, as soon as he had fallen asleep the third time, accomplished my object. He was taken up; but, as his mother was lifting the pugnacious young gentleman out of the bed, he had become so fully sensible of what was passing that he began to suspect I had something to do with his disturbance, and hit me quite a severe blow in the side with his hard little fist. I, however, after this episode, slept soundly till morning.

Before I left the house my hostess inquired of me if I knew how to write; and, upon learning that my education had extended that far, she desired me to act as her amanuensis, while she dictated a letter to a friend "way down in ole Massasip." Having a pencil and some old letters in my pocket, I told her I would take down what she desired to communicate, copy it in ink on my return to the fort, and send it for her through the post, which seemed to give her great pleasure; whereupon I seated myself, and asked her what she wished me to write. She said:

"Tell um, stranger, thar's narry fever-n'agur down this-a-way."

"Very well," I said, "that is down; what shall I say next?"

"Tell um, stranger, Davy he raised a powerful heap o' corn and taters this year."

"Yes," I said; "what next?"

"Tell um, stranger, thar's a mighty smart chance o' varmints in these yere diggins."

And thus she went on throughout the entire letter, which she "'lowed was a peart hand write." I transcribed it literally in her own words on my return home, and forwarded it to its destination in Mississippi, and I sincerely hope the good woman has received an answer ere this.

While marching a battalion of my regiment from Little Rock to Fort Towson during a very warm day in the autumn of 1848, I made a halt at a respectable-looking farmhouse near the Choctaw line in Arkansas, and, seeing a woman sitting out upon the portico, I rode up for the purpose of making some inquiries regarding the roads. She returned my salutation, and very politely invited me to "'light and have a char." I dismounted, took the chair, and complimented the good woman upon the neat and comfortable appearance of her surroundings. She said "it was tollible far, considerin they had com'd thar and commenced deadnin the trees and maulin the rails only five years afore." I should have imagined, however, from the very limited extent of her knowledge of the surrounding country, that she had but just arrived, or that she had been hibernating during the five years mentioned. As our road forked near the house, I asked her which of the two would lead us to a small town on our route about ten miles distant. She replied that "she didn't adzactly mind, but she sort'r reckon'd her nigger gal mought tell me;" whereupon she called out in a loud, shrill voice, "*O-o-o-oh* Gerushe!" but, as the servant did not respond, she said,

"Whar is that nigger?" and again cried out, in a still louder and more prolonged tone of voice, "O—o—o—o—o—oh Gerushe!!!" but the strength of her lungs seemed to have been so nearly expended in the effort of giving proper emphasis to the letter *O*, that the name of the servant was called in a quick, faint, and barely audible voice. The last call had the desired effect, and soon a venerable negress, at least seventy years old, and who struck me as being pretty well advanced for a "gal," approached, and, after dropping a polite courtesy to me, asked what she could do for "missus." The latter, in a sharp, petulant, but exhausted tone, indicating that the previous effort to rouse her sable domestic had been rather too much for her, said, "You lazy, no 'count nigger, you gess tell this yere stranger whar these yere roads goes to, right quick, do ye hear?" Gerushe very promptly replied, "Wall, mass'r, I 'specs I'ze guine to tell you all about it: Mass'r Jeemes he 'lowed this yere left-hand one he guine down to Wash-un-tum, and that thar t'other one he guine to Choctaw na-shum." I then asked the woman of the house the distance to the nearest post-office, but of this she had not the remotest idea, and again referred me to the servant, who at once gave me the information. Several other inquiries which I made of the mistress of the house only served to exhibit her ignorance of and indifference to every thing that was transpiring around her. She almost invariably appealed for information to her antiquated African "gal," who seemed to be much better posted than her mistress; indeed, she appeared to be her sense-bearer, performing not only her physical drudgery, but also her mental functions.

During the course of our conversation the proprietor of the establishment, a stalwart, leather-stocking specimen of a backwoodsman, came home, leading his horse, with a deer packed upon each side, followed by several dogs, and carrying a huge rifle across his shoulder. I congratulated him upon his success in hunting, and observed that the deer must be abundant in that neighborhood. On the contrary, he said they were getting very scarce; that when he first arrived in that section "thar war right smart o' deer; they war numerous then," he said; but, although he had been out in the woods all the morning, he had only killed three, besides "bustin" two caps at another which he did not get.

He then commenced the following dialogue:

"Ar you gwine fur to jine ole Zack down in Mexico?"

"No, sir, the Mexican war is ended, and we are now *en route* for the Choctaw nation."

"Whar did ye come from, stranger?"

"We came last from Pascagoula."

"Mought you be the boss hossifer of that thar army?" pointing to the men.

"I am the commanding officer of that detachment, sir."

"Wall, Mr. Hossifer, be them sure 'nuff sogers, or is they make b'lieve chaps, like I seen down to Orleans?"

"They have passed through the Mexican war, and I trust they have proved themselves not only worthy the appellation of real, genuine soldiers, but of veterans, sir."

"Now I gest want to know one thing more, boss; be them chaps reg-lars, or be they melish?"

"I assure you that they belong to the regular army of the United States."

Then, pointing to my uniform, he added, "Apperiently, then, fightin's your trade?"

"I adopted the profession of arms at an early age," I replied.

"War you at the Orleans fight, whar our boys gin sich particlar fits to ole Pack?" (Packenham I suppose he meant).

I answered that, though a pretty old soldier, my commission did not date quite so far back as 1814.

"Wall, ole boss, you moughtn't a been thar, but you ain't no chicken now, sure." He continued: "One time me an him, Ike Thompson, we went on a sogerin spree."

"Ah! indeed; in what place did you serve, pray?"

"In severial places; but the last pop we fout at the battle of the Hoss-shoe, whar we and ole Hickry cleaned out the Ingines."

"That was a most decisive and sanguinary battle," I observed.

"I calkerlate, Mr. Hossifer, that war the most *de*-cisivest and the most san-*guin*-ariest fight you ever seen in all yer born days. We boys, we up and pitched in thar, and we gin the yaller-bellies the most *parr*-ticlar hail Columby. We chawed um all up; we laid um out cold'r nur a wedge; we *saved* every mother's son of um—we did that thar little thing, boss."

I replied that I had no doubt very many of the Indians were killed, but that I had always been under the impression that some of them made their escape; and, in fact, I was very confident that several Creek Indians were then living upon the Canadian River who participated in the battle of the Horse-shoe. He said he "rayther reckon'd not;" but, at all events, he was quite certain "ef any of the dogond varmints did git away, they war d—d badly wounded, sartin sure."

He then produced a bottle of whisky, and gave me a pressing invitation "to liquor," remarking that "he war not too proud to take a horn with a fellur-soger, even if he war a reg-lar."

After having taken the drink, he approached me, and in a serious tone said, "Thar's narry paper tuck in this yere settle-*ment*, but I hearn tell that Gin-ral Jackson ar dead; maybe you mought heer'd some talk 'bout it as you com'd 'long the road, stranger?"

I answered that I had not the slightest doubt of the fact, and that, in my opinion, it was very generally believed throughout the United States that the general had died at the Hermitage as long ago as 1845.

Quite an amusing incident was related to me as having occurred in Washington County, Arkansas, during the early settlement of that section of the state; and, although I can not vouch for its perfect authenticity, yet, as it is eminently characteristic of the habits of the people who inhabited that country when I first visited there, and as it also illustrates a prominent feature in the customs of the Virginians, I venture to relate it, even if not wholly new.

It appeared that a traveler from the Old Dominion, while *en route* for Texas, stopped at a house in Western Arkansas for the purpose of feeding his horse, and obtaining some rest and refreshment for himself after a hard ride in a hot summer's day. On entering the hospitable farm-house, he was politely invited to take a seat, and shortly afterward a jug of whisky was produced, and he was solicited by the proprietor to join him in a social glass. He most cheerfully complied with the request, but found the liquor of very inferior quality and exceedingly unpalatable. On receiving an invitation to take a second glass, he intimated that he was very fond of mint juleps, and, if there were no particular objections, he would prefer to take the next drink in that form. His host, it appeared, had never before heard of the mixture, but expressed a perfect willingness to be inducted into the mystery of compounding it; whereupon the gentleman from the Old Dominion stepped out into the inclosure in front of the house, picked some fresh mint from a large patch growing there, and with cold water direct from the spring, and some brown sugar, he soon manufactured two juleps, which, although not quite equal, perhaps, to those that can be obtained in some of the luxurious saloons of our large cities, yet were far from being unpalatable to a thirsty traveler, and certainly were a very great improvement upon the "*bald face*" in its crude, native state.

The Arkansian pronounced it excellent, and very soon called upon his guest to concoct another, which he considered still better than the first, and before they parted quite a number of the fascinating compounds had been imbibed, and the host had learned the secret of manufacturing them.

The Virginian continued on his journey toward Texas, and in due course of time set out to return. On arriving at the house before-mentioned, he concluded he would call and renew his acquaintance with his friendly old host. Accordingly, he rode up to the gate, and seeing one of the boys of the family standing near, asked him, "How is the old gentleman, your father, my son?"

The boy, with an air of the most perfect indifference, replied, "Why, the ole man's dead, stranger."

"Is it possible? How long since?"

"About two weeks, stranger."

"Ah, indeed! Pray what was the matter with the poor old gentleman, my son?"

"Waal, now, stranger, I'll tell ye what it war. Thar war an old fellar from Virgine, he com'd along this way last summer, and he jist ups and larns the ole man to drink greens in his licker, and you can bet your life on't it knocked him higher nor a kite!"

Upon the Virginian's suggesting to the boy that it might have been possible the bad quality of the whisky exercised a more deleterious influence upon his father's health than the mint, he replied,

"No, stranger, it war not the whisky, for we've allers used licker in our family, and though it made old mom powerful weak, yet it never phazed ole pop arry time—no, it war the greens, as sure as yer born."

As the Virginian had not been recognized by the young man, and did not feel disposed to incur the responsibility of having recommended the introduction of such a fatal ingredient into the family beverage, he went on his way, if not a better, certainly a wiser man than before.

Among the characteristics of the people of the United States, I know of no custom which exhibits a more marked contrast in their habits and those of their cousins on the other side of the Atlantic than that of the interchange of civilities over the social glass. Whenever friends meet, in this country, at a private house or a hotel, it is seldom that they separate without "renewing the assurances" of their mutual esteem by taking a drink together; and if they are on the "temperance list," they take a glass of beer, lemonade, or any thing else that suits their inclinations, but the person extending the invitation always expects to pay the bill. This practice is especially prevalent in the Southwestern States; and in some places, if a man takes a drink at the bar of an inn, and does not invite all those around to join him, even though they may be strangers to him, he is looked upon with contempt.

An acquaintance of mine, living in the Cherokee country, once visited Little Rock, and stopped at the Anthony House. Feeling fatigued and thirsty after a hard ride, he, on entering the hotel, went to the bar and called for a glass of liquor, when, to his astonishment, he said, "Fourteen men who were sitting around stepped up and 'lowed they'd take sugar in thar'n!" He paid for the fifteen drinks, as it was in strict conformity with the customs of the country, but he did not visit the bar again.

As is well understood, the corps of cadets of the Military Academy at West Point is composed of young men who are appointed from all sections of the United States, and occasionally may be seen among them frontier youths who, on their first arrival, have seen but little of the world, and are exceedingly primitive and unsophisticated.

I remember very well, while I was at the institution, that a young man from the remote Western borders, near the Cherokee nation, who had never in his life been over a few miles from home, received a letter of appointment to the Military Academy through the representative from his Congressional district.

His father furnished him with a horse, saddle, and bridle, and with his slender wardrobe packed in a capacious pair of saddle-bags, he set out on his long journey for West Point. After many days' hard riding (there were no railroads then) he at length arrived in Jersey City, where, after selling his horse, he took his saddle-bags on his arm, and, crossing the ferry, entered New York, with the intention of "*putting up*" at the first respectable tavern he could find.

He passed up Courtlandt Street and Broadway with his eyes continually searching for the sign-post and swinging sign which he supposed to be the universal evidence of a tavern throughout the civilized world, but his search was in vain. He found nothing but one vast conglomeration of stores, shops, and private houses; not a single tavern did he meet with. Finally, after becoming considerably fatigued in wandering about the streets, he discovered the sign of an oyster saloon, and, as he had never before had an opportunity of testing the merits of the bivalves, he entered the establishment, and, putting down his saddle-bags, informed the waiter that "he didn't mind if he tuck a few of them ar oysters hisself;" and in answer to the inquiry of how many he desired to have, said "he reckon'd about half a peck." They were accordingly set before him raw, "on the half-shell." He did not at all fancy their appearance; yet, as he observed persons all around him devouring them with much apparent relish, he selected one of the largest, and, after scrutinizing it very attentively for a moment, put it in his mouth; but no sooner had it come in contact with his palate than it was ejected, with intense disgust, half way across the room; at the same time he called out to the waiter, "Look a yere, mister, take off these yere nasty varmints, and bring me some bacon and eggs."

Soon after this he delivered a letter of introduction, with which he had been provided, to a gentleman in the city, who kindly showed him to a hotel, and assisted him in purchasing a trunk and a suitable wardrobe; and on the following morning he took the steamer for his destination, and, in due course of time, was landed upon the wharf at West Point.

Now his letter of appointment required him to report in person to the superintendent, Colonel Thayer, who was a very refined, courteous, and dignified gentleman, but, at the same time, he was exceedingly rigid in enforcing the strictest discipline, and the highest respect for rank and military authority. My young friend, after ascertaining where the colonel's quarters were situated, shouldered his trunk (he was then about six feet high, and powerfully developed), and staggered under its weight up the steep hill to the superintendent's house, put down his trunk upon the steps, and was at once admitted into the colonel's presence.

Unlike most of the cadets on their first introduction to this dignitary, he was not in the slightest degree abashed, but felt entirely self-possessed, and, taking a chair close to the colonel, and looking him attentively in the face, said, "Ole man, ar you Colonel, or Captain, or whatever-you-call-um Thayer?" To which the old gentleman very gravely replied, "I am Colonel Thayer, sir." "Wall, now, look-a-yere, *Kurn*," said the youth, "this yere hill o' yourn *am* a breather; ef it ain't, d—n me."

The colonel soon comprehended what kind of a specimen

of humanity he had before him, and directed his orderly to show him to the barracks, where he was soon inducted into the mysteries of wholesome discipline.

As it may be a matter of curiosity with some to know what success this untutored youth of the forest met with in his academical career, I add, for their information, that he applied himself zealously to his studies, attained a good standing in his class, and, on graduating, was an accomplished gentleman and scholar, who reflected credit upon the institution, and was afterward favorably known as the author of a History of Texas.

A PRAIRIE BELLE.

As I was returning from the Plains, after having explored the Brazos River to its sources in 1854, I met, near the most remote frontier house, three girls, who were accompanied by a young man, who were picking wild grapes beside the road. We learned from them that they lived but a short distance in advance, and that there was a very fine spring, with good camping-ground, near their house, and we resolved to halt there for the night.

As we had a vacant seat in our wagon, and as the party were on foot, I inquired if one of the young ladies would not like to ride with us to the house. One of them assenting, my companion, a New York gentleman, very politely extended his hand to assist her; but, instead of accepting it, she made a sudden leap from the ground over the side of the vehicle, and landed directly by his side. This extraordinary acrobatic feat of agility, which would have done credit to the Ravel family, or any other professional artistes, took us by surprise, and as we proceeded toward the house we entered into conversation with her, and were greatly diverted by the originality of her ideas, and the perfect freedom and abandon with which she gave expression to them. She appeared to be about eighteen years of age, with rather a masculine physique, her figure tall, erect, and lithe, but well rounded, and exceedingly graceful and feminine in outline, the incarnation of perfect health and vigor. Her face was thoroughly browned by exposure and exercise in the open air (she had probably never seen or heard of such a hothouse appendage as a sun-shade), and was constantly lighted up with a cheerful, happy expression, indicating an overflowing exuberance of spirits, which disseminated an atmosphere around her, the fascination of which was irresistible to those who came within its influence; and her laughing, dancing blue eyes seemed ever on the *qui vive* for fun and frolic. She wore a closely-fitting bloomer costume, with a jaunty little straw hat upon one side of her head, fastened under the chin with a pretty pink ribbon, and her luxurious natural hair curled in ringlets all over her shoulders.

She was evidently the reigning belle of the neighborhood, as well as the favorite spoiled child of her family; and she was just as wild, untamed, and free from the absurd, tyrannical conventionalities of society as the mustangs that roamed over the adjacent prairies.

My companion related to her some of the most remarkable incidents of our expedition, which seemed to interest her vastly; but, at the same time, her credulity appeared to be somewhat taxed, and would occasionally find utterance in such ejaculations as, "*Oh, git out!*" "*You go-long now!*" "*Look at him!*" etc., which seemed the spontaneous outbursts of her impulsive nature, and rather in the character of a soliloquy than seriously intended to express doubt as to the truth of the narrative.

In one instance she became intensely absorbed in my friend's account of a visit we received from the Comanches, and some of the peculiar habits of those people, and gave vent to her feelings by administering a violent slap upon his knee, and at the same time exclaiming, "*The he—e—e—ll you say, stranger!*" giving particular emphasis to and dwelling upon the most objectionable word in the sentence.

She inquired very particularly about our camping arrangements, and manifested a good deal of curiosity concerning the shape, capacity, and material of our tent. She had never seen one, it appeared, and I remarked to her that after ours was pitched, if she would honor us with a call, she would have a good opportunity of seeing how very comfortable we could make ourselves in camp. At this she turned around, facing me, applied her thumb to her nose with her fingers extended, closed one eye, and, with her countenance assuming a most ludicrously severe expression, observed, "*I'm afraid of wolves, ole hoss.*"

As I was quite unconscious of having intended any disrespect to the young lady, I was a good deal surprised at this exhibition of indignation. What signification her remark was intended to convey I have never yet learned; I certainly never for a moment imagined that any resemblance could be detected between the carnivorous quadruped so pointedly alluded to and ourselves, even had we been attired in "*sheep's clothing.*" From the savage expression her countenance assumed, however, I did not feel inclined to press her for an explanation, and changed the subject as soon as possible.

While surveying Indian reservations in the wilds of Western Texas during the summer of 1854, I encountered a deputy state surveyor traveling on foot, with his compass and chain upon his back. I saluted him politely, remarking that I presumed he was a surveyor, to which he replied, "I reckon, stranger, I ar that thar individoal."

I had taken the magnetic variation several times, always with nearly the same results (about 10° 20′); but, in order to verify my observations, I was curious to learn how they accorded with his own working, and accordingly inquired what he made the variation of the compass in that locality. He seemed struck with astonishment at the question, took the compass from his back, laid it upon a log near by, then facing me, and pointing with his finger toward it, said, "Stranger, do yer see that thar in-stru-*ment?*" to which I replied in the affirmative. He continued: "I've owned her well-nigh goin on twenty year. I've put her through the perarries *and* through the timber, *and* now you look-a-yere, stranger, you can jist bet yer life on't she never *var*-ried arry time, and ef you'll foller her sign ye'll knock the centre outer the north star; she never lies, *she don't.*"

He seemed to consider my interrogatory as a direct insinuation that his compass was an imperfect one, and hence his indignation. Thinking I should not get any important information concerning the magnetic variation from this surveyor, I begged his pardon for questioning the accuracy of his instru*ment*, bade him good-morning, and continued my journey.

On my return to Fort Smith, Arkansas, in the autumn of 1852, after having explored the Red River to its sources, and upon the occasion when it was very generally supposed that our party had all been overpowered and put to death by the Indians, I set out with two gentlemen of the party, Captain McClellan and a friend from New York, who had accompanied us for the benefit of his health, *en route* for Rock Roe, the steam-boat landing on White River, a distance of some two hundred miles.

The health of my invalid companion was not yet sufficiently restored to enable him to digest the *heavy* balls that were usually set before travelers in that country under the name of biscuit, and he laid in at Fort Smith a good supply of baker's bread and tea for our journey.

Our first halt, after we left Fort Smith, was at a plantation house some twenty-five miles out. We drove up to the gate, and I entered the house, where I found a woman lying upon a bed, suffering from a severe attack of rheumatism. I apologized for disturbing her, and remarked that I had called for the purpose of ascertaining if two companions and myself could be accommodated with dinner.

She said her servants were all out in the field, and she could not at that time think of taking them from their work. I then asked her how long she had been ill, and whether she had a good physician to attend her, etc. She replied that the only doctor she had confidence in was Dr. Shumard, and, as he had been killed by the Indians, she did not feel inclined to call upon any other. Now Dr. Shumard had been the surgeon upon my recent expedition, and had returned with me to Fort Smith.

I inquired of the lady if she was quite certain that the doctor had been massacred by the savages. She said there was not the slightest doubt upon the subject, as he was with Captain Marcy, who, with every soul in the party, were put to death by the Comanches. I then asked her if I could prove to her that Dr. Shumard was alive and well, and at that very time at his home in Fort Smith, whether she would allow her servants to come in and get us dinner, to which she most willingly assented; whereupon, making a profound obeisance to her, I said, "I have the honor, madam, of presenting myself to you as the identical Captain Marcy whom you suppose to have been killed by the Indians; and I also have the pleasure to inform you that your physician returned with me yesterday to Fort Smith, and in the best possible state of health."

She immediately screamed out at the top of her voice, "You Jim, go out into the field, and tell Sally to come here quick, and get these gentlemen some dinner; do you hear?" Sally soon made her appearance, and in a short time set before us a very excellent repast, to which we did ample justice, and, bidding our hostess good-by, resumed our journey.

On the second day out from the fort we halted for the night at a respectable-looking farm-house, where we were informed we could be accommodated with lodgings, and my New York companion readily obtained from the hostess a promise to make a nice dish of toast and a cup of tea for supper.

In due course of events our supper was announced, and we seated ourselves at the table, which, according to the custom of the country, was spread under the portico of the house.

The dishes before us consisted of fried bacon floating in grease, some corn-bread in the shape of hand grenades, and a quantity of glutinous, half-baked hot biscuit, neither of which seemed calculated to tempt the appetite of the gentleman from New York, who called for the toast. The landlady replied that "she had it on a *fryin*, and she 'lowed it would soon be done." Captain McClellan and myself exchanged significant glances at this information, but my friend from New York did not appear to appreciate the joke, and asked "what the devil she meant by frying toast." She assured him it was all right, as he would soon see for himself. When it came on the table it appeared that she had taken the loaf, cut it in two parts, placed them in a pan, and fried them in grease for about half an hour. My friend did not seem to relish this method of cooking, and explained to the hostess in detail the proper method of making toast; whereupon she said, "Oh, you want burnt bread; I thought you wanted toast."

The woman evidently did not know much more about making tea than she did of the proper method of preparing the toast.

Indeed, it is very seldom that tea can be found among these people; and, although they all make excellent coffee, very many of them never drank a cup of tea in their lives. A lady of my acquaintance, in traveling from Fort Towson to Shreveport some twelve years since, knowing the difficulty of procuring her favorite beverage in that section, had provided herself with about a pound of choice green tea, and at one of her stopping-places upon Red River requested the woman of the house to make her a cup of it. When the supper was announced my friend inquired for her tea; the woman said, "Wall, now, marm, I put them dried greens o' yourn in the pot mor'n a half hour ago, and they've been bilin ever since, and I've changed the water three times, but tain't no use, I reckon; thar so bitter now that no woman in Rackensack (Arkansas) can eat um."

After the supper was concluded a room with three beds was assigned to our use, and we congratulated ourselves on the prospect of obtaining a comfortable night's repose. Shortly after we had retired, however, I felt something, as I imagined, crawling upon my legs, and made several rapid passes with my hand for the purpose of catching the intruder; but without success; he constantly eluded my grasp; and, after many failures, the tickling sensation still continuing, I quietly got up, lit a candle, returned to the bed and pulled down the clothes, when, without the slightest exaggeration, I sincerely believe that, at a moderate estimate, at least ten thousand bedbugs greeted my eyes. There was a perfect army of them, marching and countermarching in all directions, apparently seeking whom they might devour. As the prospect for sleep did not appear very encouraging here, I took my own blanket, went out into the inclosure in front of the house, and lay down upon the grass. As I was passing out, the gentleman from New York called out,

"What in thunder is it that tickles my legs so?" I replied, "Nothing at all," and recommended him to go to sleep and remain quiet. It was but a short time, however, before both my companions joined me, and we all passed the remainder of the night upon the grass.

The people of the New England States are proverbial for their curiosity, and it is sometimes difficult to elude their inquisitive and persevering tact in gaining the information they desire. For example, I was traveling through Wisconsin during the early period of its settlement in 1838, and stopped overnight at a small log tavern in Janesville, on Rock River. The house, on my arrival, was occupied by a number of travelers, all crowded into one small room, and among them I observed a man evidently from New England, who made himself conspicuous by questioning every one as to where he was from, where he was going, what his business was, etc., etc.

During the evening he accosted me by saying, "From Madison, mister?"

Not feeling disposed to gratify his impertinent proclivities, I abruptly replied, "No, sir."

He then said, "Oh, yer from Mineral Pint, hay?"

"No."

"Goin tu Milwakee?"

"No."

"Oh, maybe yer goin tu Racine?"

"No, sir, no, I tell you." I then asked him if there were any other items of information upon which I could enlighten him. He hesitated for an instant, then continued:

"Live at Prairie du Chien, mister?"

"No."

"Mabby ye live at Gerlena?"

"No, sir."

"Where du ye make it yer hum?"

I replied "nowhere in particular," but informed him that the peculiar idiosyncrasy of my individual *penchant* rather inclined me to adopt a cosmopolitan life. This answer appeared to puzzle him greatly, and the only reply he made was to raise his hands, turn up his eyes, and exclaim, "You doan't say so, neou, du yer." He suspended his interrogatories here, but evidently resolved to watch me closely.

Now the fact is, I was at that time stationed at Fort Winnebago, and *en route* for Chicago, but I firmly resolved that the Yankee (I am one myself, and have a right to tell them their faults) should not discover it if I could possibly prevent it. Soon afterward, however, my *companion du voyage* entered, and approaching me, said, "I wish, Marcy, on your return from Chicago, you would remember me very kindly to the officers at Winnebago."

The inquisitive individual instantly jumped up, and with a most gratified expression of countenance exclaimed, "Oh, Mr. Marcy, ye make it yer hum tu Winnebago, doan't ye, and yer going tu Chicago, ain't ye?"

I was considerably annoyed at his triumph, but the only retaliation I was able to inflict upon him was to suggest that, in my opinion, it would be just as well for him if he would attend to his own affairs, and let other people alone.

Another trait in the character of the New England man which is fully as marked as their desire to obtain information is their erratic cosmopolitan propensity for locomotion and roaming. They are eminently social and gregarious in their dispositions and habits, but at the same time they are very far from being local or clannish in their proclivities, and they may be found dispersed throughout almost all the habitable parts of the universe.

At the time the army under General Taylor occupied Brownsville, opposite Matamoras, during the spring of 1846, we found it very difficult to procure supplies of vegetables and fruits, and I had, for the first time, turned my attention to the Spanish language as the only means of communicating with the Mexicans, and had, with a great deal of difficulty, mastered a few useful phrases, when one day I started out in search of supplies for our mess.

I had not gone far before I met an old Mexican (as I supposed), dressed in full Spanish costume, with slashed trowsers, gilt buttons, and broad-brimmed sombrero, and followed by several senoras and senoritas leading *buros* packed with vegetables. I halted, and pointing to a good-sized cabbage, said, "Quantus pour este, señor?" (How much for that, sir?) To which the man, to my astonishment, answered, "Abeout tue bits;" upon which I said, "You speak English very well, señor." He rejoined, "Well, I think I or-tue—I come from Massachusetts."

Upon inquiry, I learned that this man was born and raised only about twenty miles from my own native town, and that he had emigrated to Texas some thirty years before; was engaged in General Green's expedition at Mier, captured and taken to Mexico as a prisoner, and subsequently confined in the Castle of Perote for a long time, but was finally released, and found his way back to Matamoras, where he had lived ever since, adopting the Mexican costume and habits.

The propensity of the New Englanders for wandering does not seem to be confined to the male sex, as the following little incident will show.

During the summer of 1864, I was descending the Mississippi River *en route* from Little Rock, when the steamer I was upon stopped to wood at an island where a contraband wood-yard had been established under government protection.

While the steamer was receiving its fuel I walked out upon shore, where I found quite a group of log-huts erected for the use of the negroes. In the door of one of them I saw an elderly white woman standing, and entered into conversation with her. After a few minutes she asked me if I was attached to the army, and on my giving an affirmative answer, she continued, "What may I call your name?" I said "Marcy." "What, R. B. Marcy?" "Yes." "Randolph B. Marcy?" I repeated "Yes." "Are you from Massachusetts?" "Yes." "From Hampshire County?" "Yes." "From Greenwich?" "Yes." "The son of L. Marcy?" "Yes." "Well, then, I made your shirts when you went to West Point." Of course I was very much astonished, and begged to ask whom I had the honor of addressing, and how it happened that she had wandered so far from the place of her nativity. She stated that she had been sent out here by some Christian benevolent association to teach the freedmen's children, and she was, I believe, the only white female upon the island; at all events, I saw no other.

It is very true that the New Englanders seem to be possessed with an irresistible *penchant* for accumulating as large a stock as possible of useful information, nevertheless I have observed the same dominant proclivities in the character of the Southern and Western people; with them, however, they are manifested in a more direct and blunt manner.

A friend of mine, who was traveling in Alabama upon one occasion, met a man in the road who accosted him as follows: "Whar ar ye from, stranger?" He, knowing the prejudices of the Southern people against the "Yankees," although he had never been there in his life, replied, "From Richmond."

At this answer the man said, "I once know'd a heap o' people in Richmond, and I've got right smart of kin-folks thar too; maybe you mought know Jim Johnson, of Main

Street?" to which my friend was obliged to answer in the negative. "Wall, now, stranger, do yer know Jake Brown, on Broad Street?" He said he had not the pleasure of his acquaintance either. Several other interrogatories about Richmond were asked and replied to in a similar manner, greatly to the confusion of my friend, who, notwithstanding the Southern prejudices against New Englanders, resolved the next time he was questioned to tell the truth.

He soon afterward met another man, who said to him, "Whar did ye come from, stranger?"

"I came from Connecticut, sir."

"*Whar* did ye say?"

"From Connecticut."

"Connecticut? Connecticut?" repeated the man, with a puzzled look; "wall, now, stranger, I don't mind hearin o' that thar town afore, I be dogond ef I do."

Virginians are proverbial for their hospitality, and I have no doubt that very many of them richly deserve the enviable reputation they have acquired for the liberal, open-handed manner in which they entertain their guests; but I am compelled to acknowledge that in my travels I have found exceptions to this rule.

In 1849 I made a road from New Mexico, passing through Northern Texas to Arkansas, which was traveled for several years by California emigrants, thus affording a good market to the farmers along the adjacent country for their produce.

In 1854 I passed over this road again, and stopped for dinner at a plantation owned by a Mr. McCarty, from Virginia, who, on my arrival, seemed highly delighted to see me again, remarking that if I had only notified him I was coming that way, he would have given me the biggest barbecue that country had ever seen.

He complimented me by saying that I had done more for the country than any other man living, and if I would run for Congress in that district he would insure my election. I thanked him for his kind wishes in my behalf, and informed him that I should not be able to stay for the barbecue, but that, if it was perfectly convenient, we would with pleasure dine with him.

After dinner I hesitated for some time about offering compensation to our host, but finally did so by asking him how much we were indebted for our dinner. He replied, "Only six bits apiece, Cap." (The usual price in that country was two bits.)

As we were preparing to leave, he remarked, "You must give us a call on your return, *sir*, and stay overnight with us, *sir;* I want to show you a specimen of genuine old Virginia hospitality, *sir*." He then directed one of the negroes to bring up our horses, and, as we were mounting, said, "Gentlemen, don't give that boy Jake two bits apiece for taking care of your horses; don't do it, gentlemen." (We had then made no demonstrations toward rewarding the boy.)

From the price we paid for our dinner, it occurred to me that if the barbecue had come off, the Virginian's hospitality might have proved rather an expensive affair to me.

The people inhabiting the rural districts of the Southwestern States have, as the reader has probably observed, adopted many words and phrases which are not found in Webster's Dictionary, or sanctioned by any of our grammarians. They have also taken the liberty of changing the pronunciation of many words in such a manner, and applying them in such novel ways, that it is almost impossible for one not familiar with these peculiarities to comprehend their meaning in ordinary conversation. For instance, they call bear, *bar;* door, *doo;* chair, *char;* stair, *star;* crop, *crap;* etc., etc. They say, "I made right smart o' craps this year," or "How ar ye crappin on't?" etc. But I heard this word used in a still more singular connection while I was making the passage across the Gulf from New Orleans to Powder-horn, in company with Mr. Kendall, formerly of the New Orleans Picayune, and several other very agreeable gentlemen, who were *en route* to Texas.

Shortly after leaving New Orleans our attention was directed to a newly-married couple on board, who presented the most extraordinary contrast in size that I have ever met with. The man was exceedingly diminutive—I should imagine about five feet high, and probably not exceeding one hundred pounds in weight; while, on the other hand, his bride was a most buxom and ponderous personage, and, as I verily believe, weighed at the smallest calculation two hundred and fifty pounds. The contrast was so marked, and indeed ludicrous, that they were the objects of irresistible observation and comment whenever they made their appearance together.

One day I was standing upon the upper deck of the steamer while the happy pair were promenading back and forth, arm in arm, when a passenger, who was evidently a backwoodsman, approached me, and, pointing toward them, said, "Now, Cap., don't you sorter reckon that thar little man thar has a leetle bit *overcrapt hisself?*" I concurred with him in what I took to be the import of his agricultural figure, and observed that, in my opinion, the young gentleman would have his hands full in the event of any future discord which should lead to a personal encounter between them. He turned and walked away, remarking, "As sure as yer born, he's a mighty small chance of a man to have such a powerful heap o' wife."

As we were coming into the border settlements of Texas from my first expedition across the Plains in 1849, after an absence of eight months, during which time we had not heard a word from our friends at home, one of the first houses we met with upon our route was that of a planter by the name of Butt, who possessed a large force of negroes, and cultivated extensive crops. As may be imagined, our wardrobes, after a long march through an unexplored country from New Mexico, were in a somewhat dilapidated condition, and our tattered costumes were not such at this time as to give any indication that we held commissions in the United States Army, or to impress a stranger very favorably toward us.

I started out from camp at an early hour in the morning, in advance of the command, and, riding up to Mr. Butt's gate, saw a man standing upon the piazza, whom I took to be the proprietor of the establishment, and inquired if he had any corn for sale. He, in a very curt and indifferent manner, after casting a glance at me, said, "Yes, I've a plenty of corn;" and in reply to my inquiry as to whether he would sell me some, he said, "Yes, sir, if you've got money to pay for it."

I told him that, unfortunately, our finances were then pretty low, but, if it would answer his purposes, I would give him an order upon the quartermaster at Fort Washita, which I assured him would be a good voucher for the payment of the corn. This proposition seemed to strike him with surprise, and, after looking attentively at me for a moment, he came out to the gate, invited me to alight and walk into the house. He then inquired of me what part of the country I came from, and on my replying that I was just in from the Plains, he said, "Ah indeed! pray did you hear any thing from Captain Marcy as you passed through the Indian country?" Now the fact was, we had been expected for several weeks, and serious fears were beginning to be entertained by our friends for our safety. I answered his question by assuring him that I had several times met the individual he seemed to take such an interest in, and, indeed, that we had traveled together for a considerable distance.

"Is it possible?" said he. "Well, sir, can you give me any information as to his whereabouts at this time, for his wife has been at Fort Washita several weeks, in a state of considerable anxiety, awaiting tidings from him?"

I replied that I had no doubt the lady had a proper appreciation of the perils her husband had been subjected to, but that I knew him well, as we had been raised and were schoolmates together; indeed, I said, the origin of our acquaintance might be dated some forty years back. I, however, quietly intimated to him that it might be just as well for him to say nothing about the exact number of years to Mrs. M——, as I was under the impression that she was a little sensitive upon this particular subject. I then added that, according to the best of my knowledge and belief, the captain was the identical personage with whom he was conversing at that very instant. Of course he was greatly astonished, and told me that his corn, hay, house, and every thing it contained, were all at my disposal.

I frequently met Mr. Butt afterward, and am indebted to him and his accomplished lady for many hospitalities which they have extended to me.

In passing through the interior settlements of Texas, Arkansas, and Southwestern Missouri, the traveler rarely sees a church or school-house. The few places of public worship that are met with in this country are generally located in the vicinity of springs and in groves of timber, where semicircular tiers of benches are placed, with a pulpit in the centre, something in the form of a decapitated sentry-box, the whole having no other covering but the branches of the trees, surmounted by the canopy of the heavens;

and it is only occasionally, at wide intervals of time, when a circuit or other itinerant preacher happens to come around, that they have an opportunity of listening to any elucidation of the Scriptures. The consequence is, that these people have but little appreciation of the sanctity and holiness of the principles inculcated by our Christian religion, and do not, in many cases, entertain a proper respect and reverence for the teachers of this religion.

The Reverend Mr. C——, who had spent the greater part of his life in endeavoring to improve the spiritual condition of the people in Western Texas, was at one time appointed chaplain for a military post at which I chanced to be stationed, and related to me several quite amusing incidents connected with his professional career in that country.

He was a man of most unexceptionable moral and religious character, besides being an educated and refined gentleman; but, at the same time, he possessed an irascible and explosive temperament, which required the exercise of all his powers of self-discipline to keep it under proper subjection. For example, he once learned that a certain deacon of his church had made allegations which were highly detrimental to his character, and wholly untrue. This roused his indignation to such a pitch that, upon the impulse of the moment, he seized a cowhide, and started out with the firm determination of giving him a sound flagellation; but, before reaching the deacon's residence, it occurred to him that this was rather an improper proceeding for a man of his profession, and, after a little reflection, he abandoned his purpose.

While riding his circuit at one time in the sparsely-settled country bordering Red River, he wandered from his customary route, and was overtaken by night near the house of a gambler of notoriously desperate character, whose hostility to religious persons had been evinced upon numerous occasions, and was proverbial. It was generally believed that he had been guilty of more heinous practices than that of obtaining money by the exercise of the tricks of his profession, and it was even hinted that some of the travelers who had taken lodgings at his house had very mysteriously disappeared. Mr. C—— was perfectly aware of these facts, and would have preferred other quarters; but he was a valorous "soldier of the Cross," of whom it might very truly be said "that he feared neither man nor the devil," and he did not hesitate to stop. As he rode up to the door, he overheard the man observe to his wife, "There comes that d—d old parson. I suppose he wants to stay overnight; but if he thinks I am going to put up with his praying and psalm-singing, he is very much mistaken. I'll make him pay his bill in different coin from that." He paid no attention to the ill-natured remark, but, dismounting, entered the house, and informed the surly proprietor that he intended passing the night with him. To which the man replied that perhaps he would suspend his decision upon that subject until he had ascertained whether his presence would be agreeable. To this he made no answer, excepting, as he pulled off his overcoat, he observed that he had come *to stay.* When supper was announced, and all were seated at the table, the gambler seized his knife and fork, and was about commencing his repast, when the clergyman raised his hands as in the act of invoking a blessing, and, at the same time, cast a stern look of inquiry at him, which caused him to drop his knife and fork, and in an indignant tone to say, "*Let er slide, parson.*" He was evidently much annoyed at the rather arbitrary and dictatorial manner in which the clerical gentleman exercised his ecclesiastical prerogatives upon his premises, and hardly condescended to address any conversation to him during the evening. The clergyman, however, was not at all intimidated or disconcerted by these manifestations of dissatisfaction and ill-humor, and resolved, when the time approached for retiring to bed, that he would perform his customary evening family service. Thereupon he drew from his pocket a Bible, and in a very solemn and stern manner motioned to the gambler to bring him a small table. He complied with the summons, seized the table, and in a manner as if to ventilate his indignation, slammed it down in front of his guest; then, resuming his seat, commenced whistling the "Arkansas Traveler." The clergyman said nothing, but looked a severe reprimand at him while he significantly pointed his finger to the Bible. This had the desired effect. He ceased his derisive whistling, and, with a most disgusted air, said, "Well, d—n it, parson, *bile ahead.*"

The night passed quietly, the morning service was performed, and, as my friend was about taking his departure, he opened his purse and inquired the amount of his bill, and received the following laconic reply: "Not a d—d cent, parson; go along about your business; but don't come psalm-singing around my house any more, for I won't stand it."

Among the pioneers who, under the inducements held out by Mexico, first emigrated to Texas from the United States, were many worthy citizens, who entered this new field of enterprise with the design of making permanent homes for their families; but with these were commingled adventurous spirits, who sought excitement and danger; also individuals of desperate fortunes, who had nothing to lose; as well as refugees from justice, who deemed this the safest asylum to escape the penalties due to their crimes.

As a necessary consequence, society composed of such heterogeneous elements was eminently impulsive, unsettled, and lawless. During the revolution which was inaugurated and carried on by them, and indeed for years after they had secured their independence, many of the border settlers held themselves amenable to no laws save those that were enforced at the muzzle of the revolver and the point of the bowie-knife. Even as late as 1854, after the forms of statutory civil jurisdiction had been instituted under legislative enactment, and courts had been established, the authorities were, as a general rule, almost entirely disregarded, and virtually set at defiance by the lawless desperadoes along the borders, and crimes of the greatest turpitude were perpetrated almost daily.

The law officers seldom, if ever, took cognizance of cases where men were killed in personal encounters, and oftentimes the most foul and premeditated murders were allowed to pass by unnoticed.

To such an extent were these atrocities sometimes carried, that the better classes of the people, seeing the impotence of the legal authorities, and, in some instances, their probable complicity with the perpetrators of the crimes, would become roused to such a pitch of indignation that they occasionally took the law into their own hands, and executed summary justice according to the code of Judge Lynch.

Murderers were often allowed to escape trial or punishment, but it was seldom that a man who had been guilty of horse-stealing could avoid the extreme penalty of Lynch law; this was looked upon by them as the most unpardonable offense known to their legal calendar, and public sentiment was unanimous in pronouncing this a capital crime, only to be expiated at the end of the halter.

While I was stationed upon the Rio Grande, a quiet, respectable citizen, whom I happened to know, arrived at Rio Grande City, opposite Comargo, and, entering a billiard saloon, seated himself to observe the game. He had not been there long before a man who was an entire stranger to him came in and blustered around a good deal, with the evident intention of creating a disturbance. He made frequent insulting remarks to persons in the room, endeavoring to bully them into a quarrel, but they did not seem disposed to come in collision with him. At length, however, he approached the stranger, and in an insulting tone said, "Perhaps you may have something to say about it?"

"About what, sir?" he replied.

"Why, sir, about my being the best man in all Texas. I make this assertion, and would like to see the man who presumed to differ with me upon that subject."

The stranger was so much annoyed at these impertinent remarks that he replied, "In my opinion, you, instead of being the best, are about the worst man I have met with in the state." This brought on a quarrel, which resulted in both parties drawing their revolvers, and firing several shots at each other in rapid succession. The man who gave the insult was killed, and the other was so severely wounded that he could not stand.

At this juncture a notorious desperado entered the establishment, and seeing the two men lying upon the floor, demanded to know what had happened, and on being informed, drew his revolver, went up to the living man, who was stretched out perfectly powerless, and told him he intended taking his life. The man begged of him to allow him to see a friend in town for a moment, in order to make some arrangements about his family affairs. He told him he would not permit it, and, holding the pistol near his head, deliberately fired several balls into his brain, either of which was sufficient to take his life; after which he walked around the dead body of his victim for several hours, defying every body, and challenging the community to attempt his arrest. No one, however, felt disposed to encounter the fiend, and he was suffered to remain unmolested in town until the following day, when he mounted his horse and quietly rode off.

These facts were related to me by a respectable gentleman of the place, who was an eyewitness to at least a portion of the tragedy, and who made an effort to get up a party to lynch the murderer; but the friends of the latter were so numerous that he was very glad to suspend proceedings. The last time I heard of the desperado he was living at San Antonio, and, for aught I know, is there still.

My friend, Major Neighbors, whom I have several times before alluded to, related to me the following incident in his experience among the early settlers of Texas:

He was, during the revolution, attached to the army in the capacity of quartermaster, and upon one occasion had purchased a quantity of corn from a farmer somewhere in the neighborhood of Austin; but, for want of the means of transportation, could not remove it at the time, and arranged with the vendor to keep it in store until it could be sent for. After a considerable lapse of time he procured wagons and went for the corn; but, on his arrival, the person from whom it was purchased stated that he had a claim against the government, and should not allow the grain to be taken away until this claim was liquidated. The major replied that, as the corn had already been paid for, he should certainly take it, and accordingly directed his men to load up the wagons, which was done; but, as he was about leaving, the man assured him that before he reached Austin the corn would certainly be taken from him. The major comprehended the import of the threat, and told the man that he should encamp at a certain spring, where he could be found until nine o'clock on the following morning, and that he should be ready to receive any propositions he might have to make. He knew the man to be of desperate character, and anticipated trouble with him. He therefore, on the following morning, cleaned, recharged, and recapped his rifle, and awaited the issue. About nine o'clock the man rode up with several of his associates, all fully armed, and apparently prepared for battle; but the friends of the man did not seem disposed to engage in the contest, and held a little back, while the principal individual dismounted and took a position behind an unoccupied log hut, from whence he would occasionally show himself around the corner and fire at the major with his revolver, but did not hit him. The major then placed his rifle to his shoulder, and, when his antagonist made his appearance again, drew trigger; but the gun missed fire. He put on a new cap, and missed the second time. He then deliberately pricked some powder into the cone, and recapped the rifle, while, in the mean time, his antagonist was firing several shots at him, none of which took effect. Then, raising his rifle again, he fired, shot the man through the brain, and he fell dead in his tracks. His companions then approached, and congratulated the major on having performed a meritorious act in ridding the country of a bad subject, who was a nuisance to the whole neighborhood.

Major Neighbors was attached to the celebrated Mier expedition, and was taken prisoner, marched to the city of Mexico, and thence to Pueblo, where he and his companions received very harsh treatment at the hands of the Mexicans. He informed me that himself and five comrades were every morning harnessed into a cart and conducted by a guard to the city market, where supplies for the day were procured, and hauled by this novel six-man team back to the prison.

Notwithstanding the rigor of their treatment here, the major said they were generally in good spirits, and many practical jokes were perpetrated upon the simple-minded soldiers who had them in charge. The "*off lead*" man in the team before mentioned was very conspicuous in this regard; indeed, he seemed utterly unable to resist improving an opportunity for a good joke. As an instance, one morning, while they were being driven into the market, they were passing the stall of a very old Mexican woman, whose peculiarly fantastic costume, and shriveled, haggard countenance gave her more the appearance of a fiend than a human being. As soon as the *off leader* caught a glimpse of this hideous old woman, he cast a wink back at his comrades, and, suddenly raising his head and snorting like a horse, started off in a trot, sheering around her, and gradually turning his head in imitation of a horse who shuns a suspicious-looking object. All the other men entered into the spirit of the joke, and followed him around, pretending to be prodigiously frightened, and they all with one accord set out at full speed down the Jalapa Road, with the cart rattling along over the pavement behind them, and pursued by the astonished guard, calling out in Spanish at the top of their voices for them to halt. They paid no attention to the order, but continued on for nearly a mile before the guard was able to get around them and arrest their headway. The officer then came up, very much blown, and in a most excited and angry tone demanded to know what they meant by such insubordinate conduct. The "*off leader*," who was the originator of the joke, asked him if he did not observe that horrible old hag sitting in the marketplace. "Was that what frightened you so?" said the officer. "Why, certainly," he replied; "she did it, and we could not help running away: did she not scare you too?" "No," he answered, slapping his breast, "I am a soldier, and am not intimidated by such trifles." They were then taken back to the market, and as they approached near the old woman, the officer, observing, as he thought, some indications of another stampede, ordered two of his men to take the leaders by the heads, and conduct them by a wide circuit around the object of their supposed terror.

They overheard the officer report the affair to the commander of the fort on their return, and the latter affirmed, as his candid opinion, that "*los Gringos*" (Yankees) were great cowards after all.

In 1854 I had the pleasure of meeting Colonel McLeod, who commanded the expedition to Santa Fé in 1841, so graphically described by Mr. Kendall in his interesting narrative of that expedition. Colonel McLeod was at one time adjutant general of the republic of Texas when General Houston was president, and he related to me several very amusing anecdotes in relation to the general. I can not, of course, give them to the reader in his peculiarly felicitous and happy style, but I will attempt to convey as correct an idea of the substance of one or two of them as possible.

At one time a large force of volunteers had been called out to resist the encroachments of a numerous band of Indians, who were reported as advancing on Nacogdoches. These troops were placed under command of General Rusk, afterward United States Senator, and were composed of frontier rangers, every man of whom considered himself as good as the president, secretary of war, or any other dignitary in the universe.

After the troops had been assembled, they were all desirous of encountering the savages, and felt very confident of their ability to defeat them; but it appears that the president, who was at General Rusk's head-quarters, entertained a different opinion, and either entered into a treaty, or made some other arrangements by which the Indians were allowed to escape without a battle. The troops were then disbanded and authorized to return home. On the following day the streets of Nacogdoches were filled with them, and there was a general jollification; but, at the same time, it appeared that great dissatisfaction was entertained against the president for his pacific action in the matter, and some of them did not hesitate to give expression to their feelings in open denunciations of his course.

During the day Generals Houston and Rusk and Colonel McLeod were walking through the streets, when they came near a large collection of men, and in their midst was a young and stalwart disbanded volunteer, who had probably taken several drinks, and was expatiating in a most excited and vociferous manner to the people around him.

The trio halted, and General Houston said, "It seems to me, General Rusk, that you do not preserve very good order or discipline among your men."

General Rusk replied that these men were disbanded, and they were not then subject to his control. "Well, Rusk," said the general, "come along with me, and I'll show you how to dispose of such disorderly crowds." Colonel McLeod thought he would like to witness the general's method of enforcing discipline among the "*Mustangs*," and the three set off together. It was with great difficulty that they were enabled to penetrate the dense mass of men to where the unruly speaker was holding forth, but, by dint of a good deal of hard squeezing, twisting, and turning, they at length found themselves confronting the speaker, when General Houston, in a very mild and amiable tone of voice, after placing his hand on the young man's shoulder and looking him in the eye, said, "Are you not aware, my young friend, that you are disturbing the peace and quiet of this community, and that, too, sir, in the presence of the President of the Republic?" The young man, who the instant before had been screaming at the highest pitch of his voice and gesticulating in the most excited manner, suddenly ceased his harangue, and, turning upon the general, in a low but very emphatic tone, said, "*Are you Sam Houston?*"

"I am, sir," he replied.

"Are you the President of the Republic?"

"Yes, my young friend, I have the honor to bear that distinguished cognomen."

At this the young man closed his fists, and, springing like a tiger upon the general, knocked him down, while at the same time he exclaimed, "Well, d—n you, Sam Houston, you are the very man I wanted to see;" and it was with great difficulty that they extricated the poor old man from the clutches of the infuriated volunteer.

The stoical indifference with which the frontiersman submits to misfortunes of the most disastrous character is strikingly exhibited in the following incident, which is related by Captain Burton in his work on the "City of the Saints." A man, traveling upon the desert of the Humboldt, was passing a solitary wagon standing in the road, without any team attached, "and, seeing a wretched-looking lad nursing a starving baby, asks him what the matter may be. 'Wall, now,' responds the youth, 'guess I'm kinder streakt. Ole dad's drunk; ole mom's got the *hy*-sterics; brother Jim be playing poker with two gamblers; sister Sal's down thar a courtin' of a *en*-tire stranger; this yere baby's got the diaree the wust sort; the team's clean guv out; the wagon's broke down; it's twenty miles to the next water—I don't care a —— ef I never see Californey.'"

Another illustration will suffice to establish the philosophical and recuperative nature of these people:

Governor ———, of ——— Territory, was questioned by an Eastern friend regarding the character and resources of the country over which his official jurisdiction extended. The governor, who was of sanguine temperament, replied that it was generally regarded as possessing advantages over almost any other of our new Territories; indeed, he said he had never seen or heard of but one man who was not captivated with it, and that individual did not remain long enough to thoroughly appreciate its merits. The person he alluded to was bound for Bannock, and had met with a good many accidents upon the road, such as losing his cattle, breaking his wagon, and in various other ways, which would have disheartened most men; but he was by no means discouraged, and pushed forward with unabated vigor until he lost all his animals except one ox and a small cow. These, as a dernier resort, he yoked together, and they constituted the only remaining motive power for his wagon. Still he was undaunted in his purpose to accomplish the journey he had undertaken, and, as an evidence of this fact, he had, with a piece of charcoal, written in large characters upon the side of his wagon, "*Bannock or bust.*" At length, however, the severe labor proved too much for the poor cow, and she died; and, as if to complete the catalogue of his disasters, his only remaining animal took it into his head to stampede, and he was then left without any means of transportation. About this time the governor was passing, and observed the man sitting over a small fire in rather a disconsolate mood, but apparently endeavoring to keep up his spirits by whistling "Hail Columbia!" The inscription upon his wagon, however, had been erased, and a new one substituted in its place, as follows—"*Busted, by thunder!*"

CHAPTER XIII.

MOUNTAINEERS.

Mountaineers.—Jim Bridger.—His Troubles with the "Danites."—Sir George Gore.—Tim Goodale and Jim Baker.—Bear Fight.—Singular Duel.—Mariano.—Mr. Clyburn.—His Adventures in the Mountains.—His Return to the Settlements.—Narrow Escape on Rock River.—Indian Law.

SCATTERED here and there throughout the wilds of the Rocky Mountains are still remaining a few of those semi-civilized white men called "mountaineers," who wandered from their homes in the Border States early in life, and enlisted in the service of the different fur companies. Many of these peculiar and interesting people have spent the greater portion of their lives and grown gray in the rough and adventurous life incident to their occupations as hunters and trappers, and the history of their experiences teems with thrilling incident and reckless personal adventure.

At the time the American and Northwest Fur Companies were at the height of their prosperity, and when beaver fur was worth ten dollars a pound, these men were employed in Montreal, St. Louis, and other places on the frontier for a term of years, and from the time they left the settlements until their return they seldom tasted bread, sugar, tea, coffee, or vegetables. Like the prairie Indians, almost their only subsistence from one year's end to another consisted of fresh meat, and even this was only supplied by the precarious results of the chase. The rifle furnished their entire commissariat, and, as a necessary consequence in a locality where game did not abound, they were often subjected to great suffering from hunger.

Notwithstanding the privations and perils to which these people were constantly exposed, and the slender pecuniary profits which they derived from their avocations, strange as it may appear, I have yet to see the first one of them who did not become fascinated with the life, and it is seldom if ever they can be prevailed upon to abandon it. It seems to possess for them a charm of excitement and romance which no other occupation can supply.

I have known several of these men who returned to the settlements after years spent in the Indian country, intending to abandon their roving life; but they soon became restless and discontented, and, after a brief period, went back to the mountains and resumed the habits of the trapper.

Among these people, one of the most interesting specimens it has been my fortune to meet with, and one who occupies an exalted position among his confrères as a successful trapper and hunter, and who has no superior as a reliable guide and bold Indian fighter, is the well-known veteran mountaineer *Jim Bridger*, who has passed the major portion of his solitary life in the Rocky Mountains, far removed from all intercourse with civilized society.

When I first met him at Fort Laramie in 1857, he was a man about sixty years of age, tall, thin, wiry, and with a complexion well bronzed by toil and exposure, with an independent, generous, and open cast of countenance indicative of brave and noble impulses, which are characteristics of the hunter generally. His history, pregnant as it is with scenes of startling personal incident, interested me supremely.

Bridger was a native of the "Old Dominion," and had come to the head waters of the Missouri about thirty-four years before, and was there engaged for many years in trapping. From thence he wandered south into California, and ultimately established himself upon Black's Fork of Green River, one of the two principal tributaries of the Colorado of California. Here he erected an establishment which he called Fort Bridger, and here he was for several years prosecuting a profitable traffic both with the Indians and with California emigrants. At length, however, his prosperity excited the cupidity of the Mormons, and they intimated to him that his presence in such close proximity to their settlements was not agreeable, and advised him to pull up stakes and leave forthwith; and upon his questioning the legality or justice of this arbitrary summons, they came to his place with a force of "avenging angels," and forced him to make his escape to the woods in order to save his life. He remained secreted for several days, and, through the assistance of his Indian wife, was enabled to elude the search of the *Danites*, and make his way to Fort Laramie, leaving all his cattle and other property in possession of the Mormons.

From Laramie he, for the first time in thirty-one years, returned to the States, and laid his case before the authorities at Washington, and he was on his return when I met him. As may be imagined, he did not entertain the most friendly feelings for the "*Latter-day Saints*," and he would not probably have gone very far out of his way to have *saved* their *sculps*, as he termed the savages' battle trophy.

Bridger had been the guide, interpreter, and companion of that distinguished Irish sportsman, Sir George Gore, whose peculiar tastes led him in 1855 to abandon the luxurious life of Europe and bury himself for over two years among the savages in the wildest and most unfrequented glens of the Rocky Mountains.

The outfit and adventures of this titled Nimrod, conducted as they were upon a most gigantic scale, probably exceeded any thing of the kind ever before attempted on this continent, and the results of his exploits will compare favorably with the performances of Gordon Cumming in Africa.

Some conception may be formed of the magnitude of his equipment when it is stated that his party consisted of about fifty persons, comprising secretaries, steward, cooks, fly-makers, dog-tenders, hunters, servants, etc., etc. He was provided with a train of thirty wagons, besides numerous saddle-horses and dogs.

I met Sir George at St. Louis soon after his return from the mountains, and found him affable and communicative. He related to me several of his adventures with the Indians, and showed me his guns of various descriptions and calibres, suited to the destruction of all kinds of game, and upon them I observed the names of Joe Manton, Purdy, Westley Richards, and other celebrated makers.

He informed me that during his protracted hunt he had slaughtered the enormous aggregate of forty grizzly bears, twenty-five hundred buffaloes, besides numerous elk, deer, antelope, and other *small* game. He had brought back with him a host of trophies, which would be abundant vouchers for his performances on his return home.

Some persons will probably think it a very strange infatuation that a nobleman like Sir George, possessing an income of some $200,000 per annum, should voluntarily withdraw from all society, and retire to the wilderness among savages for two long years, exposed to all the perils and privations consequent upon such a life; but I assure the denizens of cities that he required no sympathy from them, as he was one of those enthusiastic, ardent sportsmen who derived more real satisfaction and pleasure from one day's successful hunting than can possibly be imagined by those who have never participated in this exhilarating and healthful amusement. Besides, he returned home with a renovated constitution, good health and spirits, and a new lease of perhaps ten years to his life, and, finally, he had seen something of life out of the ordinary beaten track of the great mass of other tourists.

Bridger often spoke to me about Sir George Gore, and always commended him as a bold, dashing, and successful sportsman, a social companion, and an agreeable gentleman.

Sir George's habit was to sleep until about ten or eleven o'clock in the morning, when he took his bath, ate his breakfast, and set out generally alone for the day's hunt; and Bridger says it was not unusual for him to remain out until ten o'clock at night, and he seldom returned to camp without augmenting the catalogue of his exploits.

His dinner was then ordered, to partake of which he generally extended an invitation to my friend Bridger, and after the repast was concluded, and a few glasses of wine had been drunk, he was in the habit of reading from some book, and eliciting from Bridger his comments thereon. His favorite author was Shakspeare, which Bridger "reckon'd was a leetle too highfalutin for him;" moreover, he remarked that he "rayther calculated that thar big Dutchman, Mr. *Full-stuff*, was a leetle bit too fond of lager beer," and suggested that probably it might have been better for the old man if he had imbibed the same amount of alcohol in the more condensed medium of good old Bourbon whisky.

Bridger seemed deeply interested in the adventures of Baron Munchausen, but admitted, after the reading was finished, that "he be dogond ef he swallered every thing that thar *Baren* Mountchawson said, and he thout he was a durn'd liar." Yet, upon farther reflection, he acknowledged that some of his own experience among the Blackfeet would be equally marvelous, "*ef writ down in a book.*"

One evening Sir George entertained his auditor by reading to him Sir Walter Scott's account of the battle of Waterloo, and afterward asked him if he did not regard that as the most sanguinary battle he had ever heard of. To which Bridger replied, "Wall, now, Mr. Gore, that thar must 'a bin a considdible of a skrimmage, dogon my skin ef it mustn't; them Britishers must 'a fit better thar than they did down to Horleans, whar Old Hickry gin um the forkedest sort o' chain-lightnin' that prehaps you ever did see in all yer born days!" And upon Sir George's expressing a little incredulity in regard to the estimate Bridger placed upon this battle, the latter added, "You can jist go yer pile on it, Mr. Gore—*you can*, as sure as yer born."

Two veteran mountaineers, Tim Goodale and Jim Baker, accompanied me as guides when I made my expedition over the Rocky Mountains from Fort Bridger to New Mexico, during the winter of 1857–8, to procure supplies for our little army in Utah, and I am under great obligations to them for the valuable assistance they rendered me in overcoming the formidable obstacle presented by the deep snows we encountered upon the lofty summits of those sierras, and I shall never cease to regard them with the liveliest interest and friendship. Tim Goodale was an intelligent man, of fair education, and had traveled across the continent several times to California. He had lived for many years among the Indians, and had trapped beaver upon the head waters of the Missouri, Columbia, and Colorado. He was an intimate friend of Kit Carson, and they had often spread their blankets together in their mountain bivouac.

Baker was a man of more limited experience and education, but a generous, noble-hearted specimen of the trapper type, who would peril his life for a friend at any time, or divide his last morsel of food.

He was born in Illinois, and lived at home until he was

eighteen years of age, when he enlisted in the American Fur Company, went to the mountains, and had remained there ever since. He had married a wife, according to the Indian custom, from the Snake tribe, and had lived with the Indians for several years, adopting many of their habits, ideas, and superstitions. He firmly believed in the efficacy of the charms and incantations of the "*medicine-men*" in curing diseases and divining where their enemy was to be found, predicting the results of war expeditions, etc. Unfortunately, however, for my friend Jim, he would occasionally allow himself to take a glass of whisky beyond what he could discreetly carry, and, when in this condition, would sometimes commit *faux pas*.

When I first met him, I inquired if he had traveled much over the settled part of the United States before he came out into the mountains, to which he replied, "Right smart, Cap." I then asked whether he had visited New York. He said he had not. "Have you been in New Orleans?" "No, I hasn't been to Horleans, Cap., but I'll tell you whar I have been: I've traveled mighty nigh all over four counties in the State of Illinois!" and this, it appeared, was the extent of his wanderings before leaving home.

Jim seemed fond of his squaw and children, and usually treated them very kindly; but his friend, Tim Goodale, informed me that, upon one occasion, when he had taken a *drop* of liquor too much, he came into his lodge, and expressed serious doubts regarding the faithfulness of his wife; whereupon Tim assured him that he had no grounds for his suspicions, and endeavored to convince him of his injustice, but without success. Jim was very indignant, seized his hunting-knife, and, with an oath, said, "I'll cut off one of her ears, Tim;" and it was with great difficulty that his friend prevailed upon him to desist from carrying his purpose into execution. This was one of the Indian methods of punishing a truant spouse, and it seemed to Jim the most appropriate for the present occasion.

When we reached the settlements in New Mexico, after passing over the mountains, Baker concluded he would, for the time being, cast aside his leggins, moccasins, and other mountain gear, and adopt a civilized wardrobe; accordingly, he supplied himself with a complete outfit, and when I met him shortly afterward he had undergone an entire metamorphose. I remarked that I should hardly have known him, so great was the change. He did not appear to appreciate the compliment, however, and said, "Confound these yere store butes, Cap.; they choke my feet like hell." It was the first time in twenty years that he had worn any thing but moccasins upon his feet, and they were not prepared for the severe torture inflicted by the breaking in of a pair of badly-fitting new boots. He soon cast them aside, and resumed the softer foot-gear of the mountains.

Jim Baker had been in at the death of many a grizzly bear, and related to me a number of thrilling accounts of his encounters with this formidable quadruped. On one occasion, while he was setting his traps, with a companion, on the head waters of Grand River, they came suddenly upon two young grizzly bears, about the size of well-grown dogs. He remarked to his friend that if they could "pitch in and skulp the varmints with their knives," it would be an exploit to boast of. They accordingly laid aside their rifles and "went in," Bridger attacking one and his companion the other. He says the bears immediately raised themselves upon their haunches, and were ready for the encounter. He ran around, endeavoring to get an opportunity to give a blow from behind with his long knife; but the young brute was too quick for him, and turned as he passed around so as always to confront him face to face.

JIM BAKER'S FIGHT.

He knew if he came within reach of his paws that, although young, he could inflict a formidable blow; moreover, he felt great apprehensions that the piteous howls set up by the cubs would bring the infuriated dam to their rescue, when their chances for escape would be small. These thoughts passing rapidly through his mind made him exceedingly nervous, and anxious to terminate the combat as soon as possible. He made many desperate lunges at the bear, but the animal invariably warded them off with his fore paws like a pugilist, and protected his body at the expense of several severe cuts upon his legs. This, however, only served to exasperate him, and at length he took the offensive, and, with his mouth frothing with rage, he bounded toward Baker, who grappled with him and gave him a death-wound under the ribs. While all this was going on his companion had been furiously fighting the other bear, and by this time had become greatly exhausted, and the odds were turning decidedly against him. He entreated Baker to come to his assistance at once, which he did; but, much to his astonishment, as soon as he entered the second contest his companion ran off, leaving him to fight the battle alone. He was, however, again victorious, and soon had the satisfaction of seeing his two antagonists stretched out lifeless before him; but he firmly resolved never again to make war on a bear with a hunting-knife, saying that he would "never fight narry nother grizzly without a good shootin-iron in his paws."

Like the mountaineers generally, Baker was liberal to a fault, and eminently improvident. He had made a great deal of money in trading and trapping, but, at the annual rendezvous of the traders, would spend the earnings of a season in a few days' jollification. He told me that during one season he had been particularly successful in accumulating a very large amount of furs, from which he realized the handsome sum of about nine thousand dollars, and he resolved that he would abandon his mountain life, return to the settlements, purchase a farm, and endeavor to live comfortably for the remainder of his days. He accordingly made his preparations to leave, and was upon the point of departure, when a friend invited him to visit a monte bank which had been opened in camp. He was easily persuaded to take a little social parting amusement with his old friends, whom he might never meet again, and accepted the invitation, the result of which was that the *aguardiente* circulated freely, and the following morning found him without a cent of money; he had lost every thing. His entire plans were thus frustrated, and he returned to the hunting-grounds with the Indians, where he had remained ever since.

The last time I saw Jim was on my return to the States from Utah. He had established a little store at the crossing of Green River, and had for some time been doing a fair business in trafficking with the emigrants and trading with the Indians; but, shortly before my arrival, a Frenchman had made his appearance there, and set up a rival establishment, which divided the limited trade, and very materially reduced the profits of Baker's business.

This engendered a bitter spirit of competition and hostility, which soon culminated in a cessation of all social intercourse between them; and, about the time of my arrival, it had reached such a pitch that I found Baker standing in his door, with a pistol loaded and cocked in each hand, pretty drunk and immensely excited. I dismounted, and asked him the cause of all this disturbance. He replied, "That thar yaller-bellied, toad-eatin *parly-voo* over thar, and me, we've been havin a small chance of a skrimmage to-day, we have, Cap." I remonstrated with him upon his folly, but he continued: "The sneakin polecat, I'll raise his har yet. I'll sculp him, Cap., ef he don't quit these yeare diggins."

It appeared that they had an altercation in the morning, which ended in a challenge, when they ran to their respective cabins, seized their revolvers, and from the doors, that were only about one hundred yards apart, fired at each other. They then retired into the cabins, took a drink of whisky, reloaded their pistols, and again renewed the combat. This peculiar duel had been kept up for several hours when I arrived, but, fortunately for them, the whisky had produced such an effect upon their nerves that their aim was very unsteady, and none of their many shots had as yet taken effect.

I took away Baker's pistols, telling him that I was greatly astonished to find that a man of his usually good sense should make such a fool of himself. He submitted quietly, saying that he knew I was his friend, but he did not think I would wish to have him take insults from a cowardly Frenchman.

The following morning at daylight Jim called at my camp to bid me good-by, and expressed great regret at what had transpired the day before. He said this was the first time since his return from New Mexico that he had allowed himself to drink whisky, and when the whisky was in him he had "narry sense."

Another peculiar specimen of the mountaineer genus who accompanied me over the mountains was a half-breed Frenchman and Indian by the name of Mariano. He had spent all his life among the Indians, and for many years had been in the service of the American and Northwest Fur Companies. Besides the French, Spanish, and English, he spoke the languages of several of the Indian tribes with whom he had lived.

He was an intimate friend of the old patriarch mountaineer Jack Robinson, and when I met him their lodges were pitched in the same valley.

While we were making our slow progress up the western slope of the Rocky Mountains through snow from three to five feet deep, at the rate of two or three miles a day, I found Mariano's experience in the high northern latitudes, and the ready resources which he always had at hand for every emergency, of great service to me.

For example, he found a substitute for tea in the wild mint which abounded in the line of our march, and a fair imitation of tobacco was supplied by the inner bark of the red willow.

Mariano's qualities have been more fully shown in another part of the book.

While traveling in Wisconsin in the winter of 1835, I fell in with a remarkably interesting and intelligent man by the name of Clyburn, who accompanied me from Sheboygan to Green Bay.

At that early period in the settlement of this now densely-populated state there was not a house between the two places mentioned, and the only approximation to a road was a narrow Indian trail, without a tree cut down or a bridge made upon it.

I found Mr. Clyburn a very pleasant traveling companion, and he very kindly whiled away the monotony of our long and solitary ride through that dense wilderness by relating to me several thrilling incidents in the history of his highly eventful career. As his character for honor and veracity are fully established, and will, I dare say, be vouched for by the early settlers of Milwaukee, the reader may rest perfectly assured that every word of his narrative has the impress of reality and truth.

He informed me that at an early period in his life (somewhere about the year 1820 I think it was) he enlisted at St. Louis to serve for five years in the private fur enterprise organized by General Ashley, and with this company he went immediately to the head waters of the Missouri, where he followed the vocation of trapper and hunter during the entire term of his enlistment.

It was the practice of the agents in charge of the business at that time to establish a grand dépôt for the deposit of goods and the reception of furs, after which the employés were sent out in pairs and distributed over the best trapping-grounds throughout the mountains, each two men having a certain district of country assigned to them for the season.

Mr. Clyburn and a companion were at one time assigned to a district within the country frequented by the Blackfeet Indians, who had always manifested a most implacable spirit of hostility to the whites, and made war upon them whenever they met.

The two companions, however, exercised the greatest possible precaution in carrying on their trapping operations, setting and visiting their traps only at early dawn and late in the evening, and lying concealed in some solitary mountain glen during the daytime. Thus they continued their business during the entire season without having been at all molested by their Indian enemies, and they were richly rewarded for their labors by unusual success. They had accumulated a large amount of valuable furs, which they packed upon their horses, and started to return to the dépôt with them. After traveling a short distance, they determined to cross a stream which lay in their route, and had already entered a grove of timber that covered the bottom lands, when all at once, to their perfect amazement and horror, they emerged directly into a huge encampment of Blackfeet Indians. Mr. Clyburn, who was, under all circumstances, cool and self-possessed, motioned to his companion to follow him, and rode directly up to the chief's lodge, telling him by signs that they were friends, had come into his camp to pass the night, and claimed his protection, thinking that this appeal to his hospitality, one of the most prominent of the savages' virtues (if they possess any traits of character that are worthy that appellation), might touch his pride, and possibly induce him to spare their lives. The chief received them very coldly, told them to dismount and sit down, and ordered some of his wives to unpack their horses and give them supper. He then required them to give an account of themselves, and imperiously demanded to know how they dare presume to intrude upon his hunting-grounds, to all of which they gave the most discreet replies they could invent upon the spur of the occasion; but the chief was evidently very far from being satisfied or kindly disposed toward them. The squaws set some buffalo meat before them, and their savage host in a very surly and dictatorial manner told them "*to eat;*" but, although they had been traveling a long time, and, under ordinary circumstances, would have done ample justice to the fare, yet their surroundings upon the present occasion were of such a character as almost entirely to take away their appetites. They, however, in order to do away with any exhibition of alarm on their part, forced themselves to swallow some of the meat, then lit their pipes and commenced smoking. Shortly after this, Clyburn, who understood a little of the Blackfeet language, overheard the chief tell some of his warriors that he and his companion must be put to death. Now the encampment was situated directly upon the river bank, and the chief's lodge where they were seated was about a hundred yards distant. As soon as Clyburn learned the fate which the Indians had in store for them, he immediately resolved upon the course he should pursue, and very quietly, in a low tone of voice, informed his friend what he had overheard, at the same time directing him, as the only chance for saving their lives, to keep constant watch upon his own movements, and to do precisely as he did. He waited until nearly dark, when he found an opportunity at a time the Indians seemed off their guard, and had their eyes turned in another direction, to spring to his feet, and with lightning speed to run rapidly toward the river. His friend followed, but the Indians instantly gave the war-cry, and, seizing their arms, pursued them closely, firing many balls and arrows, some of which passed in most disagreeable proximity to his person. He, however, had the good fortune to reach the river, and jumped in, diving deeply, and striking out with desperate strides for the opposite shore, which he reached in safety, and hid himself under the shelving bank. Here he awaited in great anxiety for some time, until the Indians had given up the search and returned to their camps, when he crawled out and endeavored to get some trace of his friend, but none was found, and he was never heard of afterward, so that he must have been murdered by the savages.

My friend Clyburn was now reduced to first principles. He had lost all his horses, guns, and traps, besides the proceeds of a year's labor. Indeed, he now found himself totally destitute of every thing except the clothes upon his back. He was very far from being discouraged, however, and started at once for the rendezvous, where he arrived a few days afterward, and, providing himself with another outfit and companion, he returned to the trapping-grounds with as good a heart as ever. This kind of life he pursued until the expiration of his term of service, when, unlike the most of the mountaineers, he resolved to go back to his home, and for the future lead a civilized life. Accordingly, after bidding adieu to his friends, he embarked in one of the fleet of Mackinaw boats which were annually sent by the company with their furs down the Missouri River to St. Louis. In the course of their trip they arrived at the upper end of a narrow peninsula, made by a very long detour in the river, which rendered it necessary for the boats to pass many miles around, while the distance across the neck of the peninsula was comparatively very short. Thinking that perhaps he might find game here, he obtained permission from the man in charge of his boat to go ashore and take a hunt while the fleet was making the passage around the bend, expecting to re-embark at the lower extremity. He accordingly passed several hours in hunting, without giving much heed to time, believing that he could easily reach the designated point before the arrival of the boats. On reaching the river bank, he seated himself and quietly awaited their coming, but he remained here one, two, and three hours without seeing them.

Thinking that possibly they might have been delayed from some cause or other, he did not yet feel at all alarmed, but after remaining here hour after hour in anxious expectation until night, he began to think that the fleet must have passed before he arrived, and that he was left alone in the wilderness. He knew full well that the life of a trapper was of but little moment in the estimation of those in charge of the boats when put in comparison with the importance of securing a speedy transit for a year's accumulation of the company's furs, and he was also perfectly conscious of the fact that he had no reason to expect that they would make any halt on his account.

He, however, still clung to the hope that the boats might yet be above him, and, after making a fire, took his station upon the bank to await their coming; but the night passed and no boats appeared, and he was now reluctantly compelled to abandon all hopes of ever seeing them again. He possessed a very good general knowledge of the country, and, as near as he could calculate, he was at this point about a thousand miles from the fort at Council Bluffs, the nearest place where he could expect to reach a white man's habitation. He had his rifle, with eight charges of powder and ball, and with these he must provide himself with subsistence during the long and solitary journey before him, or perish in the attempt. It was a most appalling and desperate alternative, yet he was not to be discouraged by trifles, and he at once set about making his preparations for departure.

He struck out from the river bottom upon the prairies, and took his course for Council Bluffs, traveling day after day and night after night, and he says that, for several days and nights after he set out, he was under such a fearful state of anxiety in regard to his situation that he could neither sleep nor eat. He husbanded his ammunition with great care, only expending a charge when he became very hungry and was sure of his game. He would then eat all he could upon the spot, and carry with him the remainder. In this manner he continued on until he wore out his moccasins and leggins, when the sharp prairie grass cut his feet and legs so badly that he suffered intense pain therefrom.

Days and weeks passed by, his eyes eagerly sweeping the field of vision in all directions. Not a solitary human being made his appearance during the whole time. At length, after expending all his ammunition and consuming his last morsel of meat, he became greatly famished, and the only nutriment he now had was derived from a few grasshoppers and spiders which he met with in his track; but these were very far from satisfying the cravings of his voracious appetite. He continued to press forward as long as he had a particle of strength remaining, hoping every moment to see some evidences of proximity to the fort, but on every side of him was nothing but one vast expanse of dreary, desolate prairie solitude; and, finally, he became so much exhausted and so lame that he could go no farther, and was forced to the conclusion that he must die upon the prairie. The dread anticipation of such a death, in his enfeebled and famished state, induced a condition of mind bordering upon insanity, and, to add to his torture, the wolves now began to mark him as their victim, and followed on his track for several days, lapping the blood which dropped upon the grass from his lacerated feet and legs.

In his delirious moments he would imagine himself raised from the earth, and carried with giant strides through the air. The wolves seemed to be transformed into savage Blackfeet warriors, who were bent upon his destruction, and he underwent all the mental torture their actual presence would have produced. Still he staggered on, until exhausted nature entirely gave way, and he sank down upon the ground, expecting never to rise again.

He fell into a most profound sleep, which he thinks must have continued many hours, and when he awoke, to his astonishment, he felt very much refreshed. His mental aberration had left him; but it was with the greatest difficulty that he succeeded, after several efforts, in rising to his feet and slowly resuming his painful journey. His iron will and indomitable firmness of purpose, however, aided by a powerful physique, enabled him to conquer obstacles which would have disheartened most men at the outset, and he again pushed forward with renewed vigor toward the fort. He traveled on without any sustenance until at length he became weary and exhausted again, and once more sank down powerless upon the ground, and he now abandoned all thoughts of ever rising again. He expected to die there, and consigned his soul to his Maker. Yet another deep sleep soon came over him, on awaking from which he again felt somewhat refreshed, and endeavored to rise to his feet, but found himself unable to do so. At this time he was near the summit of a hill, and he thought if he could reach the crest he might perhaps be able to discover something that would afford him relief. Accordingly, he put forth all his remaining powers, and, with the utmost difficulty, succeeded in crawling upon his hands and knees to the summit of the elevation, which proved to be a bluff bordering the Missouri Valley; and who can conceive of his joy and astonishment when, on raising his eyes, he beheld, directly in front of him, and only about half a mile distant, the flag waving from the fort at Council Bluffs? His feelings on beholding this welcome haven may be more easily imagined than described. He was like a man who has been brought from death unto life; and the consciousness of his safety, after the horrible state of mental anxiety and torture to which he had been subjected for weeks, overwhelmed him with the most intense and heartfelt emotions of joy and gratitude. He prostrated himself upon the earth, and gave vent to his feelings by weeping for a long time, and then offered up sincere thanks to the Almighty for his deliverance.

In the course of a few hours he was enabled to crawl toward the fort, where he was kindly received by the officers, and nursed for several weeks before he was sufficiently restored to resume his homeward journey.

After all the scenes of danger, privation, and suffering through which Mr. Clyburn had passed, he was delighted to revisit once more the home of his childhood, and he confidently anticipated that the remainder of his days would pass in peace and quietness; but in this he was greatly mistaken, as the following narrative will show.

He had, in 1834, taken up his abode among the first settlers at Milwaukee; but the population soon increased to such an extent that the place became too crowded to suit him, and he was desirous of purchasing a farm in the beautiful valley of Rock River; and, as the government was about bringing those lands into market, he, with a friend, set out upon an expedition to explore that region, and make selections of lands. They engaged a man to transport their luggage to the bank of Rock River, where they cut down a tree and constructed a "*dug-out*" (canoe), in which they embarked, and started on their voyage down the river.

As night approached they arrived at an old Kickapoo village, which was then abandoned. It was raining at the time, and as the bark lodges offered good shelter, they determined to take up lodgings for the night in one of them. Accordingly they made a landing, and commenced carrying their baggage ashore, and the transfer was nearly completed, when, as Clyburn went into the lodge, and was in the act of striking a light, he heard his companion give the Indian salutation of "*boo-joo*" to some person outside. On going out he met two Indians, an old and a young man. They shook hands with him, apparently in a friendly manner, and informed him that they were Potawatomies. Remnants of this tribe, as well as of the Kickapoos, Chippeways, and Winnebagoes, then ranged over that section of country, but they were supposed to be perfectly peaceable and well-disposed toward the whites.

As soon as he had passed a few words with the Indians, Clyburn told his friend to kindle a fire in the lodge, while he would go out and collect some wood for the night. He went out, picked up an armful of wood, and was returning, when suddenly he heard a rifle-shot in the lodge, and, at the same moment, a cry of distress from his companion, and instantly afterward the two Indians bounded out of the lodge and fired a shot at him, which broke his arm. He dropped the wood and ran at the top of his speed into the woods, with the Indians after him in eager pursuit. Fortunately for him, it was now night, and, under cover of the darkness, he was enabled to elude the search of his savage pursuers. He concealed himself under a log, and heard them prowling about near him for some time; but they finally gave up the search and went away. He then, with great difficulty, managed to bind up his shattered arm with his handkerchief, and started back toward Milwaukee. It was raining very hard during all the night (I remember it well, as I myself bivouacked in the woods near Sheboygan on the same night), and Mr. Clyburn soon became exhausted from the loss of blood, and very wet and cold. He attempted to strike a fire, but, in consequence of his broken arm, was unable to hold the flint and punk. He continued on, however, and the next day (I think it was) had the satisfaction of reaching his home at Milwaukee.

A note was immediately dispatched to Fort Dearborn, Chicago, the nearest military post, and an officer, Captain Baxley, with a suitable force, was sent out to apprehend the perpetrators of the deed. They found the body of the murdered man, and arrested several Indians whom they discovered near the locality. These were taken to Fort Howard, Green Bay, where I was then stationed, and placed in close confinement until they could be confronted by Mr. Clyburn, who was laid up for several weeks with his wound, and had just recovered sufficiently to travel when I met him at Sheboygan. Although he had only seen the two Indians concerned in the murder for a moment, yet, on his arrival at Fort Howard, he recognized them again instantly among a dozen others.

The Indians then acknowledged themselves to have been the guilty parties, and were tried for murder before the first court ever held at Milwaukee. They were convicted, the old man sentenced to be hung, and his son to imprisonment for life. I was myself a witness upon the trial, having heard the confession of the Indians at Green Bay.

The sentences of these Indians, owing, I believe, to some flaw in the proceedings, were not executed. The stoical imperturbability of the savage character was strikingly illustrated when they received the information of the result.

The sheriff called the old man out of his cell and asked him if he was aware that the day appointed for his execution had arrived. He, without changing the expression of his countenance in the least, replied that he did not think the time was so near at hand, but that he was ready, and, shaking hands with us, bade us good-by. The sheriff then told him that he was not to be executed, and was free to go where he pleased, all of which he received with apparently perfect indifference.

The reason assigned by these Indians for committing the murder was that a relative of the old man's wife had been killed by a sentinel at Fort Winnebago, and she, with the instincts of her race, gave the old man no peace until he had assuaged her thirst for revenge with the blood of a white man. One of the peculiar characteristics of the Indians is that they never make allowances for accidents. If a man, for example, by the accidental discharge of a gun, happens to kill one of their people, they hold him just as much responsible for the result as if he committed a willful act of murder. Their legal code makes no distinction between justifiable homicide and murder in the first degree.

While I was at Green Bay, a Frenchman, who was hunting deer in the night with a torch-light, seeing before his canoe two eyes glistening like those of a deer, immediately raised his rifle and fired. He was, however, horrified, on approaching the object, to find that, instead of a deer, he had shot an Indian directly through the brain. He recognized the man, and, taking the body in his canoe, carried it to the lodge of his brother, to whom he related all the circumstances, expressing great regret at what had happened. The Indian, instead of pardoning him, seized his rifle, and killed the Frenchman upon the spot.

CHAPTER XIV.

CAPTAIN MARTIN SCOTT.

Captain Martin Scott.—The Coon Story.—The Bear-hunter.—The Horse-race.—Courting Days.—Rifle and Pistol Shooting.—His Duel.—Expedition with Explorers.—Hunting in Texas.—Wonderful Dog.—"Tally Ho!"—Return Home to Bennington.—His Death.

WHEN I first joined my regiment (the 5th United States Infantry) at Fort Howard, Green Bay, in the spring of 1833, I was assigned to "D" Company, then commanded by Captain Martin Scott, of *coon* notoriety.

The coon story has been so often related that it is probably familiar to many; but as some may not have heard it, and as I shall have a good deal to say about Captain Scott, whose peculiar reputation it aptly illustrates, it may not be amiss to give a brief repetition of it here.

The story, as I understand, first appeared in a newspaper published in Utica, New York, in 1840, and the purport of it was something like the following: Captain Scott, with several friends, were supposed to have been hunting in the woods, and had become separated. As they were passing along, one of them discovered a raccoon sitting upon the highest limb of one of the tallest trees, and fired at him, but missed the object and went on. Soon another of the party made his appearance and delivered a shot, but with the same result; and after this, several others took shots at him, but all were equally unsuccessful; the coon was not harmed. After a while, however, Captain Scott passed that way, and, seeing the raccoon, drew up his rifle, and was in the act of pulling trigger, when the coon said to him, "Who are you?" He replied, "My name is Scott." "What Scott?" inquired the coon. "Why, Captain Scott." "Are you Captain Martin Scott?" said the coon. "The same," was the answer. "Then," said the coon, "you need not shoot; I'll come down."

This officer had served for many years at our most remote frontier posts, and he had always borne the reputation of having been the best shot of his day. His ambition consisted in owning the best horses, dogs, and guns, and he was a thorough sportsman and hunter, besides being a faithful and gallant soldier.

At an early day, when he was a boy only twelve years of age, living at his home in Bennington, Vermont, a bear made his appearance in that neighborhood, committing great havoc among the farmers' sheep, and creating much alarm among the timid inhabitants of the surrounding country.

So great was the excitement produced by the advent of this savage intruder that the people of several towns turned out in mass to hunt him down. They organized into parties to scour all the adjacent mountains and woodlands on a certain day, and were to assemble at the hotel in Bennington after the day's hunt was over.

Now our young hero felt an earnest desire to participate in this exciting sport, but he was perfectly well aware that his father would not give his consent to such a proposal if it was suggested to him. He therefore very quietly got up before daylight on the appointed day, took an old smooth-bored gun of his father's, loaded it, and started out alone into the mountain where the bear was last heard from. He wandered about nearly all day, but without discovering any signs of the animal, and at length turned toward home; and, as he was descending the mountain, he came to a shelving rock, and was just in the act of passing over it, when suddenly he came upon the bear lying apparently asleep just beneath where he stood. He at once raised the gun to his shoulder and fired, and he fortunately lodged its contents in the vitals of the beast, killing him instantly. He then started for the tavern, where many of the hunters had already congregated, and were relating to each other the history of the day's experience. He told them that he had killed the bear, but they did not believe it possible, and it was with great difficulty that he finally persuaded some of the men to go with him to verify his statement. When they reached the place where the animal lay, they were amazed that so small a lad should have had the temerity to attack such a monster. He was a huge fellow, and they were obliged to construct a stout litter to carry him into town. When they arrived at the entrance of the village they mounted Martin upon the top of the bear, and thus carried him in triumph through the street; and on passing his father's house, the old gentleman came out, and, in a very abrupt manner, said, "Come down from there; what are you doing up there, sir?" The men replied, "Let the boy alone, for he has killed the bear;" and thus they went on to the tavern, where they celebrated the event with great feasting and rejoicing. After this they dubbed Martin the Bear-hunter, and he has often said to me that this was the happiest day of his life.

Like other boys, young Scott was very fond of visiting places of amusement, such as horse-races, trainings, town meetings, etc., and, as he was a good rider, he was sometimes selected to ride races by the sporting fraternity of that section.

In those days (before the time of horse-fairs) horse-racing was looked upon by the New Englanders as a most immoral and pernicious practice, and young Scott was never allowed to make his appearance at such places with his father's consent.

Upon one occasion, an unknown horse was brought to Bennington by some sportsmen, who offered large wagers upon his running against any other horse that could be produced. Now a certain Deacon R——, of that place, was the owner of several fine horses, and among them was one that was considered very fleet, but those disposed to contest the wager so confidently offered on the strange horse were perfectly well aware that a Presbyterian deacon could not openly sanction and give countenance to such diabolical immorality; yet those who knew him well verily believed if there was any one trait in the deacon's character that was not in strict accordance with the requirements of his church and with the sanctity of his ecclesiastical functions, it was the weakness he manifested for owning the fleetest horse in the country.

The men proposing to take up the gauntlet so defiantly thrown out by the backers of the new horse entered the deacon's favorite horse for the race, but with the express stipulation that the race should come off in the night-time, and should be kept a profound secret except to those directly interested. The terms having been satisfactorily arranged, Martin Scott was selected as the jockey for the deacon's horse; and on the night designated for the contest, he stole very quietly into the stable, and, muffling the horse's feet, led him out and took him to the race-track. The judges were then posted, the riders mounted, and the horses were off. It was a single straight dash of a mile, and both horses were put to their speed, and kept constantly down to their work from the word "go." But, as they approached the "coming-out" place, the strange horse began to gain a little upon his antagonist, and at this moment of interest and excitement to all parties concerned, it looked as if the deacon's horse was to be beaten, when suddenly from behind a board fence near the track jumped up Deacon R——— himself, who in a very loud and excited manner screamed out, "Put the whip to him, Martin! put the whip to him, I tell you!" Martin was perfectly astounded and almost paralyzed at this unexpected apparition, but, with nervous desperation, he made several vigorous and well-timed applications of his whip, which caused the horse to redouble his efforts and win the race by half a length, at which the deacon, in the excitement of the moment, took off his hat and gave a lusty cheer; but, instantly afterward recollecting himself, and considering the ludicrous *rôle* he had been enacting in this somewhat farcical performance, he assumed an indignant air, and approaching Martin, who was holding the horse in great trepidation, said, "Martin Scott, you young reprobate, you have stolen my horse, sir, and, unless you instantly lead him back to the stable, and give him a good rubbing down, I'll report you to your father, sir!"

When young Scott arrived at the age of sixteen he fell in love with a young lady in a neighboring village, and received her permission to pay his addresses; but his father's opinions upon the subject, being somewhat austere and dictatorial, did not accord with his own, and compelled him to conduct his courtship in a clandestine manner. He was in the habit of waiting until his father went to bed, when he would take a horse from the stable, pay a visit to his lady-love, and return home before daylight. After one of these weekly visits, he had just put his horse into the stable, and had made some little noise in doing so, which awakened his father, who ran out toward the stable, thinking that some person was attempting to steal his horse. Martin saw him approaching, and, unable to elude his observation, ran into a corn-house near by and ascended a ladder into the loft, with the old man close upon his heels.

It was dark at the time, and he hid himself in one corner of the loft; but his father groped around until he was satisfied that the next instant he would be in his grasp, and he saw but one method of escaping detection, which he instantly resorted to. He leaped upon the poor old man, and gave him a blow which knocked him down, and thus secured an opportunity to make his escape to the house.

The old man soon recovered himself, however, and called out, "Martin! Martin! come here quick; there are robbers about, and one of them has knocked me down." Martin turned, and, running back to the corn-house, aided his father for a considerable time in searching for the supposed robber.

As he was plowing in the field one day during the year 1814, the postmaster of the village brought him a letter marked "War Department, Adjutant General's Office," and directed to Ensign Martin Scott, on opening which he found a commission for himself as ensign in the United States Army. He had made no application for the appointment, and its being conferred upon him was a mystery which was never solved to the day of his death. He accepted his appointment, and forthwith joined his company at Sackett's Harbor.

He was shortly afterward sent to the Western frontier, where he found ample scope for the development of his proclivities as a sportsman.

His reputation for accurate rifle and pistol shooting was well deserved, and I am not aware that he was ever excelled, if, indeed, he was ever equaled by any of his contemporaries.

One of his performances with the pistol, which I have often heard vouched for by officers who had witnessed it, and which appears to me to require more skill in the use of the arm than any other feat I have heard of, was in taking two potatoes, throwing them into the air successively, and putting a pistol ball through both of them as they crossed, one going up and the other coming down.

Some of his performances in rifle-shooting I have witnessed myself, and for great accuracy I must acknowledge that they exceed any thing of the kind I have ever before seen. One of the many instances where I have been present at his shooting will, I presume, suffice to illustrate this.

He proposed to me, upon one occasion, that we should take an old-fashioned United States yager that he had, and determine which could load and fire three shots in the shortest space of time, and make the best target. Accordingly, a playing-card, with a spot or bull's-eye in the centre about the size of a dime, was attached to a log of wood, and placed at seventy-five yards from where we proposed to stand. Captain Scott then took the rifle uncharged, with the powder-flask at hand, and the balls and patches in his mouth, and he made the three shots "off-hand" in one minute and twenty seconds. I then myself went to the target, and found one round hole directly through the centre of the bull's-eye. I was surprised at the precision of the shot, but observed to the captain that the other two had entirely missed the target. He shook his head and called for an axe, when we split the log, and found the three balls in one mass, all having passed through the same round aperture directly in the centre of the card.

The captain was also a very excellent marksman with a bird-gun, and, although I have seen him fire numerous shots, I do not remember ever to have known him to miss his bird.

At a very early day, but a few years after the close of the war in 1814, he was attached to the expedition under the command of General Atkinson, which ascended the Missouri River and established a military post at Council Bluffs, which at that time was very far beyond the remotest border settlements. The war had not improved the morals of the army, and its effects were still seen among the officers, many of whom were addicted to cards and liquor, and a man who did not participate in these dissipated pastimes was considered as wanting in that spirit of social congeniality which, according to their code, was indispensable to an officer.

Captain Scott had never in his life drank a glass of ardent spirits, played a game of cards, or used tobacco in any form. He was liberal in his intercourse with his brother officers, but was exceedingly parsimonious in his own personal expenses, and took good care of his money. This was not in accord with the views of the officers around him, and they soon gave vent to their feelings by petty slights and annoyances, and by a gradual withdrawal from his society. This finally culminated by all the officers, with three exceptions, putting him in coventry. He submitted to their unjust persecution and insults as long as possible, but at length it came to such a pass that he could endure it no longer, and he took counsel with his three friends as to the course he should pursue. They were unanimous in the opinion that there were but two alternatives left to him: one was to throw up his commission and leave the service at once, and the other was to challenge the first man who should insult him. He determined to adopt the latter course.

The officers were soon apprised of what had been decided upon, and as Captain Scott was a much better pistol-shot than any of them, they did not feel disposed to risk an encounter against such odds.

One of their friends, however, who was then stationed at another post, was a celebrated shot, and had brought down his antagonist in several duels. They dispatched a messenger for him, and, on his arrival, he took the first opportunity to insult Captain Scott at the mess-table, and a challenge immediately ensued. The preliminaries were arranged in due form, and the parties came upon the ground. In giving me the history of this affair, Captain Scott said that he had always opposed dueling from principle, and he would not have believed that he could, under any circumstances, have been drawn into one, but here he was; and he acknowledged that he was very considerably agitated, and had determined to throw away his shot by firing into the air, when he heard his antagonist remark that he had a very disagreeable job on hand that morning, which was to shoot a d—d Yankee. This, he said, roused his indignation to the highest pitch, and made him perfectly cool and collected, and he firmly resolved to punish his adversary.

They took their positions and fired: Captain Scott received a slight flesh-wound, but his adversary fell to the ground, shot through the lungs. He was carried to the hospital, and ultimately recovered. It is mentioned as a curious circumstance that previous to this duel he had the consumption, but the wound he received is supposed to have effected a cure of that disease, and he lived for many years afterward.

At the next meeting of the officers at the mess-table, Captain Scott took occasion to inform them that he should in future hold them personally responsible for any and every insult offered to him. They did not seem disposed to contest the matter any farther, and he was soon restored to his proper social position.

The invincible determination of purpose and stubborn perseverance with which he contended against obstacles are strikingly shown in the following narrative, which I received from his own lips.

Somewhere about the year 1825 (I am not certain about the precise date), the Scientific Exploring Expedition, conducted by the naturalist Say, was organized by the government, and Captain Scott, then stationed at Fort Snelling, was selected by the Secretary of War to command the escort. It so happened that he was not a favorite with his commanding officer, who determined that another officer should be assigned to this desirable duty. Accordingly, on the arrival of the scientific gentlemen at the fort, he informed them that he could not furnish their escort from his weak command, but that he would send Captain Scott to Prairie du Chien for the necessary force, the distance between the two places by river being something like three hundred miles, and the only means of transit at that early day by Mackinaw boats. With these the captain started, and, as he had favorable winds, he made a rapid trip, secured his men, and returned to Fort Snelling in an almost unprecedentedly brief period; but what was his antonishment, on his arrival, to find that the expedition had set out immediately after his departure with an escort from the garrison of Fort Snelling, commanded by another officer. The expedition had been off about two weeks, and was then probably some two hundred and eighty miles on its way to Pembina. This, however, did not discourage Scott, and he demanded from the commanding officer the privilege of following and overtaking the party. This could not consistently be refused him, but at the same time he was only allowed an escort of four men, with one old horse, that was never known to go over about twenty miles without breaking down, to transport his supplies. With this outfit he started. As he had anticipated, the horse gave out and was abandoned the first day out. They were obliged to pack their luggage upon their backs, and in this manner continued on rapidly day after day, until at length their provisions were all exhausted excepting a few biscuits, which were divided equally. No game was seen for several days, and their only subsistence for a considerable time was confined to one biscuit per man daily. Even these were finally consumed, and for two days they had nothing. They wore out their shoes, and became so lame that it was with difficulty they could walk. The captain saw that, under such circumstances, his prospects for overtaking the main party were small. He therefore ordered all his escort to turn back to the fort, and alone pushed forward again. After a few days' rapid and toilsome marching, he overtook the party near Pembina, assumed command of the escort, and retained it throughout the remainder of the expedition.

For several years after the establishment of the post of Fort Snelling, all the lumber was procured by the labor of the troops, and it had been the practice every year to send an officer with a detachment of men to Rum River, where they passed the entire winter in cutting "saw-logs," and rafted them down to the falls in the spring. This service was any thing but agreeable to the officers, and Rum River was designated by them as "Botany Bay;" and some of them even had the temerity to whisper it about that, by a most astonishing coincidence, whenever an officer incurred the displeasure of the commanding officer, it invariably became his next detail for service at "Botany Bay." However this may have been, it is quite certain that Captain Scott passed the following winter at *Rum River.*

Although Captain Scott possessed his firmness of nerve and accuracy of sight up to the day of his death, yet his qualities as a hunter were seriously impaired by age.

During the winter of 1845–6, while General Taylor's army occupied Corpus Christi, Colonel Garland, Captains Scott, McCall, and myself, went about a hundred miles up the Nueces upon a hunting expedition. Our hunt, after we reached the ground, lasted four days, and the result was we bagged twenty-seven deer, seventy-three wild turkeys, four tiger-cats, besides quite a number of geese and ducks, and of these Captain McCall and myself killed the greater part. Captain Scott only killed one deer and a few turkeys.

I soon perceived that he considered his reputation as somewhat damaged by these disparaging results, and, as we were returning to Corpus Christi, he remarked to me that it might be just as well not to mention to the officers at camp which one of us bagged the greatest amount of game, as this would not probably please the other two gentlemen. I replied that it would be exceedingly unbecoming in me to boast of my own exploits, therefore I should, of course, say nothing upon the subject.

On our arrival at the encampment with the extraordinary quantity of game, the officers collected around us, and manifested a great desire to ascertain which of the four had excelled in the hunt. I made an evasive answer, stating that we had not been particular about keeping accurate count, but that there was not probably much difference. The question was then put to Captain Scott, who, after my generous reply, thought he must say something magnanimous in return, and he answered that he was not altogether certain as to which had bagged the most game, but of one thing he was quite sure, and that was that he had seen a great many deer-hunters in his day, but that he had never met with one who could *crawl*, and *sneak*, and *squirm* up to a deer like Marcy. I appreciated the motive which dictated the remark fully, but, at the same time, I regarded the intended compliment as somewhat equivocal in its import.

The captain was not upon all other occasions as magnanimous as he might have been toward those who attempted to come in competition with him as marksmen or hunters.

While at Green Bay in 1833, I had procured a rifled pistol, which description of arm had only been in use a short time then, and Captain Scott, having never before seen one, was incredulous in regard to my assertions as to its performances. The barrel of this pistol was about twelve inches in length, and would throw a ball fifty yards with as much accuracy as a rifle. Scott did not believe it, however, and often bantered me to give a specimen of its powers; but, not feeling disposed to subject myself to the ridicule of this celebrated sportsman by incurring the risk of making a possible failure in the presence of spectators, I declined, until one day he proposed that we should go out alone and try it, to which proposition I assented. In order fully to appreciate the sequel of our target excursion, it must be remembered that the captain was exceedingly economical, and estimated a dollar at its full value. He had that morning treated himself to a new and high-priced pocket-knife, with which he cut out a piece of paper about four inches square, and fastened it to a board by sticking his knife directly through the centre of it. I made a shot standing fifty yards distant, and struck the lower part of the paper. He expressed some astonishment at the precision of the shot, but gave it as his opinion that it was accidental, and doubted if it could be done again. I assured him that it was by no means the result of chance, and that, in all probability, I should make a better shot the next time; indeed, I added that he must not be surprised if I struck his new pen-knife (only the end of the handle was exposed). He replied, "Never mind the knife; don't let that give you the slightest uneasiness, sir; go ahead and make your shot; I'll be responsible for the knife." Whereupon I raised the pistol and fired again, and at the same instant the paper fell to the ground. Upon examination, we discovered that the ball had hit the knife in the end of the handle, and split it into at least a dozen pieces. Scott made no comments, but, looking daggers at me, abruptly turned and walked off to his quarters, and it was some days before he received me into favor again.

Captain Scott was at one time, while stationed at Prairie du Chien, in possession of a wonderfully sagacious dog, a cross of the setter and pointer. I never saw the animal myself, but several of the officers of my regiment had frequently witnessed his astonishing performances, and those of them who are now living will doubtless vouch for the truth of what I relate.

The captain would, for example, while sitting in his quarters at the fort, with the dog at his feet, say to him, "Mark, I want you to go over to the island and ascertain if there are any woodcock there, and come back and tell me." The dog would instantly go to the river, swim to the island, and, after having hunted it over, return, and, if he had found birds, run up to his master, then to the gun, wag his tail, and make other demonstrations of joy, which made it perfectly apparent that he had been successful. Scott would then tell the dog to get the canoe in readiness, and, strange as it may appear, he would take the cushion in his mouth, carry it to the river bank where the canoe was moored, place it upon the seat, return for the paddle, carry that to the canoe, then go back to Scott, and look up in his face with an expression which indicated that all was ready.

The captain had at the same time another dog, which he called Turk. These dogs, from their first acquaintance, had never been on friendly terms, and they had many severely contested encounters, which finally resulted in Turk's gaining and retaining the mastery. Mark was emphatically a vanquished dog, and, by his meek and submissive demeanor in the presence of his adversary, he admitted as much.

Upon one occasion Turk had gained possession of a

bonne bouche in the form of a beef's bone, which he was quietly enjoying by himself upon the parade-ground, when Mark chanced to pass that way, and scented the choice morsel. The longing, anxious look which he cast toward the bone, as he circled around at a respectable distance, told how desirous he was to participate in the feast; but his experience had taught him that an attempt to contend with his powerful adversary would only result in his own discomfiture. He therefore prudently resolved to resort to strategy in order to accomplish his ends. Accordingly, he ran furiously outside the stockade inclosure and set up a tremendous barking, as if something very extraordinary had occurred; upon which, as usual, all the dogs in the fort hurried out of the gates to see what was the matter, and among them was Turk, who, in the excitement of the moment, abandoned his bone. As soon as this was done, Mark very quietly slipped back, seized the prize, and carried it to a hiding-place where he could enjoy it at his leisure.

Mark was by no means a dog of regular habits, and would often steal away from home and pass the night among his canine companions of the opposite sex. For this he was invariably punished, his master compelling him to stand upon his hind feet, with his fore paws resting against the wall, while the castigation was administered with a cowhide. In one instance, after having absented himself all night, he returned home with a most dejected and penitent air, and, seeing his master looking very angry at him, he immediately went to the wall, placed himself in the position he had been required to assume when he received his previous punishments, and at the same time turned his head around and looked at Scott, as much as to say "I am ready."

In the course of time Mark waxed in years, and was no longer able to endure the work required in hunting, and

Captain Scott took him home to Bennington to pass the remainder of his days in quiet retirement, and here he continued to make himself useful even in his dotage by going to the pasture every night and driving home the cows. It certainly appeared as if this animal was endowed with something beyond mere brute instinct, as he seemed to comprehend the relations existing between cause and effect.

Captain Scott was so very fond of his dogs, that I have known him, upon the death of a favorite one, to walk his room in great apparent distress of mind during the entire night, and afterward place the body in a coffin, and, with his boy Jack leading his hunting-horse draped in black, follow it to the grave, and bury it with as much care and ceremony as if it had been a child.

He generally kept a pack of hounds, and would occasionally take out his friends to participate in a deer or fox drive; but, upon these occasions, he invariably insisted that every one should conform strictly with the most approved rules of the chase. He was himself thoroughly posted in all the technicalities of sporting lore, and he lost all respect for those persons who misapplied or ridiculed the proper use of sporting nomenclature. Thus he never failed to correct a man who called a line of geese "*a flock of geese*," a bevy of quails "*a brood of quails*," a herd of elk "*a gang of elk*," etc. He was an uncompromising stickler for the correct and literal application of sporting language upon all occasions, but more especially when in the field.

This peculiarity of his was forcibly illustrated while our army was lying at Corpus Christi in 1846. He proposed that we should take his hounds and go out into a place called the Rincon, where the large jackass rabbits were abundant, and have a drive. Quite a number of officers joined the party, and we started out under the guidance of

Captain Scott, who was the acknowledged master of the hunt.

On arriving upon the ground near where the game was supposed to be, the captain stationed the gentlemen around upon the skirts of an extensive chaparral thicket, and prepared to send in the dogs to drive out the rabbits. He gave his last instructions, and specially enjoined upon every one, on the instant a rabbit should make its appearance, to give the view halloo of "*Tally ho.*" Now it so happened that among the officers engaged in the hunt was Captain F. B——n, who was distinguished for his propensities as a practical joker, and never was known to let an opportunity escape for indulging in his favorite amusement.

The hounds were unleashed and taken into the chaparral, and in a very few minutes they gave tongue most vociferously. All were waiting upon their posts with eager anxiety to catch the first glimpse of the game as it emerged from the brush, when suddenly, near the position of Captain B——n, bounded out a mule, with some twenty dogs in full cry at her heels. At this instant of excitement we heard a prolonged cry from the stentorian lungs of Captain B——n of "*Sally whoa! Sally whoa! Sally whoa!*"

The appearance of the terrified mule, and the ludicrous metamorphose of Captain Scott's "view halloo," turned the whole thing into a farce, which brought forth irresistible peals of laughter from every one in the party excepting Captain Scott. He did not smile; on the contrary, his face flushed, and assumed a most indignant expression. He called off his dogs, and, looking daggers at Captain B——n, went back to camp. Immediately after this he sent a challenge to Captain B——n, and it was with great difficulty that their friends could adjust the matter to his satisfaction without an exchange of shots.

With the exception of the money he expended in horses,

dogs, and guns, which were always of the very best description, Captain Scott, as I remarked before, was very economical in his own personal expenses; he, however, did a great deal toward supporting several members of his family who were not very well to do in the world, and contributed liberally toward this worthy object during his whole life. Upon one occasion, after he had been absent in the Far West for quite a number of years, and had accumulated a considerable sum of money, he obtained a furlough for the purpose of revisiting his friends in Bennington. He had left there a poor farmer's boy, and he resolved to make a respectable appearance on his return. He owned two of the finest horses that I have ever seen, and a negro boy for whom he paid five dollars a pound, and whom he subsequently set free.

Captain Scott was seated in a beautiful new gig, drawn by his magnificent white horse, followed by *Jack* dressed in livery as an outrider, and mounted upon his thoroughbred horse Dandy, and the rear of the cortège was brought up by some twenty full-blooded dogs of various breeds and descriptions. In this order he drove through the quiet streets of Bennington and halted at the village inn, where a great crowd of inquisitive citizens were soon assembled, all manifesting the keenest anxiety to learn the name of this distinguished stranger. No one, however, recognized him as he entered the house and took his seat by the window. He did not remain long before he saw his brother passing with a yoke of oxen, whereupon he went out and accosted him, saying, "You have a very fine pair of oxen there, sir; do they belong to you?" His brother, not recognizing him, answered that they were very good cattle, but belonged to one of his neighbors, and that he was not able to purchase them.

The captain then inquired what they could be had for,

and when his brother mentioned the sum, he took out his purse, handed him the amount, telling him that he liked his appearance so much that he would make him a present of the oxen. This most extraordinary liberality astonished his brother, who could hardly believe it possible that a man should show such munificence to a stranger. He, however, took the money, and expressed his profound gratitude to his benefactor.

The captain then asked him where he lived, and remarked that he would, if he had no objections, like to make him a call, to which his brother replied that he rented a small farm near by, and that it was only by the most rigid economy and industry that he could manage to support his family and pay his rents, but that, of course, he would be glad to receive a visit from one who had shown such generosity to him. He then inquired of his brother what price the owner put upon the farm, adding that he believed he should like to present him with that also. His brother now looked attentively at him, and for the first time recognized him. They went home together, both exceedingly happy.

As those persons who are not familiar with the history of Captain Scott may have some desire to know what became of him, I will add, for their information, that he was killed while gallantly leading forward his command in that most sanguinary battle of the Mexican war, "Molino del Rey."

Although, like the most of us, he had his faults, yet, upon the whole, Captain Martin Scott was a pleasant companion, an honorable man, a kind brother, and a gallant soldier. I most sincerely respect his memory, and with all my heart say, "Peace be to his ashes."

THE END.

www.ingramcontent.com/pod-product-compliance
Lightning Source LLC
LaVergne TN
LVHW021136110826
845150LV00005B/1042

* 9 7 8 1 4 2 5 5 4 8 6 1 2 *